This book has been a labor of love . . . and th[...]
For the many years we have known Sarah, we have seen the reality of this journey in her own life: her hunger to know God, deeply, intimately; and her passion for prayer and journaling. And the result is this scholarly yet personal account as her own story is interwoven in God's greater Story. And what a beautiful blending of the two!

As Sarah reminds us again and again through the Scriptures of the unfailing love of God, we are given an *Invitation*, so personally and so powerfully, to come into his presence and enjoy Life and intimacy with him."

—John and Linda Willett
NC Area Director with Search Ministries, former Grace Brethren and Westover Church Pastor, Lecturer with Family Life Marriage Conferences (Campus Crusade for Christ)

At last, a practical, daily help that inspires, challenges, invites and demonstrates how to enter God's presence though His Word. It works!

—Dr. Richard H. and Shirilee Little
Retired Presbyterian Pastor, Author and Lecturer,
Seventeenth Moderator of the Evangelical Presbyterian Church

The Invitation presents with clarity and understanding the benefits received by those who answer God's invitation to come into his Living Presence through prayer and to record scripture and insights spoken to the heart.

Sarah provides daily journal examples of her truthful responses to scripture with such transparency. She provides a powerful motivation to her readers as she reveals the pathway to intimacy with God.

—Phyllis Stern
Regional Speaker Trainer, Stonecroft Ministries Cary, NC

The Invitation provides some very refreshing points of view, good analogies, contemplative questions, and good spiritual challenges that will truly assist the believer in making a significant contribution to their Christian growth and walk.

—Dr. Sharon Johnson, Editor

You are an inspiration, Sarah. Your book was like a polishing cloth to silver—it cleans and makes it shine. Your words purified me to see the Lord shine and enjoy him more.

—Amy Maxwell, Proofreader

Alissa,

Thank you for all your love and support. I will always remember our time together discussing listening prayes!

I love you!

Sarah

THE
INVITATION

Come Boldly

to the

Throne

of

Grace

DISCOVER PRAYER AND JOURNALING

SARAH BUSH

WinePress WP Publishing

WinePress Publishing, PO Box 428, Enumclaw, WA 98022 functions only as book publisher. As such, the ultimate design, content, editorial accuracy, and views expressed or implied in this work are those of the author.

Interior Illustrations by Sandra Snarski.

Some names in this book have been changed to protect the privacy of various individuals.

ISBN 13: 978-1-57921-966-6
ISBN 10: 1-57921-966-7
Library of Congress Catalog Card Number: 2008927379

May My Prayer
Be Set Before You
Like Incense.
May Your Words
Be Bound on My Fingers and
Written on the Tablet of My Heart

—Psalm 141:2, Proverbs 7:3

THIS BOOK IS dedicated to my faithful and loving husband, Eric, who has been my pillar of support.

The moment I shared my dream of writing this book with him, he said, "Go for it." Throughout the years he has encouraged, exhorted, and spent hours with me working until the manuscript was finally completed.

His incredible faith in God and his belief in my ability to create this work have enabled me to persevere and finish. Eric, I could not have done it without you.

CONTENTS

Part IV: Glory Beyond the Sacred Temple

PREFACE

T O HAVE BEEN the vessel chosen by God to create this book
is truly a blessing. By no means, does this book encompass the
expansive scope of prayer and all its mysteries. Nor is it meant to be
a doctrinal tome, dissecting all the different theological aspects of
prayer. My heart's desire is for these pages to serve as both inspiration and practical advice, for God's people to be drawn closer to
God through prayer and journaling. My hope is that prayer will
increase as people come to an eternal perspective in all areas of their
life while they encounter the living God, see his faithfulness, and
find him worthy of their trust as they record their life journeys.

My spiritual journey began when I was thirteen. My father shared
the gospel of Jesus Christ with me and gave me my first Bible. Since
my youth, I have been actively involved in a Bible believing church;
however, many of my richest experiences come from private moments with God while studying in his Word and communing with
him in prayer.

I remember, soon after making my commitment to the LORD, sitting on the floor by my bed reading scripture and struggling to pray
each morning. I asked the LORD, *Please give me the desire to pray, to
get up early, and to spend time with you.* God has certainly answered
my prayer. He created in me a new heart, a heart committed to
him, and a heart with a passion for prayer. As God revealed his

spiritual gifts to me of mercy and encouragement, I found great joy in sharing these gifts through intercessory prayer.

Over the years, I have had a habit of recording prayer requests and journaling; recording answers to prayer, tracing life's lessons, and how God reveals his presence in my life. I have used various types of journals and intercessory prayer lists, but I was not able to locate a book combining both prayer requests and journal together. This endless search led me to create this book and the companion prayer guide and journal, *Grace for the Journey*. It is my fervent prayer that these books be used by God to aid those who desire a more zealous prayer life and build confidence by seeing how God is at work in their life.

For fourteen years I gathered quotes and ideas, piecing this book together, unsure if God had called me to do this seemingly insurmountable task. With each step and each prayer for direction, God faithfully guided and encouraged me to finish this work.

At one point, wondering if I could finish, and losing focus, I read Colossians 4:17. ". . . see to it that you complete the work you have received in the Lord." It was God's personal instruction for me. This is my 'work' for now—my gift of encouragement to others.

In our fast-paced society, blown back and forth by the tyranny of the 'urgent,' our need for time alone with God is often neglected. As a member of Moms in Touch International, an active participant on the prayer team at church, and a women's ministry speaker and teacher, I have come in contact with many Christians who desire a resourceful prayer guide and journal to enhance and simplify their daily prayer lives. Recognizing how foundational prayer is to our faith, and seeing the value of journaling in support of our prayer life, I endeavored to bring the spiritual and practical together to help on our journey to sanctification.

My dream is that God would use these materials as a ministry of reconciliation—to restore the human heart in intimacy with the Designer and Creator of our soul. By placing a spiritually stimulating book and a practical prayer guide together, may you see and remember God's faithfulness and mature in your faith as you record your prayers and life journey. I hope this book will provide a greater understanding of prayer, and provide some structure and direction to your prayers so you can better know God's unfailing love and believe in the purpose and benefits of prayer. For those of you who are tentative about your ability to pray or who are unfamiliar with journaling, my hope is that these materials will be a source of confidence in building faith, a life of prayer, and an appreciation of the practical effects of journaling. In addition, it will equip those of you who do believe in the power of prayer and journaling, but lack the accountability to create consistency and discipline. Individuals who seek achievement may discover a balance of goals and grace.

My prayer for each person who opens this book is that you come to understand that God is the great provider. Through his Word and through prayer we are granted access to faith, salvation, his plan for our redemption, his very thoughts. May his invitation, "Come to me," become very personal to you. I pray that your heart will be turned toward God and set free to worship with a stronger commitment to prayer and a love for Jesus; I hope you discover life in your God-given purpose—to help build God's kingdom and give him glory. May you, too, ". . . know this love that surpasses knowledge—that you may be filled to the measure of all the fullness of God" (Eph. 3:19). May the love of Christ compel us to pray, that we who live, no longer live for ourselves but for him who died for us and was raised again (2 Cor. 5:14–15).

—SJB

ACKNOWLEDGMENTS

My first expression of thanksgiving goes to my Lord and Savior, Jesus Christ. If it was not for his saving grace, I never would have come to the understanding of the truth and the eternal treasures of prayer.

I am thankful to my loving husband, Eric, who believed in me and encouraged me every step of the way to accomplish this calling on my life—to write. I am thankful to my children—Nathaniel, Hannah, and Abigail—who have also encouraged me and kept me accountable by asking their curious and innocent questions concerning the book.

I am thankful to my parents who left a legacy of loving God and living for him, who always prayed for me and encouraged me, and who continue to be examples to me.

To all the members of my family, I appreciate your love, words of support, and prayers.

To my River Oaks Community Church family, my small group, my prayer team, and to so many other friends that are too numerous to mention; thank you. You each have been faithful sojourners by my side. You have taken time to pray with and for me, approaching the throne on my behalf and on the behalf of my readers. You have faithfully encouraged me, given me insight and ideas, and kept me persevering.

THE INVITATION

Thank you to my editors, Linda Gilden and Sharon Johnson.

Last but not least, thank you to those who have worked at the WinePress Group to bring this book to reality.

God bless you all!

INTRODUCTION

T HE MAIL ARRIVED this afternoon. In it was the usual—bills, credit card applications, coupons, and then my eye caught an envelope personally addressed to me. The fancy calligraphy piqued my interest. Inside was an elaborate wedding invitation. Don't you love receiving this kind of mail? As a woman my mind started pondering what I would wear and who else will be attending. The invitation gave me something to look forward to—to anticipate. It communicated that my presence was important. We have hope when we have something to look forward to—especially when others we know and love will be there with us.

God's long-standing invitation welcomes us into his holy presence. God desires a response in the human heart by faith through the vehicle of prayer, and reading his Word. Journaling allows us to more easily see how God is at work in our lives. These disciplines cultivate a surrendered heart intended for God's purpose. By bringing hope to individuals in developing a vibrant relationship with God and discovering their individual and unique purpose, God's kingdom is being built, and his glory revealed.

The Invitation presents a biblical foundation of prayer to teach, encourage, and give us endurance during these difficult days as we search for hope. Our journey begins in the Garden of Eden explaining the fall of man, but God does not leave us abandoned. He continues to pursue mankind with his love as we look at several Old Testament covenants made with great men of faith—Noah, Abraham, and Moses. Exploring these covenants will demonstrate God's ordained relationship with mankind. The building of the Tabernacle was God's plan for the Israelites to meet with him. We will look closely at the responsibility of the priesthood and the role of the altar of incense, both provide more evidence of God's design for our lives of prayer. Together with other Old and New Testament readings, we will explore the benefits and value of journaling as an aid to our spiritual walk.

The Invitation offers assurance as Jesus affirms we were designed for a life of prayer in the New Testament covenant of grace. Jesus lives to intercede for us, reconciling us to God, and leading us to discover our purposes. Following his example, we should live to pray, approaching the throne of grace with confidence.

Throughout the book, I have added a few of my personal journal entries to share as a testimony of God's ever-present work in my life and to give you some ideas if you are new to journaling. In several chapters there are questions for your journal response called *Today's Prayer Journal Task*. An appendix includes resources listing recommended reading, scripture references, and prayers for your time of worship, along with a sample Daily Prayer page from the journal.

The companion book is a prayer guide and journal, *Grace for the Journey*. This book is your response to *The Invitation*, containing Daily Prayer and journal pages. The Daily Prayer pages are given for individual prayers consisting of prearranged scripture verses and available space for listing personal needs, immediate family concerns, and vocational requests. Each day provides a journal entry page with available space to write personal thoughts, life lessons, insights, and your journey. Weekday Prayer pages are designed for prayer requests with a specific, daily prayer guide listing a variety of topics and scripture verses each day.

If you are a new believer, new to prayer, or new to journaling, keep it simple. I recommend you read *The Invitation* while using the companion prayer guide and journal, *Grace for the Journey*. Begin your journey by simply praying through the Daily Prayer page first. Write your thoughts on the journal page as you reflect on God's work in your life and your reading responses. When you have gained confidence add to your devotional time the Weekday Prayer page.

This book and its companion, *Grace for the Journey*, are about freedom in Christ. The apostle Paul encouraged us with these words in his teachings showing us that while we are under God's law, we are no longer in bondage to the law, "For the kingdom of God is not a matter of eating and drinking, but of righteousness, peace and joy in the Holy Spirit, because anyone who serves Christ in this way is pleasing to God" (Rom. 14:17–18). These books are meant to be tools to equip you by recording God's work in your life, and your testimony of answered prayer. Writing your prayers and recording your journey will help you remember where you have been and see how God is taking you closer into a relationship with him.

God will honor your efforts made to enter his rest. Our fumbling prayers offered on trembling knees, earnestly pleading, are heard. Our God has ears that hear, eyes that see, and a heart that loves. How much our heavenly Father will give good gifts to those who ask! Why would we not take everything to him? A favorite hymn says it well,

Trust Him When Thy Wants Are Many

Trust him when thy wants are many;
Trust him when thy friends are few;
And the time of swift temptation
Is the time to trust him too!

Trust him when thy soul is burdened
With the sense of all its sin;
He will speak the word of pardon,
He will make thee clean within.

Trust him for the "grace sufficient"—
Ever equal to thy need;
Trust him always for the answer,
When in his dear name you plead.

Trust him for the grace to conquer—
He is "able to subdue";
Trust him for the pow'r for service;

Trust him for the blessing too.

Trust him when dark doubts assail thee,
Trust him when thy strength is small,
Trust him when to simply trust him,
Seems the hardest thing of all.

Trust him! He is ever faithful;
Trust him—for his will is best;
Trust him—for the heart of Jesus
Is the only place of rest.

Trust him, then, through clouds or sunshine
All thy cares upon him cast;
Till the storm of life is over,
And the trusting days are past.[1]

As we live our lives trusting in God, we are set free to accomplish more than we ever dreamed. Obedience in praying and reading God's Word are the keys to discovering God, living in joy, and accomplishing God's purposes. Journaling helps in your ability to rejoice at his hand at work in your life, giving you vision and hope. It is proof that you are God's child and he is your loving, heavenly Father, who is intimately involved in every detail of your pursuit of his presence. With commitment and discipline, we gain joy in the LORD.

May you touch the world around you through prayer. As the final trumpet sounds, may your golden bowl in heaven be filled and over-flowing. May it flow as a glory of grace around his feet and his robe and rise as a sweet aroma unto him. May you hear the words, "Well done, good and faithful servant! You have been faithful with a few things; I will put you in charge of many things. Come and share your master's happiness!" (Matt. 25:23). Let us boldly approach the throne of grace with a surrendered heart intended for his purpose and with confidence in his unfailing love for us; may we to discover our purpose, finding mercy and grace in our times of need. Let us begin our journey—that we might continue to explore and understand our relationship to "the Invitation."

PART I

THE INVITATION

THE KING REQUESTS your presence.

You have a long-standing invitation to dine with an honorable King, a Host of Hosts, whose heart is full of gracious hospitality, warmth, and affection. A King who longs for you to *come* and join his banqueting table filled with a luscious array of all kinds of delightful delicacies. To refuse his invitation is unthinkable!

God anticipates your company as his distinguished guest. He wants to robe you in royal linens and crown your head with glory. You were created for a relationship with this King who wants you to know and love him. He welcomes you into his presence with love. He wants to share the riches of his kingdom.

CHAPTER 1

YOU ARE INVITED TO COME!

H AVE YOU EVER wanted to be loved and accepted by someone unconditionally, forever, no matter what? It is a natural
God-given desire. These longings are intended to make us yearn
for more of God.

Our very survival may depend more on the healing power of
love, intimacy, and relationships than we care to admit. When we
feel alone, life is miserable, long, and tiring. Lonely people may suffer from physical, emotional, and mental illness. Research shows an
association between loneliness, lack of social support, and stress.
As stress levels increase over long periods, they contribute to severe
emotional and physical effects: fatigue, depression, thoughts of
hurting others and ourselves, and many other physical symptoms.
So the opposite would be true, "A heart at peace gives life to the
body" (Prov. 14:30).

The young man responsible for the deaths of over thirty people
in the tragedy at Virginia Tech on April 16, 2007, felt alone and
rejected although surrounded by a sea of people. His mind dwelled
on the lies of the enemy who deceived his heart, convincing him
he was indeed alone and unwelcome. His choice to believe the lies
led him to act with insanity. To end his misery he took the innocent
lives of people around him and then his very own. Lies that creep in
our minds and hearts telling us we are alone or we have no purpose

are far from the truth. God desires for his people to know they are loved and live in fellowship with him.

God promises repeatedly in his Word that he is with us. We are not alone. "What a man desires is unfailing love" (Prov. 19:22). God extends an invitation to us to *come* into his presence to enjoy the company of his fellowship. He desires us and persistently woos us to come closer to him. God wants us to walk with him in the light of his truth and love.

God has also graciously provided us with companions to walk beside us if we so choose. As we take a look at our earthly relationships, they can either deter or help us find out what a relationship with God is all about.

Growing up in the southern United States, I often wonder where the days of southern hospitality have gone in my busy life with three children and many commitments.

My dear neighbor is a true southern belle and her door is always open. With the most gracious welcome in her slow, gentle, southern drawl she says, "Hey, Sayruh! How are you? Won't you come on in? James made some extra coffee. Come, sit down and let me get you some."

Entering her home she gives me her full attention, as if I were the only person who existed. Time stops and she is fully present with her whole heart and attention on me. At that moment, I am the only one that matters. As conversation dabbles beyond the update about the kids and my family, I begin to feel safe and willing to confide in her. This warm southern hospitality conveys a welcoming picture of God's heart toward us.

God's heart is full of love and compassion which he longs to pour out on his creation. He wants to spend individual, unhurried time with each person. Before the creation of the world, God had each one of us in his heart and mind for his pleasure (Eph. 1:4). Did you know God's thoughts toward you are precious and more numerous than the grains of sand on every beach of the universe? (Ps. 139:17–18). God extends his invitation. He asks us to "Come" and stay awhile. He is always fully present and offers a safe place to confide our hearts. Out of his great love, God has forever initiated a relationship with us.

The Bible's theme of love is a thread though every story and every chapter. God loves us infinitely! Our obedience in prayer is a perfect response to the love of God. As we grow closer to him, his love will transform our prayer life, "for Christ's love compels us" to pray (2 Cor. 5:14). An effective prayer life always comes from an overflow of our love for God. The way to obtain the burning passion of God's heart is to draw closer to him so he can communicate his love and desires to us.

When I was a young mother with three children under the age of four, there were many days when I only had one nerve left and my children were pushing all the right buttons, Matthew 11:28–29 become one of my favorite passages of scripture. I have grown to love the Amplified version which says, "*Come to Me*, all you who are weary and burdened, and I will give you rest. I will ease and relieve and refresh your souls. Take My yoke upon you and learn of Me, for I am gentle (meek) and humble (lowly) in heart, and you will find rest, relief and ease and refreshment and recreation and blessed quiet for your souls."

In my journey with the LORD, I have grown to know God as one who has unquestionable hospitality. He welcomes us into his presence with warmth and kindness. The word "come" is used over 1300 times in the Bible in various forms. The invitation "come to me" is used twelve times by Jesus. In the Hebrew, *come* means *korban*, to draw near to God or come closer. *Deu'te* in the Greek means *come here*.[1]

God promises that when we listen to him our souls will delight in the richest of fare. God invites us to come, "*Come to me*; hear me that your soul may live" (Isa. 55:3).

If a relationship is built on mutual communication, how does Almighty God plan on building a relationship with us? God is spirit and we are created in God's image, with a spirit. Throughout scripture God is portrayed with human traits, yet is not limited to them. Scripture references to human traits are given so we might better understand our Creator. God is described to have eyes that see, fingers that write, ears that hear, a sense of smell, and a mouth that speaks. In God's perfect design of mankind, we were created with these same senses so we could experience him and his creation. We were created to know and experience God. The need for communication is at the heart of the relationship. God has ordained that we are designed for a life of prayer. The King's love is so immense and profound, he extends his invitation and desires that we come into his presence and be his honored guest for eternity.

Throughout this book we will glance at God's plan since the time of creation. Moving through the Old Testament we will witness God's pursuit of mankind through the covenants made with the great men of faith—Noah, Abraham, and Moses. We will explore the Tabernacle and God's intentional dwelling with us. Then we will gain knowledge that God desires to dwell so close to us that he came in the form of a man, God's Son, the exact representation of his being so we could know, love, and fellowship with him for eternity. All these intentions of God's heart prove we are created for relationship.

Today's Prayer Journal Task

- Do you live your life feeling lonely or unsatisfied?
- Are you refreshed reading Matthew 11:28–29?
- What is our first responsibility? Just "Come!"

Designed for a Life of Prayer

Presenting a biblical overview of prayer, I value the importance of the foundational readings of the Old Testament. The Old Testament scriptures were written to teach us, give us endurance, encouragement, and hope for our lives. These written accounts will bring understanding of God's character, our true relationship, and his redemptive plan and purpose for a life of prayer in his people.

Let's travel back to the beginning when God created Adam and Eve. They possessed in their hearts the desire to walk and talk with God in the garden free from fear.

> God made man a little lower than the heavenly beings and crowned him with glory and honor. He made him ruler over the works of his hands; he put everything under his feet.

> —Psalm 8:5–6

God purposely created mankind with greater value and purpose than any other creature on earth.

Unfortunately, the pure relationship between God, Adam, and Eve was corrupted. The hearts of Adam and Eve were deceived by Satan. Satan made them think God was holding back something good and not telling them the full truth. Satan deceived Eve, and therefore, Adam—as he can do to us today. He convinced her that she could know more power and wisdom than God, rather than be transparently known by God.

Adam and Eve disobeyed God. They took a bite of the forbidden fruit from the tree of the knowledge of good and evil. Sin entered the heart of the human race. Suddenly aware of their nakedness, they hid from God. God called to them, "Where are you?" (Gen. 3:9). Finding them lonely and afraid, God, in his mercy, covered their shame with the skin of a sacrificed animal. From that moment on, we have sought after the unfulfilling things of this world to satisfy our needs rather than turning to God. Because of our sinfulness we are unable to initiate a relationship with a Holy God. But God, in his goodness, has made provision so we are welcomed into his presence.

Where are you spiritually? Have you responded to God's invitation?

God, in his sovereignty, before time began, had a plan for our redemption. He longs to restore us to the unstained, unhindered, perfect relationship he initially designed for us. His purpose and plan to dwell with us, talking and walking in the routine of our days, is apparent now just as it was then in the cool of the garden with Adam and Eve.

Throughout the Bible, God's plan of redemption unfolds. The great men of faith, in their relationships with Almighty God, were sure of what they hoped for and certain of what they did not see (Heb. 11:1). God, in his mercy, gave many symbols representing his presence; these symbols portrayed his immense desire for communication and relationship with us. At different times, in different places, God gave his people glimpses of his plan.

Symbols can bring great revelation to our limited understanding of the many attributes of God and our consequent relationship. What are some of the things we know about God?

- God is confident and sufficient. God does not *need* us to commune with him.
- God created us for his pleasures, to know him.

- God desires that we know him intimately. "'You are my witnesses,' declares the LORD, 'and my servant whom I have chosen, so that you may know and believe me and understand that I am he'" (Isa. 43:10a).
- God wants us to communicate, participate, and accomplish his purpose in giving him glory. We are designed for a life of prayer.
- God initiated covenant relationships with mankind to share his love.

CHAPTER 2

THE COVENANT PROMISES

Noah

DISCOVERING HIDDEN treasures in the Old Testament brings me encouragement and joy! To see how God interacted with others throughout history, teaches us valuable lessons revealing God's pursuit of mankind. God's heart of love initiates covenant relationships with Noah, Abraham, and Moses. God reveals his dedication to commune with his creation.

During Noah's generation, Noah was the only God-fearing man around. Noah habitually talked and walked with God. God spoke to Noah and told him to build an ark with exact specifications because he was going to send a flood to wipe out all the corruption on the earth. By faith, having never seen rain, Noah finished building the ark and God said, "But I will establish my covenant (promise, pledge) with you, and you shall come into the ark and your sons, your wife and your sons' wives with you" (Gen. 6:18 AMP). Noah's obedience led to the salvation of his family and the human race.

Once the flood ceased and land was discovered, God said, "Come out of the ark, you and your family" (Gen. 8:16). Noah built an altar in honor of the LORD, and taking some of the clean animals, he sacrificed burnt offerings. The LORD smelled the pleasing aroma and promised to never flood the earth again for generations to come. He spread a rainbow across the heavens proclaiming his promise. The altar remained as a permanent reminder of God's presence.

In this promise, or covenant, God initiated the first everlasting verbal covenant with Noah, communicating his love and plan for our redemption; a people who will eventually give us a messiah are preserved. The meaning of *covenant* is "a formal, solemn, binding agreement or promise between two or more parties especially for the performance of some action, to recover damages for breach of such a contract."[1] God blessed Noah and gave him everything he needed, commanding him to fill the earth. God promised, "This is the sign of the covenant I am making. Whenever the rainbow appears in the clouds, I will see it and remember the everlasting covenant between me and all living creatures" (Gen. 9:12, 16).

The covenant promise is still for us today. God has shown me his presence and love displayed through many beautiful rainbows. The reminder of God's faithfulness after seeing a spectrum has been a recurring theme in my life. Even though the rainbows were seen infrequently, I often saw them as affirmation or a nod of approval, that I was right where I was supposed to be—often after major decisions, moves, or in the presence of friends and family.

Recently, as I stepped out in faith to write this book, God has shown me a rainbow almost daily. As I began to look expectantly for the rainbows as a sign of his presence and affirmation, they were not always seen strewn across the sky, especially since we were in a time of drought in North Carolina. But God surprised me everywhere; from the sun shining through a plastic tumbler cup to the reflection of a rainbow on the garage floor off my kids' bicycle reflectors. Once, sitting in my car at a stop light, I saw a spectrum of colors on the "Access Ahead" sign when there was no sun shining. I noticed a prism shining through a neighbor's lamppost at night.

Last spring, while I attended a book festival there was a beautiful stone wall at the park, and I sat down a few minutes listening to a poetic musical group sing a song about pursuing your dreams. While watching the people, I noticed in the distance a rainbow painted on the side of a delivery truck. Deep in my heart I knew it was for me. I smiled—thinking God has such a sense of humor. Many other days I have received rainbows of promise, and on particularly difficult days, the most special ones were from my daughters' art work.

As my husband and I pondered the repetition of the rainbows, he reminded me what they truly mean. "God is with you," he said.

The next morning after our discussion, I opened my Bible. As the Christmas season approached I wanted to refresh my heart by reading about the birth of Jesus. There on the pages of Luke 1, Mary was reminded as the angel said to her, "Greetings, you who are highly favored! The Lord is with you." Daily now I look for him with great expectation. I know God is there waiting for me to notice him. Every time I see a rainbow I say within my heart or to my children in a quiet confidence, "There's a rainbow! God is with (us) me."

Abraham

God initiated a relationship with Abraham, another man whose faith was recognized as righteous. When called by God to move to a place he did not know, Abraham obeyed—traveling through many destinations before he made his home in a foreign land. The LORD blessed Abraham for his obedience. God in his graciousness told Abraham to look at all the land he could see. God would give it to him and his offspring forever. God promised Abraham that his offspring would be as numerous as the dust of the earth and the stars in the sky. All people on earth would be blessed through him.

Although Abraham was seemingly past the age of fathering children, he believed God's promise that he would have a child and numerous descendants. He made an altar honoring God and fell asleep. God confirmed the promise between himself and man. "When the sun had set and darkness had fallen, a smoking firepot with a blazing torch appeared and passed between the pieces (of animals). On that day the LORD made an unconditional covenant with Abraham"— (Gen. 15:17–18), solidifying the promise to give the land and blessings to him and his descendants.

In ancient days covenants were made through sacrificial customs. The stronger partner of the two parties named the terms of the covenant and the weaker partner agreed to the terms by slaughtering an animal and positioning it so that blood would flow on the path. The weaker partner committed his life to the agreement by walking through the blood of the sacrificed animal. In this sacrifice with Abraham, God guaranteed the covenant with his life by walking through the blood, solidifying his unconditional promise to Abraham. God's extraordinary and significant act extends his commitment to bless us from generation to generation. God proves his faithfulness by keeping the Abrahamic covenant.

After Abraham had been blessed with a long-awaited son, God tested Abraham's faith by calling him to take his only son, Isaac, whom he loved so much, and sacrifice him as a burnt offering. Abraham willingly obeyed God's call saying, "Here I am." As they approached the site and built an altar, Isaac asked where the lamb was for the burnt offering. Abraham answered with bold faith that God *himself* would provide the lamb.

In reverent fear of a Holy God, Abraham attempted to sacrifice his son. However, God kept his promise and intervened by providing a ram caught in the brush; a beautiful foreshadowing of God's provision, a sacrifice temporarily offered for his son. "He (Abraham) believed God, and it was credited to him as righteousness" (Gal. 3:6). God pronounced that all generations on earth would be blessed because Abraham had obeyed. The covenant blessing is foundational in understanding God's provision for us to be able to enter God's presence in prayer.

Moses

Moses, another man pursued by God, was born a Hebrew, but raised by Pharaoh's Egyptian daughter. Moses left Egypt searching for his identity. After forty years of living in the desert, Moses encountered God in an unusual way. God's presence dwelt within a burning bush. God initiated a conversation with Moses and called out to him using his name twice, reinforcing his terms of endearment, "Moses! Moses!" As if Moses didn't observe the radiance of the all consuming fire, God enlightened Moses that he was standing in his presence on holy ground. By faith from a pure and willing heart, Moses responded to a Holy God, "Here I am" (Exod. 3:4).

Israel had lost their freedom and became slaves in Egypt. God informed Moses that he had heard the cry of his people. He desired to send Moses as his messenger to inform the Israelites of their impending deliverance. Moses apprehensively asked God what he should reply if the Israelites inquired who sent him. To foreclose any insecurity, God said to Moses, *"I AM WHO I AM. This is what you are to say to the Israelites: 'I AM has sent me to you'"* (Exod. 3:14).

In this moment, the LORD God proclaims in two simple words, "I AM," that he is all-sufficient, all-powerful, immutable, and sovereign for all time. The eternal King of kings and Lord of lords for all generations continues to be and encompasses all the Hebrew names of God, ever present for his people. Jehovah, the Self-Existent One who reveals himself with purpose to be known by mankind is complete—not lacking anything to accomplish his purposes. It was the name of God, Jehovah, or Yahweh that was known by the Israelites and given with authority.

Those powerful words, "I AM has sent me to you," gave me strength beyond myself as I wrote down my thoughts and ideas for this book. For over a year I struggled with my interactions with other people, especially when speaking before groups, even on occasion to individuals. These insecurities drove me to examine my heart.

Journal Entry Sept. 28, 2007

Thank you, LORD for encouraging me and meeting me at the speaker's training seminar yesterday. On the way in the car, I was asking myself, "Why in the world am I going to a speaker's training seminar?"

As I was driving I was preparing for my interview for our women's outreach. I kept thinking about my studies recently, when God called Abraham, Moses, and Isaiah; all three said to the LORD, "Here I am." God told them to "Go!"—All three obeyed and went to unfamiliar, uncomfortable places.

Once I arrived at the training, I couldn't believe it . . . The opening speaker said that she changed her devotion from prayer to . . . Exodus 3:4. When God called Moses. Moses replied, "Here I am."

The seminar speaker asked, "Are you content with your ministry? 'Now, go!' Maybe it's time to step out of your comfort zone." She even quoted Moses' excuses . . . "But I can't speak." The same verse I had been memorizing for several months, "Who made man's mouth? Is it not I the

LORD? Now go; I will help you speak and teach you what to say."

—Exodus 4:10–12

She continued to say, "God gently leads and we don't think we hear him correctly. What is God asking you to do today?"

The speaker ended by saying, "Be in contact with God. Be open. Listen. Be trusting. Be excited."

As I reflect on the words I AM—all the names of God: I AM your Comforter, Shield, Shepherd, Loving Father, All Powerful One, Merciful; I AM your Strength, Grace, and Compassion, I AM Forgiveness, Savior, King. I AM . . . Prince of Peace, Almighty God.

We lack nothing—he is Our Provider of all things! Even the words of my mouth!

Oh, LORD—Keep showing me, step by step. I am sad to leave one ministry, to start another, but I know you have put it on my heart to slowly relinquish the duties of my ministry so I can focus on the book and speaking. Thank you for your patience with me! "For I have been slow of heart to believe" . . . that you would call me to write and speak. But to speak about you thrills my heart—to share my passion for prayer and journaling!

God gently revealed my insecurity. Just like Moses, my excuses were the same when God called me to speak, "LORD, I am inadequate and stumble over my words." And, as the LORD said to Moses, he reminded me of my utter dependence on him for everything, especially my words. My excuses were peeled away and my heart sought his help in continual dependence to go and speak when he opens the door of opportunity.

As the story continues, God directed Moses to go to Pharaoh and tell him to let God's people, the Israelites, go, so they could worship God. Pharaoh refused to listen. After the traumatic discipline of the plagues, God used Moses to deliver the Israelites out of slavery in Egypt and away from Pharaoh.

God revealed his love to the Israelites by performing many miraculous demonstrations of his power, protection, and presence. When the Israelites were fleeing Egypt, God displayed his mighty power by parting the Red Sea, and delivered them from Pharaoh's army. As they continued their journey, the LORD went ahead, ceaselessly guiding them in a pillar of cloud by day and a pillar of fire by night, so that they could travel by day or night. God used a visible sign of his leading and presence as the Israelites moved from camp to camp in search of the Promised Land.

The whole Israelite community literally traveled in the wilderness to a place named Sin, physically and spiritually. The Israelites began romanticizing the past as they grumbled and whined against Moses. They would have rather died in Egypt where they had plenty of food than travel in the desert experiencing God.

The LORD heard their grumbling and the entire Israelite community was invited to come before the LORD. God would provide for their needs and then they would know the great I AM, the LORD their God. Each morning God promised to rain down bread from heaven. The life-giving provision communicated hope. The people were to go out each day and gather enough manna for that day; leaving the responsibility to the Israelites to gather their food daily according to their need. God faithfully administered his mercy and grace in perfect measure.

God initiated additional provision for Moses by extending his presence. He invited Moses to Mount Sinai to approach God in his glory. The LORD said to Moses, "Come up to me on the mountain and stay here, and I will give you the tablet of stone, with the law and commands I have written for their instruction" (Exod. 24:12).

When Moses went up on the mountain, the cloud covered it, and the glory of the LORD settled on Mount Sinai. For six days the cloud covered the mountain, and Moses waited. On the seventh day the LORD called to Moses from within the cloud. To the Israelites the glory of the LORD looked like a consuming fire on top of the mountain. Moses entered the cloud and he stayed on the mountain forty days and forty nights. During this time, God wrote the words of the covenant on the tablets—the Ten Commandments.

After receiving the Ten Commandments or Book of the Covenant, Moses returned from the mountain with the covenant for the people. After Moses' mountain top experience, he found, to his disappointment in a little over a month's time, the Israelites had rebelled and had begun worshiping other gods. Moses saw the people were running wild and Aaron had lost control. So Moses stood at the entrance to the camp and said, "Whoever is for the LORD, come to me" (Ex. 32:25–26). From out of the twelve tribes of Israel, only the Levites rallied to him. Those who followed were set apart for an extraordinary purpose.

To cover the sins of the people, God required an animal sacrifice. Moses obeyed and built an altar. He made an offering and read the Book of the Covenant out loud to the people. Moses sprinkled the blood from the sacrifice on the people to seal the covenant.

> "Israel's earliest concept of God was based on the covenant, the contract made on Mount Sinai. Through their spokesman, Moses, God said to the Israelites, 'You will be my people, and I shall be your God.' . . . Thus the Jews related to a covenant God who had initiated the contract, who had talked to Israel first, begotten her as a people, and given her a sense of identity."[2]

Moses received the external covenant written on tablets made of stone by the fingertip of God. These ten laws were sent to the Israelites not as a set of regulations for the Israelites to earn their salvation, but as a demonstration of God's love, protection, and provision. God longed for the Israelites to dwell in his presence.

Through the covenants with Noah, Abraham, and Moses, God established his commitment to provide his love, grace, and blessings on his people for all generations. God was looking for those who were humble and reverently responsive to his presence when he spoke. By faith these men responded by building an altar and offering a sacrifice of shed blood to God. He asked the Israelite nation and each man, woman and child of faith to come worship him. God intentionally wanted to provide a more consistent, intimate place to meet. This more permanent "meeting place" communicated the glorious premise of God's heart—his love for us and our design for relationship. By God's redemptive plan he was providing a way into his presence for eternity.

CHAPTER 3

THE TABERNACLE—GOD'S DWELLING PLACE

T HIS IS WHAT the LORD says, 'Heaven is my throne, and the earth is my footstool. Where is the house you will build for me? Where will my resting place be?'" (Isa. 66:1). As the most valuable of his creation, God longs to meet with us. The establishment of God's earthly tabernacle is foundational to understanding the responsibility of the priesthood and the role of prayer.

To provide accessibility to a holy, approachable God for all the people, God initiated a relationship with the human race, providing a way on his terms to enter into his presence without being consumed. The first covenant between God and Israel had regulations for divine worship; it involved creating a sanctuary here on earth that was movable as God directed the Israelites from place to place.

God called Moses to establish the first tabernacle or tent of meeting as an invitation for anyone searching for him. God commanded Moses, "Make this tabernacle and all its furnishings exactly like the pattern I will show you" (Exod. 25:9). The Tent of Meeting or tabernacle was "a copy and shadow of what is in heaven" (Heb. 8:5).

> The tabernacle had to meet God's standard rather than a human one. The Hebrew word for sanctuary is *miqdash*, meaning a consecrated or holy thing or place; a hallowed part, like a chapel, an asylum; an area devoted to the

sphere of the sacred. It is derived from the word *qadhash,* which means to be clean, to make clean, to pronounce clean (ceremonially or morally); to hallow, to dedicate, to purify. The Hebrew word for tabernacle is *mishkan,* carrying the basic meaning of residence.[1]

The emphasis was on being set apart and holy. Through the establishment of the earthly tabernacle, a copy of the heavenly one, God promised to move about the Israelites to protect them. But, the one condition—the most serious requirement in preparing and maintaining God's dwelling—was that the place of meeting must remain holy and free of any shameful offense to God. Without sanctification no one could enter his presence.

God promised to be with the Israelites and give them a sense of identity and belonging. "I will put my dwelling place among you . . . I will walk among you and be your God, and you will be my people" (Lev. 26:11–12). "The same Hebrew verbal form used for God's walking back and forth in the Garden with Adam and Eve, also describes God's presence in the tabernacle."[2]

God revealed to Moses the instructions on how to build the tabernacle. Moses explained to the whole Israelite community what the LORD had commanded: "Have them make a sanctuary for me, and I will dwell among them" (Exod. 25:8).

God provided for what he wanted to accomplish. The Israelites' hearts were compelled to serve God. By giving all the materials they had acquired during the deliverance of the Egyptians at the Red Sea, the tent or tabernacle could be constructed. Moses utilized these items to create the exact representations of what had been shown to him on the mountain—earthly symbols, constant reminders of the heavenly tabernacle.

Everyone, donating from what they had, brought their freewill offerings to God morning after morning. Moses received the offerings from each man whose heart prompted him to give . . . gold, silver, and bronze; blue, purple, scarlet yarn, and fine linen . . . acacia wood and olive oil for the light and the fragrant incense. Many valuable linens, metals, and jewels were needed—each having symbolic meaning within the tabernacle.

The tabernacle was constructed by the people whom God gifted and called to fulfill his purpose. All the Israelites with various talents and skills were to make everything the LORD had specifically commanded—details from the outer court walls to the interior pieces of furniture. God desired a willing contribution from each man, giving of themselves for the sheer joy of working, sharing, and taking ownership in the final outcome, enjoying his presence.

The Tabernacle

West

Altar of Incense

Holy of Holies

Holy Place

South

North

Laver

Outer Court

Brazen Altar

Gate

East

The only entrance to the tabernacle was located on the east side where a thirty-foot gate made of blue, purple, and scarlet yarn and finely twisted linen was hung. Each color of the yarn had significant meaning. Blue symbolized the heavenly throne of God over their heads; purple represented royalty; scarlet was a reminder of the sacrifice. The walls and ceiling were constructed of linens. The ceiling received special care, with finely embroidered cherubim within the linens (Exod. 26:1). These angels were a visual reminder of God's nurturing protection and comforting security within God's presence while one was worshiping in the tabernacle. "I long to dwell in your tent forever and take refuge in the shelter of your wings" (Ps. 61:4).

The perimeters of the tabernacle were 150 feet in length and 75 feet in width, approximately half the size of a football field. Each item of furniture was designed and placed specifically within the tabernacle walls; the bronze altar and the laver or bronze basin stood in the outer court of the tabernacle. The altar was made of incorruptible acacia wood and was covered with bronze to signify strength. Designed with horns on each corner, it was anointed and used for the offering of sacrifices. The bronze basin or laver allowed for cleansing before and after the sacrifice. The lamp stand, the table for the bread of the Presence, and the altar of incense were located in the first room called the Holy Place. The most interior room containing the Ark of the Covenant was called the Holy of Holies.

When the tabernacle was completed God invited the people into his presence. The outer court was as close as the masses could get to their Holy God. The priests from the tribe of Levi were the only appointed ones who could enter into the outer room to carry on their ministry in the tabernacle. Only the high priest would enter the inner room once a year, and never without blood which he would offer for himself and for the sins the people had committed.

The Responsibilities of the Priesthood

The work assigned to the Levites, maintaining and caring for the furniture in the tabernacle, were similar to the terms used to describe the work and care allocated to Adam in the garden (Gen. 2:15, Num. 3:7–8). The *work* was meant as worship, and not only service. Vigilant care was required; watching and waiting at a moment's notice, as God directed the Israelites to move out from their camp, packing up the Tent of Meeting.

Aaron, who was appointed as priest, came to the altar and sacrificed a sin offering to make atonement for himself and the people. To make *atonement* means to make reconciliation by bringing God and mankind together, presented as a blood sacrifice covering man's sin.[3] The LORD had commanded him to do this so that the glory of the LORD could appear to them.

Sacred garments were crafted for the priests to give dignity and honor; these symbols of consecration allowed them to serve the LORD in the sanctuary. Each time the priest entered the tabernacle they were required to wear over their heart, a breast piece adorned with twelve stones representing the twelve tribes of Israel. A gold plate on his turban was inscribed with the words, "Holy to the LORD." This was a reminder of his irreproachable role as priest. As the priest entered further into the tabernacle, God Almighty's holy presence grew more prevalent.

As God's requirement, the constant cleansing of sin needed to occur as the priest assisted at the bronze altar and washed at the basin. It was mandatory for the priests to be holy, not to profane God's name. They had to have their entire body washed once to serve as priests. At the bronze basin, they were required to wash their hands and feet repeatedly after the sacrifice offering, signifying cleansing. Only high priests having met the requirements could enter further into the tabernacle.

After a perfectly unblemished sacrifice was offered, the LORD appeared in glory. God gave his approval by consuming the offering with flames as a visual reminder of his holiness, power, and presence. God purified the altar and the sacrifice with his awe-inspiring fire. Every morning the priest was to add firewood and arrange the burnt offering on the fire. As a sign of God's constant presence, the fire

was kept burning on the altar continuously; it was not allowed to go out.

Five types of sacrifices could be offered according to the individual or corporate need, but God first required a payment for sin according to his standard. Each individual desiring atonement made a personal sacrifice by providing an unblemished lamb, goat, bull, pigeon, or dove for the burnt offering. The offender slaughtered the head of the animal and blood flowed. The participant acknowledged the cost of the sacrifice made for their sin.

As the priest entered the holy place, he took care to see that the beautifully designed furniture was properly arranged against each wall of that room:

- The golden lamp stand
- The table of the bread of Presence
- The altar of incense

The golden lamp stand was made of one piece of pure gold hammered out with a base, a shaft, and three branches extending with seven flowerlike cups on each side. The Israelites were to bring olive oil as an offering and the wicks of the lamp were to burn continually, providing light in the tabernacle.

Along with the lamp stand was the table of the bread of the Presence constructed of imperishable acacia wood and overlaid with pure gold. Rings and poles were assembled to aid in the carrying of the table. The craftsmen were to make twelve plates and dishes of pure gold, as well as pitchers and bowls for the pouring out of offerings.

God commanded the priests, "Put the bread of the Presence on this table to be before me at all times, twelve loaves, Sabbath after Sabbath, as a lasting covenant" (Exod. 25:30, Lev. 24:3, 8). Aaron and his sons were to eat the bread as a holy part of their share in the offering. The preparation denoted an invitation of acceptance and fellowship.

The golden altar of incense was also located in the Holy Place. The altar of incense was to be made of acacia wood and covered with gold. Horns were designed on each corner with rings and poles to carry it. After the sacrifice was offered at the bronze altar, the coals stained with blood where taken and placed under the altar of incense. Any other unauthorized fire was unacceptable and resulted in death for those responsible. The altar of incense was placed in front of the curtain that concealed the Holy of Holies. "Prayer  was the great principle piece of service with which they honored God. The incense could not be accepted without prayer."[4]

The Holy of Holies contained the Ark of the Covenant, the Israelites' most sacred possession. The Ark of the Covenant or Testimony contained the gold jar of manna, Aaron's staff, and the stone tablets of the covenant. Above the Ark were the gloriously emblazoned cherubim shading the cover of the Ark. At this most intimate place of the Tent of Meeting, God promised "There, I will meet you and speak to you" (Exod. 29:42). In the Hebrew the word *meet* is *ya'adh*, meaning *to appoint, fix, (a place or time); to betroth, give in marriage, to meet by agreement, to come together.*[5]

The Ark of the Covenant represents the very presence of a Holy God. "Here the LORD would speak to Moses face to face, as a man speaks with his friend" (Exod. 33:11). The Ark would be set apart for his glory as "the LORD reigns . . . he sits enthroned between the cherubim" (Ps. 99:1).

The LORD warned Moses and Aaron not to come into the Most Holy Place whenever they wished; if they did, the encounter would result in death. Instead, Aaron was given specific instructions when and how he was to enter the sacred area. He was to put on the sacred garments, go into the sanctuary with the sacrifice and make atonement. He took a sensor full of burning coals from the altar before the LORD and two handfuls of finely ground fragrant incense with him behind the curtain. He put the incense on the fire before the LORD, and the smoke of the incense concealed the atonement cover above the Testimony so he would not die. He took some of the bull's blood with his finger and sprinkled it on the front of the atonement cover.

Once the offerings were prepared for sacrifice the LORD instructed Moses to take fragrant spices and make an aromatic blend of incense grinding it into powder or oil. It was to be pure and sacred. Moses would place the incense in front of the Ark of the Covenant where God promised he could be found. The incense was holy. In the tabernacle the incense became a dominant aroma that filled the rooms and obscured the unpleasant odor of the burning sacrifice.

The Fragrant Incense

Understanding the construction of the Tent of Meeting and the role of the priest is foundational in deciphering God's initiative to dwell with us and his developing an intimate relationship. While each symbol and piece of furniture within the tabernacle was meant to serve a certain purpose and have significant implications, throughout this book we will look more closely at the altar of incense.

All through history, incense has had a variety of uses, most generally being burned for aesthetic enjoyment and as a fragrance to obscure less desirable odors. For religious purposes, burning incense was an act of consecration as a sacrificial offering to deity. The more well-known incense in biblical times were frankincense and myrrh. These were given to Jesus at his birth, and were applied on his body following his death. Incense was required to be pure, and it was forbidden to burn anything on the golden altar besides pure incense.

Recently, a dear friend returned from a trip to Israel. She shared about the many fragrant plants that were blooming in the spring. She brought me a small bottle of incense called Spikenard

Magdalena. The ingredients included myrrh, cinnamon, and Iris.[6] The myrrh and cinnamon are from the trunks of certain small trees. She had no idea how God had used this gift of encouragement affirming the underlying theme within my book.

God emphasized the aroma and fragrance when he instructed Moses to take the fine spices: liquid myrrh, fragrant cinnamon, fragrant cane, cassia, and a hin (about four liters) of olive oil and make these into sacred anointing oil, a fragrant blend. Moses used this oil to anoint the Tent of Meeting, the ark of the Testimony, the table and all its articles, the lamp stand and its accessories, the altar of incense, the altar of burnt offering and all its utensils, and the basin with its stand. Moses consecrated the entire sanctuary with fragrant oil so it would be most holy, and whatever touched the objects also became holy. The time and care spent by the priests in preparing the Tent of Meeting was an unhurried daily commitment in absolute reverence with the expectation of encountering God's presence. This fragrance brought pleasure and joy to the people, reminding them of God's presence. "You love righteousness and hate wickedness; therefore God, your God, has set you above your companions by anointing you with the oil of joy. All your robes are fragrant with myrrh and aloes and cassia . . ." (Ps. 45:7–8).

Every morning in the tabernacle, Aaron would burn fragrant incense on the altar while he tended to the lamps. He was also required to burn incense in the evening. For generations incense would regularly burn before the LORD. The incense was kept in golden bowls—a sweet offering unto the LORD. The LORD "appointed some of the Levites (priests) to minister before the ark of the LORD, to make petition, to give thanks, and to praise the LORD, the God of Israel" (1 Chron. 16:4).

Do you enjoy the smell a refreshing fragrance of a perfume or lotion when someone whisks by you or gives you a hug? Often when this happens our senses are triggered and we recall someone who wears the same fragrance. Our sense of smell can powerfully activate our minds and emotions.

I can still remember perfumes my college roommates wore. As we often shared clothes, I could on many occasions smell the perfume that had permeated their clothes. Through the years, whenever I encounter one of those fragrances my mind travels back to great times and friendships.

Occasionally when my daughter and I are out shopping and as we walk by others, she will say, "Oh, that smells like Grandma's perfume!" I wonder if the fragrance makes her heart warm with fond memories of Grandma. Writing about visiting her grandma, my daughter's friend wrote, "I remember when you made us pancakes. They had one of those happy feeling smells."

Several years ago for Christmas, I bought myself some fairly expensive hand lotion and placed it under the tree—labeled "From: Santa – To: Mom." At first, I tried to preserve it to make it last as long as I could by only wearing it on special occasions. Now, a few years later, I have decided to live life and enjoy it. I love putting it on almost every day as a practical reminder of a spiritual truth, that in Christ my prayers and life are a sweet fragrance to God.

Similarly in the Tent of Meeting, day after day the priest stood to perform his religious duties; again and again, offering the same sacrifices with the same incense. In this ritual the priest could make atonement for the person's wrongdoing and he would be forgiven. This was the covenant of blood that God commanded the Israelites to keep. "Without the shedding of blood there is no forgiveness of sins" (Heb. 9:22).

This constant repetition of sacrifice showed that the most excellent way into the Most Holy Place had not yet been made known. This sacrificial system was an illustration indicating that the gifts and sacrifices being offered were not able to clear the conscience of the worshiper. They were only applied as external regulations until the appointed time of a new system. Israel's faith was based on the acceptance of the sacrificial atonements as they looked forward to the Messiah's arrival. All of these directives were a foreshadowing of the only permanent sacrifice for sins.

A Settled Temple

With stubborn hearts the Israelites continued wandering, continuously relocating the Tent of Meeting. God's plan was to establish a more settled residence. After Moses' death, Joshua was commissioned to lead the Israelites into the Promised Land. Many years later under the reign of King David, after many battles of war, the LORD had finally granted him rest from all his enemies. When King David was settled in his palace:

"He said to Nathan the prophet, 'Here I am, living in a palace of cedar, while the ark of God remains in a tent.'"

> Nathan replied to the king, "Whatever you have in mind, go ahead and do it, for the LORD is with you." That night the Word of the LORD came to Nathan, saying: "Go and tell my servant David, 'This is what the LORD says: Are you the one to build me a house to dwell in? I have not dwelt in a house from the day I brought the Israelites up out of Egypt to this day. I have been moving from place to place with a tent as my dwelling.'"

> —2 Samuel 7:2–6

After Nathan informed the king of God's instructions, King David made preparations for the building of a new, more permanent, earthly temple. But God revealed that he would build, establish, and bless his house *himself* forever. God declares, "I will build a house for you" (2 Sam. 7:27). Having confirmed his covenant, David found bold courage to pray for the glory of God's name and asked God's blessing of good things on his family; a crown through whom God's Kingdom would be established forever.

The Word of the LORD had come to David telling him that he would not build the temple because his hands were the hands of a warrior. But David would be appointed to other work, writing psalms and enlarging the borders of Israel. When David's son, Solomon, became king, he was told he would rule with peace. Solomon was chosen to build the temple with the exact specifications which had been passed down from his father. The temple was designed to serve all nations as a place to worship God.

In awe, Solomon asked, "But will God really dwell on earth with men? The heavens, even the highest heavens, cannot contain you (him). How much less this temple I have built!" (2 Chron. 6:18). Solomon's temple became a permanent structure housing all that had formerly been inside the Tent of Meeting.

After the Ark had been put in place in the newly constructed tabernacle, the priests consecrated themselves and sang praises to the Lord. "Then the temple of the Lord was filled with a cloud, and the priests could not perform their service because of the cloud, for the glory of the Lord filled the temple of God" (2 Chron. 5:13–14). God proclaimed, "I have chosen and consecrated this temple so that my Name may be there forever. My eyes and my heart will always be there" (2 Chron. 7:16). "May the glory of the LORD be praised in his dwelling place!" (Ezek. 3:12).

Again we witness God's trustworthiness in keeping his promises from one generation to the next. Both father and son have their individual gifts and callings from God to build his Kingdom. What God calls men to achieve for his glory, he accomplishes through us and for us. He works through obedient yet imperfect vessels!

God had placed the desire on David's and Solomon's hearts to construct a permanent dwelling place for God to meet with them and make his presence and provision available. Yet time after time, the Israelites followed after false affections and continued to worship foreign gods. They refused to pay attention to God; stubbornly they turned their backs on him, closed up their ears, and chose to make their hearts hard. They would not listen to the law or to the words God Almighty had sent by his Spirit through the earlier prophets.

The prophet Malachi confronted the priests for offering blemished sacrifices. God asked, "Where is the respect due me . . .? It is you, O priests, who show contempt for my name" (Mal. 1:6). Using Malachi, the LORD spoke in relatable terms and asked the priests if it would not be wrong for them to bring the blind, crippled, and diseased animals as gifts to their governors? He rebuked their careless actions and selfish attitudes they had shown by bringing impure offerings. With righteous indignation, God announced he was not pleased and demanded they shut the temple doors and not light useless fires on his altar. The Israelites' spiritual life was not in good condition. Living in half-hearted devotion, they dishonored God in his own temple.

Like the Israelites, I wander and struggle at times with a lack of love and joy in my heart. Several years ago, traveling on a twelve-hour trip from North Carolina to Connecticut to visit my sister-in-law at her peaceful home for vacation on the beach, tensions were high in our minivan. Because of the typical stress of traveling, my kids had exasperated my husband and me. Animosity was building and we were at odds, hardly speaking to each other.

One evening during our trip, when I was still bitter and in a failing-to-forgive attitude, we met my sister-in-law's neighbor for dinner. This woman was very pleasant, quite happy, and enjoyable to be with. She laughed and loved life.

Later during my visit, in my misery, I learned she was an atheist. I was dumbfounded to say the least. This woman who had no faith in God, did not know his love or believe in it, demonstrated more joy, contentment, and freedom than me—a woman who knows and believes in the God who is love himself.

In my own misery and self pity, I was choosing to live unhappily. I was deeply convicted to embrace the truth and extend forgiveness that I had already received, but which I needed to acknowledge by asking. I had forgotten the gospel. Unfortunately, I humbly confess, I was not a light and witness of God's love to this lady. As Christians we would win the world if we truly believed, and lived in the love, forgiveness, and freedom that we receive freely from God.

As God did with me, in the delivery of his correction, he reminded the Israelites of his covenant—a blessing of life and peace for those who revered his name. Israel continued to defile the sanctuary the LORD loved by choosing to worship other gods.

The LORD Almighty was very angry and declared, "The days are coming when I will send a famine through the land—not a famine of food or a thirst for water, but a famine of hearing the Words of the LORD" (Amos 8:11). But God would not turn his back on them completely. God would not break his covenant. Knowing he was God of the covenant, he would not destroy all mankind again. He had set his affection on Israel. In perfect faithfulness God kept his covenantal promises that were made to Noah, Abraham, and Moses.

Tragically for the people of Israel, the LORD's glory departed from the temple and settled on the mountain east of Jerusalem. Four hundred years later, when men's hearts were starved to hear a Word from the LORD, God's time for man's redemption had come. God, in his mercy and grace, decided to send his whole heart, in the form of a man, his Son. Isaiah gave the prophecy that "The LORD himself will give you a sign: the virgin will be with child and will give birth to a son, and they will call him Immanuel which means, 'God with us'" (Isa. 7:14, Matt. 1:23).

Jesus came to earth so that we could know the heart of God. "No one has ever seen God, but God the One and Only, who is at the Father's side, has made him known" (John 1:18). "For God was pleased to have all his fullness dwell in him (Jesus), and through him to reconcile to himself all things, whether things on earth or things in heaven, by making peace through his blood, shed on the cross" (Col. 1:19–20). Now the glory of God was revealed through his Son as the Word became blood and flesh and made his dwelling among us.

From the beginning of creation God has gone to incredible lengths to dwell with us.

God purposed and planned to walk and talk in the garden with Adam and Eve. God revealed his glory and extended his heart to Israel through the establishment of the covenants and the tabernacle with an invitation to come into his presence and enjoy the company of his fellowship. Considering the work and care specified in the garden and the priests' offerings in the tabernacle, we see that we were designed for worship and fellowship with God. God's final provision of entering his presence was accomplished by sending his Son. God's grace provides you an invitation to participate in his fellowship.

CHAPTER 4

GOD'S *WORD*
WITH US

I N THE NEW Testament, Jesus brings affirmation to the invitation of God's heart. The previous use of foreshadowing in the Old Testament points us toward the new covenant of grace. In the life of Jesus we see the culmination of the covenant promises, the tabernacle, and our true relationship with God. The voices of the prophets, the incredible history of ancient Israel, and God's drawing of man, culminates in Christ. All scripture affirms that God longs to dwell with us. Through the gift of Jesus, and his death on the cross, God offers an eternal invitation of continual access into his presence and the provision of his living Word with us.

The previously mentioned Old Testament covenants, laws, the role of the priests, the offerings, and the design and function of each piece of furniture in the tabernacle contain rich symbolisms pointing to Christ. The gradual unveiling of Jesus though scripture will be fully uncovered as we travel through the book. Christ is revealed as the true tabernacle in the New Testament. Revelation of the fulfillment of the tabernacle will give you a glimpse into God's heart. He has made a perfect way to meet with us.

In the New Testament we see Jesus—God in the flesh—meet many people. Their encounter with him changes their lives forever. Do you remember the little man named Zacchaeus who climbed the sycamore tree to see Jesus as he entered Jericho? Do you ever feel like Zacchaeus? So small spiritually, always making mistakes, peering in on Jesus' encounter in other peoples' lives? Zacchaeus was a greedy, disrespected tax collector who lined his pockets with extra funds from other people's money. Jesus actually invited himself to Zacchaeus' house for dinner where Zacchaeus quickly welcomed him into his home, and then, into his heart.

As people condemned Jesus for spending time with a sinner, this offender began surrendering his agenda and was planning to seek reconciliation with his payees. Jesus knew the crowds might turn against Zacchaeus and to protect him Jesus took the initiative. Jesus' presence alone produced a change in the heart of Zacchaeus. There is no record of any exchange of words as they walked to Zacchaeus' home, but we do see a man become transformed after spending time with Jesus. Jesus came to save us from sin, to rescue people who do not have it all together, to heal the wounded heart, to comfort people who need his care, and to give hope to people who need love.

Jesus lived his life among us and he showed us the love of the Father, reaching out to us no matter our spiritual, physical, or economic condition. He lived his life among us, showing us the forgiveness, freedom, healing, power, and glory of the Father.

When Jesus' ministry on earth was nearing completion and he was preparing to return to heaven, he entered the tabernacle in Jerusalem before his triumphant entry to the cross. Jesus observed the buying and selling of merchandise in the temple courts and he cleansed the temple in righteous anger and said to the people, "My house will be called a house of prayer for all nations? But you have made it 'a den of robbers'" (Mark 11:17). Jesus' actions physically represented what was getting ready to happen spiritually—the cleansing of the actual temple illustrated the spiritual condition of our hearts.

The state of our hearts and the role of prayer are deeply important as we walk though the rich symbolisms of the tabernacle and understand the covenant promises of grace and mercy; all of these truths certainly affirm that Almighty God initiates a relationship with us. God's invitation of grace precedes us and produces a response in our hearts. As seen in all other scriptural covenants made with God, God's covenantal intention is that we are joined with him in love and eternal fellowship by redemption through his Son. In his presence, we will be changed.

This is the glory of living on this side of the gospel. "The God who made the world and everything in it is the LORD of heaven and earth and does not live in temples built by (human) hands" (Acts 17:24). He longs for his presence—his very own Word to dwell in temples made by his very own hands. Will you respond to God's loving invitation by faith and become all that he designed for you? You are his sacred dwelling place.

God Writes, We Write

Did you know God is a God of books? The more I explore the writing arena, the more I find God teaching me about his passion for the written word. He is the Author of our faith and our lives. Each of our days were written in his book before one day came to be (Ps. 139:16). God is so personal—he has a list of our tears recorded in his scroll (Ps. 56:8). King David states "Here I am, I have come—it is written about me in the scroll" (Ps. 40:7). Is your name written in God's scroll, the Lamb's book of life? We can have assurance that our names are written there if we believe and receive God's Son. Paul exhorts his fellow workers in the cause of the gospel by reminding them their names are written in the book of life. Revelation warns that those whose names are not recorded in this significant book will be cast away from God's presence.

Why do you think God has all these books? God must enjoy books. He is an Author! He could have libraries of books, stories that extend into the heavens—stories about us. I love books! Don't you love a new book? Having been an elementary teacher, I especially enjoy children's picture books. I think most importantly God writes because he loves us. I would think God loves the colorful stories of our lives. The Bible is one lengthy love letter; every book, every chapter, every page is written with messages of love toward us.

God is a supernatural deity so he does not forget anything; we know he does not need books and records for his recollection. God's creation is for his pleasure and he loves to share it with us. Like the Bible, I wonder if God's records are essentially for us. I wonder if God will show us the records of our tears; the day our children were born, or when a loved one crossed the threshold of this life. Maybe opening the Lamb's book of life, God will graciously show us names written there in response to our prayers and witness, those from our lineage to future generations.

God's spoken Word became his written Word, and living Word for us. Do you grasp the fact that in your hands you can hold the Words of Almighty God? I remember God told Moses, "Write this on a scroll as something to be remembered . . ." (Ex.17:14). The scriptures have been recorded and preserved for hundreds of years so we could know God. The term "unfailing love" is used 32 times in the Old Testament. Again, God has made every effort to make himself available, accessible, and approachable. Jesus came to fulfill God's Word. "In the beginning was the Word (Jesus), and the Word (Jesus) was with God, and the Word (Jesus) was God (John 1:1). God's Word has brought us eternal life. God has life-giving purpose for us to possess a record of his written Word. God writes to record his love. God writes to express his love. And each generation still longs to read his message of unfailing love. The Bible remains the number one seller!

> My heart is stirred by a noble theme as I recite my verses
> for the king; my tongue is the pen of a skillful writer.
>
> —Psalm 45:1

Throughout the book, I have shared a few journal entries to give you a taste of God's hand in my daily walk with him. Journaling has become a method of communication between God and me. The daily discipline grows precious over time. I have been journaling for twenty-seven years, some years more consistently than others. I tend to look back through my journals when I need to find something in particular and I can't remember the details. While writing this book it has been refreshing to read my journals and review my journey with God. I am convinced that journaling is an important part of the "seed" being firmly planted and bearing fruit. Taking the time to reflect on my journey with God contributes to the growth of my faith and the direction of my life. Journaling facilitates my discovery.

Journaling is a beneficial tool in the spiritual journey. Writing is a resource available to us to express our hearts and record God's guidance and work in our lives. Therefore, it builds our faith as we recall, remember, and rely on God's faithfulness. Significant scriptures, heartfelt prayers, and God's personal work in our lives can be retained more effectively in our hearts by journaling.

Journaling can be a sojourner companion, providing unlimited opportunity to discover treasures within God's Word and yourself. Writing daily during your time with God opens the door to a safe place to record personal experiences, process thoughts, clarify decisions, discover purpose in life, find healing, strengthen faith, and restore joy.

People possess different types of learning styles: auditory, visual, and manipulative. I know for myself that journaling helps me to retain God's Word as I write; I meditate and pray over scripture and lessons. Journals can provide a consistent place to reread what I am learning until it is memorized and meshed into my soul. As a mother of three children, my non-stop lifestyle spins my mind into forgetfulness. I desperately need to write things down to learn well and recall anything.

We have an inside family joke that when I die my family has permission to burn my mountain of journals in a huge blazing bonfire! My life would certainly be an open book at that point! But truly one reason we journal is to leave a legacy of love. Journals are a witness of God's work in a person's life . . . a journey of grace . . . left behind.

Today's Prayer Journal Task

- How do you record the monumental events of the hand of God working in your life?
- Describe how these encounters leave an impression on your soul?
- Are you able to recall in detail significant moments of blessings, joys, and trials, remembering God's grace in your life?
- If not, how can daily journaling help you see your spiritual growth?

Your Sanctuary

For an emerging prayer life and to begin journaling, it takes a step of faith and courage. As you pray and begin to work through the companion journal, I'd like to share further insight on journaling to equip you for the journey. Journaling is a work produced by faith as an object of remembrance.

As we grow to understand and receive God's unfailing, unconditional love, we want to come before him with surrendered hearts—yielding, teachable, and willing to openly share with him our thoughts and concerns through prayer and journaling. Once we experience and see that solitude with God is attainable and beneficial, prayer and journaling come more easily.

Our hurried, busy world is filled with entertainment and constant noise: TVs in every room, computers in our laps, and electronic devises in our ears—iPods, MP3 players, cell phones, and shorthand of texting. With teenagers in the house, at times all of these electronics are sending messages at the same time! We work at jobs in cubicles where no privacy can be found. We are becoming a society that is uncomfortable with solitude. Creating solitude these days is a physical condition free of noise and distraction, but solitude is also a state of mind and heart in which you are comfortable before God. This inner place represents your sanctuary.

Do you have a quiet place to meet God, a quiet place to retreat? Atmosphere is vitally important as you take time to pray, read, and journal. A quiet, calm environment helps to focus your attention on what God may be communicating to you.

As I run for exercise, I discovered I like to go early in the morning. It is quiet with less traffic. Even starting out a half hour later, the traffic starts to distract and agitate me; breathing all the fumes, dodging cars at intersections, and their constant motion zipping by seems to quickly wear me out.

There are parallels between my physical running and my spiritual life. I enjoy praying early in the morning. It is quiet with fewer distractions to interrupt. As a mother, time alone is a rare commodity. The day gets away unless I get up early to read my Bible and pray. "The practice of being still is not easily learned, but it is essential if we are to worship and walk with God effectively. We need to take time on a daily basis to be still before God. The words, 'be still,' create a mental image of focusing on God in complete peace and relaxation without distractions. Reality is that being still before God requires serious concentration on our part."[1] Ask God, "Teach me to be still" and he will.

In the Psalms, David knew the importance of finding a serene place to renew his mind, soul, spirit, and body. Psalm 23 says, "He leads me beside quiet waters, he restores my soul." Meet him at the water's edge to clear your mind and restore your soul.

To begin journaling, locate a peaceful place for your sanctuary—peaceful in every sense—physically, spiritually, emotionally, and mentally. Breathe deeply, clearing your mind and preparing your heart for entering God's presence. Listening is vital with a Bible open and your journal at hand. Remember to take your time; relax, being fully present as the distinguished guest. "Let us not be in a hurry to leave the King's presence" (Eccl. 8:3).

If you are uncomfortable with your surroundings completely quiet, you may enjoy the variety of candle light and music softly playing during your prayer time. "Studies have shown Baroque has a calming effect on the body, is conducive to creativity and learning, and was written as an open doorway to the mystery of God."[2] To enhance my learning, and to seek a tranquil setting, my favorite place, my own personal sanctuary for peace and quiet is my swing underneath my deck. It is secluded with a view of the woods, enormous oak trees, and azaleas blooming in the spring.

By recording your own thoughts and emotions, carefully listening for the condition of your heart, you are caring for yourself and taking time to nurture your soul. Slow down and listen to your inner voice, thoughts, and feelings. These are processed best when they are written down, allowing time for reflection. Listening, journaling, and prayer can be taught, but the breakthroughs and discoveries they lead to depend on the work and consistency of doing them day after day, week after week. Over time a sense of homecoming will be established. Your heart will long for the solitude until it becomes a necessary and integral part of your life.

Be authentic when you write—the sound of your voice thinking. Keep your thoughts aligned with the Word of God for your life. Write what you hear, recording on your paper your immediate thoughts and prayers as if you were speaking them, communicating as directly as possible. Talk to God just as you would to a close friend. Feel free to elaborate without the need to edit your thoughts and prayers. Your journaling does not have to have fancy inspirations, just be real, who you are, and true to yourself and God.

Respond in writing as the Holy Spirit prompts you. Your journal belongs to you. Do not worry about aesthetic standards, grammar, punctuation, or eloquence. Be careful not to make premature judgments concerning your entries. Step by step, one day at a time, you will grow in and through the process of journaling. Just like running, some days you'll have a good run and other days you will think it was awful, but every run has benefits. The more frequently you write the more effective and purposeful your entries will become. The more you journal, the more you can journal, and your enjoyment should begin to grow.

Use the KISS principle—keep it short and simple, date it, write out your prayers, thoughts, words, or verse that touched you deep within. Keep it brief and to the point. "Journal straight from your heart."[3] Pray, asking God to give you understanding as you read a passage of scripture. The Holy Spirit is your Counselor and he will teach you new truths, nuggets to be found when something has penetrated your heart. God's Word does not grow old and deeper understanding can be learned from familiar passages. Be still and listen, and know he is God (Isa. 41:10).

Make journaling your own! Write down your prayers, special quotes, illustrations, and stories that are meaningful to you from favorite authors and speakers. Record lessons that you may be learning from your Bible studies. Write part of a Psalm to praise, a Proverb for direction, or a verse from Ephesians as an antidote for depression.

As you finish working through your prayers for each day, you may have read a scripture that touched your heart or as some say, "jumped off the page." You knew it was personally for you. Write down a few thoughts or write out a prayer relating to the scripture that spoke to you.

God's Word is "alive and active. It penetrates dividing soul and spirit; it judges the thoughts and attitudes of the heart" (Heb. 4:12). God has given us the Holy Spirit to help us understand his Word and what he has freely given us. God's Word through the revelation of the Holy Spirit helps us to correctly evaluate the condition of our hearts, pointing us to the gospel of grace, and results in sanctification. We can trust in God's promise that all Scripture is inspired by God and he will use it to instruct, admonish, and guide us. His Word strengthens and gives us what we need most.

God may draw out feelings, attitudes, motives, or conflicts that need healing. The skill and capacity to listen to God and your own heart is awakened by journaling. Get to the heart of the matter. Expressing your heart, recording God's teachings to you personally—how you feel about those insights—are all a means to discover the many plans God has for you.

If God has repetitively led you to a verse, write it down. Meditate on it, mulling it over in your mind, memorizing it until it is applied in your heart. If you do not understand a scripture, ask him, "What does this verse mean? How can I apply it to my life?" He is the Master Teacher of his Word. God may use another person, a Bible study, or a revelation through his Spirit to provide clarity and direction. Remember scripture is always consistent and supported by other scripture. Be patient. Some revelations may come years after the question.

When you look back over the weeks, months, and years, you will notice the repetitions written down. You will begin to observe a theme or a purpose that God is working in you.

Be creative when you journal.

- Draw pictures if you desire to express yourself.
- Write poetry.
- Draw a symbol of a hand to signify a prayer.
- Put a sunshine around the word "But" when it appears before the word "God" when he overcomes opposition or declares a promise.
- Put a question mark for something you don't understand that you need to come back to ponder. Ask God to show you the answer.
- Place a smiley face representing the joy of seeing God's sense of humor.
- Write "TYL" for Thank You LORD before and after answer to prayer.

- Write "PTL" for Praise the LORD.
- Draw a heart for something you love.
- Draw a tree for areas of growth, new life . . . or a stump when you're being pruned.
- Draw a music note for a song you sang with a few words.
- Draw a bubble around a new truth or scripture revelation. Transfer the scripture verse to a memory index card and place these on a mirror, window seal, or in the car.

Shorter, more frequent entries develop the discipline of journaling. Over time familiarity grows, provoking a greater desire of continuing the daily dialogue with God. The amount of time journaling may lengthen as you grow more comfortable with the discipline. After some experience journaling your thoughts, you will begin to record what is meaningful and significant to you. Details of life, revelations from scripture, memories, responses to life, and your awareness of God's presence can be written in your journal. Journal any time of day that works best for you with the least interruptions. Some days, you may want to come back to your journal entry and add more thoughts, share an experience, lyrics from a song, or a remark from a friend that ministered to your heart.

Given that prayer and journaling are my passions, talking with people about these topics brings me joy. Recently, I spoke with a woman at a speaker's training conference about her journaling experience. She said she just recently reestablished the discipline of journaling. She shared with me some simple questions listed below that might be helpful for anyone who is new or starting to journal again. If you are uncomfortable listing people's names, than implement the idea or use initials. God knows who it is, so you can be free to write.

Take time to be alone with God for prayer, Bible reading and journaling—establish your sanctuary. Only then, will you find a storehouse for everything you need, because all God possesses he shares with us—faith, strength, love, wisdom, and joy! Seek silence, not only to hear or learn from God through the counsel of his Holy Spirit and the reading of his Word, but to possess a renewed, contented Spirit-awareness of his love that you can take with you all day.

Today's Prayer Journal Task

- What are you most grateful for today?
- What are you looking forward to?
- What are you praying for and expecting God to do?
- Is there sin you need to confess?

How Sweet It Is to Be Loved

For we know, brothers loved by God, that he has chosen you.

—1 Thessalonians 1:4

Knowing and believing God is who he said he is through his Word influences every aspect of why and how we respond in prayer. It is actually not so much how, when, where, or even with what eloquent or theological words we use when we pray that is important, but to know to whom we are praying. To know and glorify God are the keys to prayer. It is vitally important to spend time reading God's Word. To know his Word is to know him. His Word is life. God has given his Word as authority to sustain, guide, protect, heal, and set us free. As we pray for circumstances in our lives, his Word helps us trust in his sovereignty and love.

God's love is committed and unconditional. The invitation of God's heart is to his love. God's covenant promises are not only kept to Noah, Abraham, and Moses, but he says to us, *"I love you with an everlasting love."* God showers his love on us through many ways and reveals himself through his creation.

One creation that I am particularly fond of is dogs. Dogs can be loyal creatures that teach us valuable lessons in life. Dogs live in the moment celebrating life's simplicity, balancing play and structure, paying attention to non-verbal cues (most of the time listening since they can't talk back); they don't hold grudges, and function better with a need to contribute by having purpose. One of the greatest lessons my dog has demonstrated is a depiction of God's unconditional love.

THE INVITATION

Five years ago, my oldest daughter, at the age of five, asked for a puppy. My husband and I researched all kinds of dogs. We surveyed many people as to their favorite dog. Most agreed mutts were their favorite because of their disposition and ease of care from not contracting diseases.

After seriously being in prayer concerning the purchase of a dog, I heard James Dobson on a radio talk show share about his dog and how great it is to adopt from a shelter. Then, my Bible study leader started talking about her dog in one of her lessons. She said during the lecture, "I don't know why I am talking about my dog," but I sure knew! I think God cares about every detail. If it concerns you, it concerns him.

At our house, Santa could not deliver a puppy on his sled knowing that Christmas day would be too much of a shock for the puppy, and the fact that our whole household was heading out of town to celebrate. However, within weeks after the holidays we kept our promise and in January we found a short-haired, abandoned mutt which had been brought in with a litter of St. Bernard puppies.

Our little puppy that we named Peanut is anything but a St. Bernard. She is full grown now and weighs eighteen pounds and is a short-haired, brown and tan Terrier-Chihuahua mix. The veterinarians laughed when her adoption papers listed her as a St. Bernard mix.

We all know the saying, "Big things come in small packages." This little dog has taught me some great big lessons about life. First and foremost, how much God loves me! Peanut is my shadow from the moment I get up until I go to bed. She just wants to be with me wherever I am: on the couch, outside in the yard, or in the kitchen under my feet waiting for scraps to fall.

Many days she increases the stress level with her non-stop barking; the incessant door bell ringing bothers her as friends want to come over to play with our children. I can get so mad at her that I begin yelling at her to stop barking as she runs out of the room. Even if chased, she never seems to mind. She comes back wagging her tail—jumping up and down and greets us all with such honor and excitement.

Most dogs surely seem wired to be loving and loyal. This dog has taught me the simplicity and truth of God's love that I need to believe in and receive—even though at times I feel unworthy. God's love is not based on my feelings. He is my shadow, the shade at my right hand. He watches over me. He is ever present and longs for my company wherever I may be at any given time. I am accepted no matter what I look like or what I do. He loves me just because I am me. God is "abounding in love to all who call on him" (Ps. 86:5).

God created you and me as an object of his affection. God pours out his love on us. We were created with hearts that have the ability to love in return. To love, we must believe God exists and sent his Son as an expression of his love so that those who believe in him have life. 1 John 4:9, 15–17 states:

> This is how God showed his love among us: He sent his one and only Son into the world that we might live through him. This is love: not that we loved God, but that he loved us and sent his Son as an atoning sacrifice for our sins. If anyone acknowledges that Jesus is the Son of God, God lives in him and he in God. And so we know and rely on the love God has for us. God is love. Whoever lives in love, lives in God, and God in him. In this way, love is made complete in us so that we will have confidence.

It is amazing, Almighty God, who created the universe and sustains it, wants us to come and accept his love with confidence. God lives in us when we acknowledge that Jesus is the Son of God who was sent into the world as a sacrifice for the payment of our sin, that we might live through him by his Spirit. As we participate in prayer, receive, and believe his love, we surrender our independent hearts and come to know that God is love and all his ways are loving.

Accepting God's immense love for us compels us to pray. God demonstrated his love for us in sending his son as a sacrifice for our sin . . . while we were yet sinners; while we were rejecting, rebelling, and turning our backs on him—while we were nailing Jesus to the cross. He chose to love us. Then, if that's not enough . . . saving us from our sins, Jesus proclaims his love for us when he promises, "I will not leave you as orphans; I will come to you . . . If you remain in me and my words remain in you ask whatever you wish and it will be given you." Jesus says, "'As the Father has loved me, so have I loved you. Now, remain in my love'" (John 14:18, 15:7, 9).

"As the Father has loved (Jesus)? *As* is a tiny word loaded with power. With this same intensity and degree of love God has for Jesus, Jesus loves you and me. The pure, sacrificial love of God the Father and the Son are absolute for eternity.

Why would we not want to receive this kind of love? We are created, designed, and desperate for it. Mankind is hopelessly and eternally condemned without God's grace and love. God's love for his Son is perfect, holy, true, and vast; therefore, so is the love he has for us. It is our responsibility to receive this love.

In our humanness, we attempt to earn God's love and acceptance. At times this complicates and burdens our lives. We receive love when we "come" and "remain"—stay put, soak up the Word, listen, obey, and remember him. Jesus promised, "All that the Father gives me will come to me, and whoever comes to me I will never drive away" (John 6:37).

Even after years of my walk, run, stumble, and skip with God, I am still learning that all of life comes down to this principle of his unfailing love toward us. Whenever I get in a "funk," a less than loving attitude, not enjoying the journey with those around me, and not accepting my mistakes, I must focus on his love to regain contentment and joy.

I often think of a little card from DaySpring that had a simple, sweet message of plucking the daisy petals off the stem. Instead of the words, "He loves me. He loves me not," it said, "He loves me, he loves me still. He loves me. He *really* loves me." This is where my mind must dwell for my heart to follow. For my heart to heal, for my heart to know and rely on this love, is life and peace.

The invitation of God's heart is to grant us with his endless benefits: fellowship, peace, rest, strength, wisdom, protection, help, wholeness, forgiveness, salvation, sanctification, and glorification. God in his compassion calls us, "give ear and come to me; hear me that your soul may live. I will make an everlasting covenant with you, my faithful love promised to David" (Isa. 55:3).

The more we pray, read his Word, listen, and obey, the more we accomplish his purposes. When we respond to God's unfailing love by faith through prayer we grow ever closer to God's heart. Prayer is one of the hardest things to make a priority, seemingly the least thing we do for ourselves and others, but yet the most vital. Begin asking God to show you his love that surpasses anything you have known. Understanding God's immense love for us demonstrated through the covenant of his grace, must come first before we can respond humbly and fervently in prayer. Pray believing! Believe in his love for you and then commit to pray daily "because your (his) love is better than life" (Ps. 63:3). God has not rejected our prayers responding to his invitation or withheld his love from us!

The Sacrifice of Love

As we consider God's unfailing love, this love cannot be separated from acknowledging the gift of his Son. God wants us to recognize and know Jesus. So great is his unfailing love that God sent a part of himself through the form of his only Son, Jesus—whose coming to earth was a sacrifice of love. He gave up his heavenly throne and all the angelic hosts singing praise unto him to come to earth as a human, yet divine. Jesus' entire life on earth, from the moment he was born in a manger, raised with the responsibility of a carpenter's son, serving in a ministry of constant demands, and laying down his life in an appalling death, was not a life of ease.

Throughout Jesus' ministry, he had no place to call home. Jesus' ministry rattled the traditions of the priesthood by not following the laws of the old covenant; but instead healing on the Sabbath, and spending time with the outcasts. He was simply stripping away the customs of religious hypocrites, preparing them for a reformed way of thinking, doing, and being.

Although the authorities protested against Jesus' teachings and claims to be God, whole towns gathered regularly to hear his teaching and many people were brought to Jesus for healing. After giving of himself, Jesus would intentionally get up very early in the morning while it was still dark and go alone to a private place, where he prayed to his Father. Prayer renewed and energized Jesus.

Reaching the end of his earthly ministry, Jesus went as usual to the Mount of Olives to pray. He knelt, crying out to the LORD, earnestly saying, "Father, if you are willing, take this cup from me; yet not my will, but yours be done" (Luke 22:42). Jesus prayed in anguish to the point his sweat was like drops of blood. The sins of the world would be placed upon him who was sinless. God in his mercy sent an angel to minister strength. The strength of love from God the Father took Jesus to the cross and constrained him there.

At the age of thirty-three, Jesus was flogged, mocked, and humiliated by the cruel punishment of crucifixion on the cross. Asphyxiation was usually the cause of death in crucifixion. During the nine hours on the cross Jesus uttered three prayers. The first prayer during the last hours of his life, "My God, my God, why have you forsaken me?" (Mark 15:34). The most heartwrenching pain for both Jesus and God were the moments of separation from each other. More excruciating than the physical pain of suffering was the fact that Jesus bore the wrath of God against all of our sin upon himself. Jesus made a costly sacrifice of love. God's wrath was appeased by love on the cross. His last gasping breaths were prayers offered for us; "Father, *forgive them*, for they do not know what they are doing" (Luke 23:34). With a final prayer of commitment, "Father, into your hands I commit my spirit" (Luke 23:46). Jesus gave up his life for us.

This is sacrificial love. Jesus died—taking the punishment of our offenses, our wrongdoing—so that we could live. The divine exchange—his life for ours. In the midst of excruciating agony, Jesus prays for our forgiveness. All our sin was paid for—our past, present, and future sins. Jesus' death fulfilled the payment required for the need of any other sacrifice. Isaiah prophesized, "Therefore I will give him a portion among the great, and he will divide the spoils with the strong, because he poured out his life unto death, and was numbered with the transgressors. For he bore the sin of many, and made intercession for the transgressors" (Isa. 53:12). Jesus' prayers offered for us were perfumed with the incense of atoning blood.

We previously took a look at the responsibility of the priest in the tabernacle offering sacrifices. The former priest only performed a temporary covering of sin until the true, only spotless Lamb was provided to make the unrighteous, righteous. Jesus is the fulfillment of these symbolic functions. The ministry Jesus established was superior to theirs, the new covenant of grace was "founded on better promises" (Heb. 8:6).

When Christ came he fulfilled the role as our perfect High Priest, he did not enter the heavenly tabernacle by means of the blood offered by animal sacrifice; but he entered the Most Holy

Place by his own blood, shed on the cross, and obtaining eternal redemption for us all.

> How much more powerful then, will the blood of Christ . . . cleanse our consciences from acts that lead to death, so that we may serve the living God! For this reason Christ is the mediator, (the go-between) of a new covenant, that those who are called may receive the promised eternal inheritance—now that he has died as a ransom to set them free from the sins committed under the first covenant.
>
> —Hebrews 9:14–15

In the Old Covenant, the priest's work—of offering the blood of the sacrifice and the fragrant incense—was never finished. It was never enough at the bronze altar; never complete until Jesus became the final sacrifice, the fragrant offering. The perfect bloodshed offered once and for all. The work completed on the cross and the victory of the resurrection over death brings us life and freedom. "But because Jesus lives forever, he has a permanent priesthood. Therefore, he is able to save completely those who come to God through him, because he always lives to intercede for them" (Heb. 7:24–25). To *intercede* means "to meet with a superior in order to plead either for or against another's case, to intervene between parties with a view to reconcile differences, to mediate, to plead or arbitrate on somebody's behalf."[4]

The promise is forever for those who come to God through Jesus. The Amplified version emphasizes complete salvation, "Therefore he is able also to save to the uttermost (completely, perfectly, finally, and for all time and eternity) those who come to God through him (Jesus), since he is always living to make petition to God and intercede with him and intervene for them." He has covered us with grace by his perfect blood and his purified prayers.

Journal Entry April 4, 2001

> Oh LORD, God, I am full of revelation—I am so excited. My cup is overflowing. As I study the book of Hebrews, I am learning about the superiority of Jesus—the final priestly offering, the perfect sacrifice; himself. In Leviticus 16 in the old covenant and old order, the priest took in the bull and goat with the incense (the symbolism of blood and

prayers), a scapegoat was let go. Jesus was the perfect bloodshed offered once and for all.

Without his blood and without his prayers we cannot be saved!

Jesus holds both positions of priest and king simultaneously. "Such a high priest meets our need—one who is holy, blameless, pure, set apart from sinners, exalted above the heavens. Unlike the other high priests, he does not need to offer sacrifices day after day . . . he sacrificed for their sins once and for all when he offered himself" (Heb. 7:26–27). By oath from the living God, Christ was appointed as priest forever. Jesus takes each prayer of ours and presents them perfumed with the incense of his atoning blood.

Jesus not only came to save us from our sins, but God sent Jesus to earth to experience life like us in every way, in order to know how to pray for us and become a sympathetic High Priest in service to God. He himself was tempted and suffered in every way like us, yet he was without sin. Now that he has experienced every situation we would ever face, he is able to help us in our weaknesses.

Jesus Christ, the Righteous One, speaks to Almighty God on our behalf. What grace and comfort to know Jesus is our merciful, faithful, and sympathetic High Priest who totally understands us, knows how to pray for us, and knows how to deliver us.

Before leaving earth, Jesus promises another helper. He comforts his disciples and tells them, ". . . It is for your good that I am going away. Unless I go away, the Counselor will not come to you; but if I go, I will send him to you" (John 16:7). And with that came a promise to receive power when the Holy Spirit comes on you; and that he himself would be in us (Acts. 1:8, John 17:26). Jesus returns to heaven and sends the Holy Spirit so we can know him and communicate with him. Again, we see proof that God intimately desires to interact with us. Invite him in, offering permanent residence in your heart!

What comfort to know we are now encouraged to approach the throne of grace with confidence for our every concern. We no longer need an earthly mediator or priest. Jesus is our great sympathetic High Priest, who sat down at the right hand of the throne of the Majesty in heaven, and who serves in the sanctuary, the true tabernacle set up by the Lord, not by man.

Do you know what Jesus is doing right now? He is praying for you, asking God to fulfill his purpose for your life. Jesus continues to give of his life as he serves us and the Father by interceding for us. He is powerful to completely save, protect, heal, and make you whole, every step of the way. Expositor's Commentary says, "Christ's salvation is a complete deliverance, no matter the need of the sinner."

Jesus, who is the fulfillment of all the Old Testament laws and regulations, came so that those who believe in him by faith would have complete forgiveness of sins. He was sacrificed for our sins so we could enter into the presence of God and no longer need to make atonement for our sin by an animal sacrifice. His perfect blood fulfilled all that God required. The permanent stain of his blood with the heavy scent of cleanliness speaks a powerful word . . . *forgiven*.

Jesus makes available a new covenant of grace to all who believe in him. In the new covenant, God's promises are 'Yes' in Christ. The old covenant was based on external regulations keeping all the law. The new covenant is based on freedom and grace. The old covenant was written on tablets of stone. The new covenant is written on the tablet of our hearts. God no longer desired to dwell in temples made by human hands, but to dwell in our hearts created by his hands, to fulfill the eternal promise to be with us. "In him you are being built together to become a dwelling in which God lives by his Spirit" in your inner being "so that Christ may dwell in your hearts through faith" (Eph. 2:22, 3:17). God has chosen you as his dwelling place.

Jesus always interceded for us whether when he was on earth or now in heaven. Jesus is talking to God about you—he's looking out for your best interest. Jesus loves talking to God about all the present and future plans he has in store for you, his promises to be fulfilled in you. I am confident in this; it will surprise you discovering all that God has planned! "No eye has seen, no ear has heard, no mind has conceived what God has prepared for those who love him" (1 Cor. 2:9).

Prayer is a true expression of sacrificial love. Jesus *lives* to pray for us! There is nothing more profound than to think that after the finished work on the cross and the victory of his resurrection, prayer is Jesus' appointed work, his purpose, and his life in heaven. He lives, thrives, and breathes to pray for us. He prays so that we might live.

Jesus' heart of love models how we are to unceasingly pray. Because Jesus lives to intercede for us, how much more should we live to intercede for others? Job proclaims Jesus as his advocate, friend, and intercessor, "Even now my witness is in heaven; my advocate is on high. My intercessor is my friend as my eyes pour out tears to God; on behalf of a man he pleads with God as a man pleads for his friend" (Job 16:19–21).

Journal Entry March 3, 2001

It has been impressed upon me—I want to be like Jesus! Living to intercede for others. My passion is prayer. This is so good! Freeing! I don't know if this is a real "gift" of the spirit. It is definitely a discipline. Yesterday, I was touched praying for MOMS group. I was blessed—knowing I could intercede on their behalf in my absence.

Beth Moore in *Praying God's Word*—"What a heavy yoke is shattered when we awaken in the morning, bring our hearts, minds and soul and all other 'needs' to the great Soul-ologist, offer him our empty cups, and ask him to then fill them with himself!"

"Let the morning bring me word of your unfailing love."
—Psalm 143:8

"No one is more pleasurable to be around than a person who has had her cup filled by the Lord Jesus Christ!" Enter his rest once again! When I feel empty I need to pray—run to his presence!

I am complete in him. "(I) You have been given fullness in Christ."
—Colossians 2:10

"Teach me to do your will, for you are my God; may your good Spirit lead me on level ground" (Ps. 143:10). Help me be stable, LORD, for my husband and children.

—This too is accomplished by entering his rest.
I hear gently within, "I AM your stability, Sarah."

Jesus models, "This, then, is how you should pray" (Matt. 6:9).

When we pray the Lord's Prayer, we *come*:

1. As God's children   "Our Father in heaven,"
2. As worshippers   "hallowed be your name,"
3. As subjects   "your kingdom come,"
4. As servants   "your will be done"
5. As recipients   "Give us today our daily bread."
6. As sinners   "Forgive us our debts, as we also have forgiven our debtors."
7. As tempted ones   "And lead us not into temptation,"
8. As victorious people   "but deliver us from the evil one."[5]

As we come to God believing and receiving his love, let us receive the covenant of grace through the gift of his Son. Accept and acknowledge the final sacrifice for our sins, once and for all, offered on our behalf. Jesus is the final sympathetic High Priest, the eternal Intercessor who is able to save us completely by his prayers offered with the incense of his atoning blood. Therefore, as he lives to intercede for us as a sacrifice of love, let us follow Jesus. Let us give sacrificially of ourselves, our time, our comfort, and live to pray for others.

Today's Prayer Journal Task

Look back over the first four chapters of this book. God is constantly pursuing you.

How does that change your perception of God in terms of:

- God's invitation and design of you for a life of prayer?
- How God has blessed you through the covenantal promises?
- Describe how God has proven the depth of his desire to meet with you by establishing an earthly tabernacle?
- Praying sacrificially for others?
- Knowing Jesus lives to intercede for you?

Part II

RESPONDING TO THE INVITATION

A QUOTE by F. B. Meyer says, "Let the first moments of the day, when your heart is fresh, be given to God. Do not see the face of man till you have seen the King." God cares about the daily condition of our hearts. The heart is central. It encompasses the most vital part or passion, what we care about the most—our innermost character or feelings. How do we respond to God's invitation to come? We respond through prayer to God's heart of love by faith. Faith is essential to a life of prayer through which we can accomplish God's purposes. Realizing we are designed for a life of prayer, and in that, we discover our purpose. As we clarify God's purpose for our lives, we find ours; it points us to the ultimate goal and, the end to be attained; the eternal companionship of God.

> My heart has heard you say, "Come and talk with me."
> And my heart responds, "LORD, I am coming!"
>
> —Psalm 27:8

"God asks us to be men and women of prayer, people who live close to God, people for whom God is everything and for whom God is enough. That is the root of peace."[1] Forever God has made an effort to dwell with us. By his grace, we begin to understand our entire purpose for existence; to grow in an intimate, vibrant, and reverent relationship with God and people.

Addressing our sinful independence, Jesus says, "You refuse to come to me to have life" (John 5:40). God makes it straightforward for us who would choose to believe in his Son; he gives us the gift of the Holy Spirit that settles in our hearts and makes a home there.

May your response to the invitation into the King's presence be one that is full of anticipation saying, "Yes! Yes, I'll come."

As we meet and talk with God it is so good to be known by him and to know him. To know him is to love him. "He will hear (you) for he is compassionate" (Exod. 22:27). As you take time to pray, read, and obey his Word, I am confident in God's promise, just as he was with Moses, so he will meet with you, but now much more so—face to face. All of us who have had the veil removed can see God is a personal presence, a living, life-giving Spirit, who—makes us more and more like him, changed into his glorious image (2 Cor. 3:18).

Principles are shared in the following chapters to enhance our understanding of God's invitation and our response through prayer, aided by journaling. Prayer's purpose is beyond total human comprehension and understanding by our finite minds. May these concepts help motivate you to begin praying and journaling along with reading God's Word, and most importantly, increase your desire for a more intimate relationship with God. God is waiting for you to walk through the doorway of faith—the doorway of no regrets!

R. S. V. P.—Your *First* Response to the Invitation

As you read this book you may have questions about your assurance of being saved and possessing eternal life. Your prayer of salvation is the most critical prayer of all. It is the most important decision you will ever make. This prayer is the vital response to the invitation from God to "Come."

- **A**dmit that you are a sinner, first.
  "For the wages of sin is death, but the gift of God is eternal life in Christ Jesus our Lord" (Rom. 6:23).
- **B**elieve Christ died for your sins.
  Jesus answered, "I am the way and the truth and the life. No one comes to the Father except through me" (John 14:6). "But God demonstrates his own love for us in this: While we were still sinners, Christ died for us" (Rom. 5:8).
- **C**ommit your life and future to Jesus Christ.
  "For everyone who calls on the name of the Lord will be saved" (Rom. 10:13).

A-B-C . . . Have you made this commitment?

Why not invite Jesus now to be your Savior, Redeemer, and Friend? Pray and confess in a simple prayer like this:

- LORD, I confess I am a sinner.
- I believe Jesus died for all my sins on the cross.
- I receive his forgiveness and I am now clean.
- I believe he was raised from the dead and is coming back, again.
- I now commit my life to you. Come Lord Jesus, and dwell within my heart.
- Fill me with your Holy Spirit.
- Thank you for saving me.
- In Jesus name, Amen.

If you have prayed this prayer for the first time, commit to seeking fellowship at a Bible teaching church and tell someone who can help you grow spiritually that you made this decision.

CHAPTER 5

ENTER THROUGH
THE DOOR OF FAITH

I Thessalonians 1:2–4, I pray for you reading this book, *I (we) always thank God for all of you mentioning you in (our) my prayers. I continually remember before our God and Father your work produced by faith, your labor prompted by love, and your endurance inspired by hope in our Lord Jesus Christ. For we know, brothers loved by God, that he has chosen you* . . .

THE FIRST COMPONENT the Israelites possessed as they built the tabernacle was faith. Their continual participation to work in the tabernacle by bringing sacrificial and fragrant offerings demonstrated trust in the promise of God's presence. Faith is the basis by which we respond to the invitation and pray. Prayer is an expression of our faith.

Communicating with God through prayer is a *work produced by faith*. Like any relationship that we value, it takes time and energy communicating for it to grow. Love takes effort. This *work* of prayer is energy released and puts power in motion. Work is sustained physical, mental, or spiritual effort to overcome obstacles or achieve an objective or result. This work produced by faith in prayer is having a belief or state of mind and heart in which trust or confidence is placed in God's promises. This labor is prompted by our love for God and from that love flows a desire to be obedient to his command to pray. Our endurance to continue in prayer is inspired by hope in our Lord Jesus Christ.

This *work* of prayer is accomplished by grace and strength by the Holy Spirit. Prayer is a step of faith in the unseen realm. We have not seen Jesus, but we believe in the testimony of the Bible and those whose spirits have identified with his Spirit. Jesus said to doubting Thomas, "Blessed are those who have not seen and yet believed" (John 20:29). We cannot worship God in truth without his Spirit.

As we surrender our hearts to Jesus, it is a promise that his Spirit will come and dwell within us. But we must be careful to continue to build our faith by reading his Word and to keep praying. Faith requires action motivated by love. Our prayers count when they are offered in love by faith to the LORD alone; otherwise, they are empty words (Gal. 5:6).

As I explore the realm of running for exercise, I am learning so much about myself and my "run" with God. It takes an effort to reap the benefits. It's a choice I make each day. Spending time daily in prayer and Bible reading is just like my need for water while I am running. I need to re-hydrate myself for endurance, or my body will shut down. I have discovered that my body cries out for water and oxygen to drink in deep. As I parallel the thought of spiritually trying to live without prayer, I realize I need more of God. It is like taking a deep breath on my runs, relaxing and sustaining, inhaling, breathing in more of Jesus, "The LORD's anointed our very life breath!" (Lam. 4:20), and exhaling, breathing out less of me. Our prayers are like breathing as we take every thought and concern to him, filtering them with Spirit and truth, to disclose for his glory.

Prayer often sets the pace for my life. When I am rushed with demands in life, prayer is what keeps the tempo of my heart at a healthy pace so I can survive. Prayer prevents me from getting too far behind, or too eager to move ahead. There is a calm assurance entering his presence each day that I can do this "thing" called life because he is by my side. He is with me. He is what my body thirsts for spiritually. A simple quote that puts prayer in perspective says, "You can accomplish more in one hour with God than one lifetime without him." We need to believe—prayer is a holy work.

There is a story in the Old Testament when the LORD heard the Israelites complaining to Moses as they were traveling from place to place as the LORD had commanded. They stopped to camp, but there was no water for the people to drink. The Israelites were no longer walking in the footsteps of faith. So they grumbled and quarreled with Moses and said, "Give us water to drink . . . Is the LORD among us or not?" (Exod. 17:7).

Then Moses cried out to the LORD asking him what he was to do with these discontented people. The Lord answered Moses and instructed him to walk on ahead and to take his staff. God was with Moses by a rock at Horeb and said, "Strike the rock, and water will come out of it for the people to drink" (Exod. 17:6) Moses simply obeyed.

Journal Entry Sept. 10, 2002

"He opened the rock and water gushed out; like a river it flowed in the desert."

—Psalm 105:41

Thank you, LORD, for giving me an analogy for this verse—the rock being our "hard" times. You are there—working-flowing-gushing out of our lives through the hard circumstances. You are alive and working to use the hard times to make me (us) depend on you, to trust you, seek you, and most of all to glorify you. You send the LIVING Water that fills and flows into our desert. You provide in our desert times. I am finally putting this past year together. What are you doing in my life, LORD? It seems to come down to one word. FREEDOM. To get to the *who* I am in Christ—healing my identity and embracing the "me" in me!—Free of the bondage of comparing, of "doing" to please others, free of what I think people think I should do. The "rock" being this hard place I am in—learning to be free to be me.

Help me walk in obedience to what you put on my heart—willing to say, "Yes, LORD" with freedom to be me. I am accepted in the beloved, no matter what I do or do not do! Thank you, LORD, for the "rock" you have placed in my life.

When life gets difficult, I think it is easier to be more like the Israelites, moaning and complaining, instead of deciding to first—believe God is with me and pray. Deep effectual prayer is hard work. God invites us to cry out to him with our complaints and he will answer. The Israelites drank from the spiritual rock that God provided for them in their desert. The living water accompanied them, and that rock was a foreshadowing of Christ. In the New Testament, Jesus says, "To him who is thirsty I will give to drink without cost from the spring of the water of life" (Rev. 21:6).

Jesus proclaimed himself as the living water who quenches our spiritual thirst. As we drink from the Rock and as we abide in him, we will be satisfied. By faith through the provision of prayer our thirst will be quenched, allowing the Spirit to flow through us to love and bless others.

Journal Entry Aug. 28, 1987 In Peru with South American Missions

We made it home from our first river trip on the tributaries of the Amazon. Our boat got stuck on the dry river bed due to the draught. To get to our destination we walked through the jungle this morning for two hours! I loved the adventure. It was muddy and there were beautiful huge trees. Our leader had a machete and he hacked his way through the tall grass as we followed behind. It was so hot and we were all thirsty. Out of the bushes appeared a little girl. She carried with her an armful of beautiful large luscious pink grapefruits! We split them among the group. The juice and flavor was the most refreshing taste quenching my thirst; God's provision in perfect proportion to our need!

When I returned to camp Psalm 16:11 was on a package I received from the states. "You have made known to me the path of life; you will fill me with joy in your presence, with eternal pleasures at your right hand." The LORD is teaching me there is joy in the simple things, the joy of a simple grapefruit.

For us to respond to the invitation, to drink of him is a step of faith. To take a drink is a simple analogy, but Jesus used it so all men could understand the principle, "Come to me." He invites us to live and be satisfied. Without the basic need of the living water being met in us, there is neither life nor joy. Through prayer (and scripture) our thirst is quenched.

Today's Prayer Journal Task

- Where do you see that "the Lord is among us" today?
- When you enter the door by faith, how does complaining hinder the work of prayer?
- What "rock" has God placed into your life that you can thank him for?
- Look for the simple things along life's path. What brings you joy?

Access to Grace

May a spirit of thanksgiving rise in our hearts, as we comprehend the covenant of grace given to us through the gospel; the purest demonstration of God's unfailing love. Love covers us by his grace and allows us to come into his presence through the sacrifice of his Son. Recalling the Old Testament tabernacle when the priest offered a pure sacrifice for the sins of the people, then cleansing with water in the bronze basin, no one could enter God's presence and live without meeting his sacred standards. Now by the provision of his grace, we are given the privilege to come anytime, at any moment, without fear of death because of the new covenant given to us through the gracious gospel of Christ. "And that's not all. You will have complete and free access to God's Kingdom, keys to open any and every door: no more barriers between heaven and earth, earth and heaven (Matt. 16:19 MSG). Let us not quickly forget the sacrifice Jesus made so that we could live with him forever.

There is an insurance commercial showing a father pushing his preschool son on the swing. In the last push, the son comes back on the swing as a teenager. As he swings back, he slams into the father and knocks the father down. The ad says, "Life comes at you fast . . ." I laugh because it is true.

Trials come into our lives and the lives of those we love so quickly that in our fleshly responses we forget the gospel. When "this" hard circumstance seems to arbitrarily interrupt my life, I repeat a little saying that brings my heart back to the truth of the gospel. "For 'this' Jesus came. For 'this' Jesus died. For 'this' Jesus lives to intercede!" It gives me a quick reminder of the suffering Jesus endured—entrusting himself to God for his glory, and I should do the same. My hope is restored knowing he is praying me through "this" hard circumstance.

Jesus paid a tremendous price to have a relationship with us, covering our lives by the power of his blood and his prayers. That is amazing grace!

One of the lessons I am learning while writing this book is his grace works in us that which is pleasing to him. When I was lacking confidence, I had to memorize scripture to help me finish this book. ". . . he said to me, 'My grace is sufficient for you, for my power is made perfect in weakness.' Therefore, I will boast all the more gladly about my weaknesses, so that Christ's power may rest on me" (2 Cor. 12:9). The word *rest* here in the Hebrew is *episkenoo*, meaning to spread a tabernacle over or cover.[1] He spreads is sufficient grace over us like a prayer shawl.

Do you believe God's grace is sufficient for you to experience the power of prayer? Many of us do not truly understand grace. Grace is the power of God to change us. It allows God to accomplish through us what we cannot do by ourselves. Be careful of statements, "Praying is just too hard!" or "I am just not comfortable praying." God frequently leads us to places that are hard and uncomfortable because he wants to exert his strength in us for his glory. We need to be careful we are thinking properly about prayer and receive the grace extended to us beyond measure.

We often lack conviction that prayer is valuable. In our human fallen nature, we are people of "immediate gratification." When we do not see the results of our prayers right away, we too easily quit, or attempt to get by with the least amount of work or time spent in prayer. We value other things as more important. Sometimes we may think we can earn our own merit and get prayers answered by doing good deeds instead of trusting for God's grace. Pray to grow in grace, trusting God's provision to enter his presence. The simplicity of a childlike trust in a loving

Father characterizes the believer who lives by grace rather than striving for perfection.

When we feel inadequate in our own ability to pray, it is a good thing. It is a humble place to be. His power is more obviously manifested through our weaknesses. We have access to the same power that raised Jesus from the dead. "And his incomparably great power (is) for us who believe. That power is like the working of his mighty strength, which he exerted in Christ when he raised him from the dead and seated him at his right hand in the heavenly realms" (Eph. 1:19–20). For us who believe, we have his power and authority.

By grace we, too, have been saved and raised with Christ and seated with him in the heavenly realms (Eph. 2:6). This is the position God designed of a believer's life of prayer before time began. The Apostle Paul writes,

> But join with me in suffering for the gospel, by the power of God, who has saved us and called us to a holy life— not because of anything we have done but because of his own purpose and grace. This grace was given us in Christ Jesus before the beginning of time, but it has now been revealed through the appearing of our Savior, Jesus Christ, who has destroyed death and has brought life and immortality to light through the gospel.
>
> —2 Tim 1:8b–10

Jesus knows our struggles with prayer, our lack of desire for prayer, our fears, insecurities, and our excuses. When we pray with open hearts and hands to receive God's abundant provision of grace, he enables us in all things at all times, and in every way, having all that we need, we will accomplish good works . . . which includes praying! (2 Cor. 9:8).

To choose to believe that we "grow in grace" and that "our hearts are strengthened by grace" is living by faith and confidence in his power working in us (Heb. 13:9 , 1 Pet. 3:18). "Grace is the majesty, the freedom, the unreservedness, the newness, and the arbitrariness in which a relationship to God and therefore, the possibility of knowing him is opened up to man by God himself . . . Grace is God's good pleasure."[2]

God promised to the Israelites, "I will pour out on the house of David and the inhabitants of Jerusalem a spirit of grace and supplication" (Zech. 12:10). By faith we believe and receive God's abundant provision of grace. "Now I commit you to God and to the word of his grace, which can build you up and give you an inheritance among all those who are sanctified" (Acts 20:32). Grace is knowing that Almighty God is able to make voluntarily available to all of us his provision of all of himself, any part, at any time, for any need.

As we remember the Old Testament symbols when the Israelites received the manna, we see in the New Testament Jesus fulfills the promise of his presence when he said to them, "I tell you the truth, it is not Moses who has given you the bread from heaven, but it is my Father who gives you the true bread from heaven. The bread of God is he who comes down from heaven and gives life to the world" (John 6:32–33). God has given us Jesus, the bread of life. Savor the bread of his Presence. Through the Son, through the Word, he "gives us each day our daily bread" (Luke 11:3). His provision for your every need is accessible. Because of what God has done we have the privilege to "approach the throne of grace with confidence, so that we may receive mercy and find grace to help us in our time of need" (Heb. 4:16). God's unlimited provision of himself is our grace for the journey.

To understand God's grace as an expression of his love totally changes the way I relate to him, myself, and others. His grace is unmerited, divine assistance, acceptance, and forgiveness to an unworthy recipient based only on his love.

Both in prayer and in life, to trust God is to relax in his gracious love and acceptance with a childlike faith. Until we know him who made us, we will not receive the full revelation of ourselves. By God's grace we can accept ourselves and our prayers as an act of faith created with human limitations, yet designed to grow in godly virtue. Self-acceptance of your individuality in your prayer life brings an established peace.

As I work with a ministry to young moms at my church, my heart goes out to the young parents with babies and toddlers. They are thrust into instant denial of self, not having a single free moment to meet their own needs. Time alone is a rarity, much less finding time to pray.

Prayer is the greatest responsibility we have as parents and grand-parents. God does not require you to set aside an hour for daily prayer, although it is a healthy goal. When time allows snatch five to ten minutes to pray and know it is a season. Pray in the shower, pray at the park, or while you're doing the dishes or folding the laundry. Extend grace to yourself because God extends it to you. One of my favorite verses when my children were young and it continues to be while they enter their teen years is found in Isaiah 40:11. It gives me comfort that Jesus understands a mother's (parent's or grandparent's) heart. "He tends his flock like a shepherd: He gathers the lambs in his arms and carries them close to his heart; he gently leads those that have young." He knows our hearts and our circumstances. He gently restores our souls. ". . . he gives us more grace!" (James 4:6).

Do you extend the grace and forgiveness that you have received to yourself and others? Our prayers have the capability of making a difference concerning the grace we breathe on ourselves and others. "He has delivered us . . . On him we have set our hope that he will continue to deliver us, as you help us by your prayers. Then many will give thanks on our behalf for the gracious favor granted us in answer to the prayers of many" (2 Cor. 1:10–11). Giving grace to others through our unconditional love and prayers gives God glory.

God's love is so perfect that he planned from the beginning of time for us to be able to have complete access to him by grace without fear. God fulfilled his highest standard through the sacrifice of his Son, covering our sins by his blood and prayers so that we can live in constant communion with him. Unlike earthy kings, God's scepter is forever raised. Enter into his presence by grace to worship.

Today's Prayer Journal Task

- How are you more aware of God's covenant of grace?
- How can the grace of God's sufficiency and power change your prayer life?
- Ask God to pour out on you a "spirit of grace and supplication."

You Are a Royal Priesthood

GOD DELIGHTS IN our communion and he accomplishes a great work in us, equipping us to be participants of his kingdom and priesthood forever. Remember when God established his earthly dwelling and tabernacle, the role of the priests who served in the temple, offering sacrifices, incense and prayers were sanctified, separated, and holy unto the LORD.

In the New Covenant of grace we are a royal and holy priesthood. As we grasp our true identity in Christ the King, we accept our identity as an heir and coheir of the royal household of heaven. "But you are a chosen people, a royal priesthood, a holy nation, a people belonging to God, that you may declare the praises of him who called you out of darkness into his wonderful light" (1 Pet. 2:9). You are chosen, a royal priesthood! With Jesus, you are an intercessor.

Our hands are designed for more than texting and typing buttons on a cell phone, changing channels on a remote control, and scrolling screens on a computer. We were designed to be a royal priesthood:

- To lift our hands in praise and prayer
- To invite others into the house of God
- To release the captive
- To touch the hurting with healing
- To consecrate our hands to God by serving others

The most powerful moment in the gospel showing God's love and grace occurred when Jesus died on the cross as the Lamb that was slain, the final sacrifice. Remember in the temple the high priest could only enter behind the veil or curtain once a year—the curtain separating the Holy of Holies was three inches thick. At the moment Jesus died, the curtain was torn as a visual phenomenon; the ending of the old covenant and the beginning of a new covenant. From that moment in history, every man, woman, and child is welcome to enter the Holy of Holies by faith in the blood of the Lamb. You are invited to come and hear directly from God. No longer do you need to hear from the priests, prophets, and pastors what the Lord has to say to you. Grace grants you free access into the Holy of Holies.

> Therefore, brothers, since we have confidence to enter the Most Holy Place by the blood of Jesus, by a new and living way opened for us through the curtain, that is, his body, and since we have a great priest over the house of God, let us draw near to God with a sincere heart in full assurance of faith, having our hearts sprinkled to cleanse us from a guilty conscience and having our bodies washed with pure water.
>
> —Hebrews 10:19–22

Do you believe the LORD has set you apart as a holy priesthood to offer your worship and life as a living sacrifice? As you come to Christ, the living foundation of God's temple, be assured you have been cleansed and stand unblemished before the LORD. You are a living stone that God is building into his spiritual temple. You are serving as his holy priest when you pray. Only through the mediation of Jesus Christ, incensed by his atoning blood, can we offer spiritual sacrifices that please God (1 Pet. 2:4–5).

What are our spiritual sacrifices? "The sacrifices of God are a broken spirit, a broken and contrite heart" (Ps. 51:17). Sacrifices offered now are our hearts surrendered, prayers offered and service to him by faith, especially those done sacrificially. Even when we are feeling blue or blah "in the belly of a whale" we can choose along with Jonah to sing with a thankful heart. "I, with a song of thanksgiving, will sacrifice to you" (Jon. 2:9). As we sing praise our focus and spirits are lifted. Music penetrates the senses and the words often remain embedded in our hearts and minds for years. One song in particular I sing daily as I commit my day to the LORD.

Live in Me

Live in me. Love through me.
I give to you my body. A living sacrifice,
Holy acceptable to Thee.

(*Chorus*)
I abide in you, LORD
And you abide in me
I am the branch and you're the vine
You give life to me
Such a mystery, how can it be
That in vessels of clay,
You choose to display
Your glory?

Hide me LORD, deep in you
Shield me I pray from all who pursue me.
Draw me in safe under your wings
Whom shall I fear, if you are my dwelling? (*Chorus*)[3]

Our hearts and our prayers are the continuing sweet fragrance that minister to the heart of God. Know that "he whose walk is blameless will minister to him" (Ps. 101:6). We minister to the heart of God! Your walking through the doors of grace brings God joy.

The tender words written in a love story from the Song of Songs, often taught from a perspective of God's heart toward us as his bride, say, "You have stolen my heart, my sister, my bride; you have stolen my heart with one glance of your eyes . . . How delightful is your love, my sister, my bride! How much more pleasing is your love than wine, and the fragrance of your perfume than any spice!" (Song of Sol. 4:9–10). As we pray honestly, and live with integrity, we are a delightful aroma to God. God knows our hearts and in contrast, scripture compares a proud and deceitful heart to the stench from an open grave.

God jealously longs for his Spirit to live in us. Our time of worship is not only for what we receive and get out of it, but it is a time to give of ourselves and spend time loving God. As we meet with him, "Our goal should not be joy, or peace or even blessing, but God himself" (author unknown).

Can you imagine Aaron and the priests of the tabernacle, dressed in their sacred garments, singing as they worshiped and worked in the tabernacle? We have much to celebrate and sing about; we are now clothed in the righteousness of our Lord Jesus Christ! "For he has clothed me with garments of salvation and arrayed me in a robe of righteousness" (Isa. 61:10). We are to receive and believe the transformation by clothing ourselves with the Lord Jesus Christ (Rom. 13:14). Daily remember to clothe yourself with righteousness, "since God chose you to be the holy people he loves, you must clothe yourselves with tenderhearted mercy, kindness, humility, gentleness, and patience" (Col. 3:12 NLT).

Offering spiritual sacrifices means we lay down our desires to take time to intercede for others, especially those who are hard to love and forgive. We need to "present everyone perfect in Christ;" to see them as God sees them. This is the goal, the end to be obtained with all his energy which so powerfully works in us (Col. 1:28–29). Look for reasons to be thankful for them in your life even if God is using them as a sharpening stone.

As we come before him in the new covenant, remember the altar of incense, "we are to God the aroma of Christ" (2 Cor. 2:15). Every person has a diverse scent, a unique fragrance, an essence of him. The foreshadowing in the depiction of the incense burning continually day and night is a beautiful illustration of the sacrificial offering of our lives, intermingled with our prayers that never cease. Your life of prayer, of constant communion, your worship and praise is a sweet aroma, pleasing to God. Our hearts and prayers offered in his presence are means to a glorious future without end.

> *Journal Entry May 23, 2001*
>
> Help me be an example to my kids and let them see Jesus in me.
>
> Let me be a sweet AROMA to them. As we learned for family night—a fragrance of the knowledge of him by living out the acronym:
>
> A—affection
> R—respect
> O—order
> M—merriment
> A—affirmation[4]

"Build an altar" of prayer in your home to bring a sweet fragrance to God. Spend a few minutes a day praying together as a family or with friends, and once a week commit to an extended time of prayer. God asked Moses to "anoint them (the priests' sons) just as you anointed their father, so they may serve me as priests. Their anointing will be to a priesthood that will continue for all generations to come" (Exod. 40:15). This priestly anointing continues in our generation as it did with Moses. Our anointing comes by the power of the Holy Spirit to those who believe. Ask for more of the Holy Spirit to teach you to live a life of uninterrupted communion.

God wants to pour out his anticipatory love as he unfolds his plans in our lives. "In the presence of the King don't ask for small gifts."[5] God gives generously beyond our imagination to all who call on him. His Spirit empowers us to have faith, creates in us the desire to know more of God through his Word, and guides us in the ability to pray according to God's will. With all God's heart and soul, he rejoices over us, and desires to bring blessing into our lives just as he promised.

God accepts you as a fragrant incense; a scent of satisfaction to his heart (Ezek. 20:41). Jesus ". . . loves us and has freed us from our sins by his blood, and has made us to be a kingdom and priests to serve—to him be glory and power forever and ever! Amen" (Rev. 1:5b–6). Thank God for giving you permanent access as an intercessor-priest of God by grace through Jesus Christ!

A Labor Prompted by Love

Once we respond in prayer with a surrendered heart to a *work produced by faith*, we simultaneously develop a *labor prompted by love*. Prayer is a labor of love. As many of us have experienced, prayer does not always come easily. As we sacrifice our time and our conveniences to pray for others, God is glorified. By interceding, our prayers offered to Christ for others, become a covering, a shield—"love covers a multitude of sins" (1 Pet. 4:8). God warned the priests to guard themselves in their spirit and not break their faith in their wholehearted devotion and reverent example as priests; they were messengers of his covenant of love. We now are priests and ministers of a new covenant inviting people to come near to God and enter in his presence.

Jesus often labored in the work of unseen prayer. I believe most of Jesus' prayers were intercessory. "Who is he who condemns? Is it Christ who died, and furthermore is also risen, who is even at the right hand of God, who is also interceding for us" (Rom. 8:34). When Jesus returned to his Father's right side in heaven, he chose to place his high priestly role as intercessor at the forefront: As Jesus fulfills the role of King and Savior, "far above all rule and authority, every power and dominion, and every title that can be given" (Eph. 1:21), he also chose to be called an Intercessor.

Unfortunately, some people doubt the effect of intercessory prayer. Prayer can falsely be perceived as unproductive and accomplishing little. If prayer does not accomplish a great deal and change hearts and circumstances within the world in which we live, then why did Jesus, the most powerful authority ever to live on earth, choose the vocational title of Intercessor? It's hard to imagine Jesus taking his seat at the Father's right hand and wasting time.

We are also called to this labor; love prompts us to have a selfless heart when we pray. Can you comprehend that Jesus took the eternal task of interceding on our behalf? Exemplified in his life, Jesus knew the power of prayer. To be transformed into his likeness, we must believe and practice the power of prayer. Believing that Jesus lives within us, we possess Jesus' power and authority. Jesus longed for others to be participants of that power and invited others to intercede.

During Jesus' last hours of life on this earth, surrendering his will was difficult. He asked the disciples to stay awake nearby. Later, when he found the disciples sleeping, he asked, "Could you not keep watch with me for one hour?" Jesus gave some final instructions to strengthen the disciples, "Stay awake and pray so that you won't enter into temptation. The Spirit is willing; but the flesh is weak" (Matt. 26:41 HCSB). Prayer was the key to resist temptation, but it's the staying awake part that I always battle too.

During Jesus' earthly ministry, scripture tells us that Jesus labors in love, praying for his disciples and all believers. Even after Jesus left his perfect heavenly home to come to earth and be sacrificed for (our) sins ". . . once for all when he offered himself" (Heb. 7:27); in prayer he continues to make a sacrifice of love for us.

Effective relationships require sacrifice. To pray fervent, effectual prayers for someone is a sacrifice of time, love, and energy. It is a true form of denying ourselves and thinking of others first. Other than the prayers of praise and thanksgiving offered directly to God, intercessory prayer possesses purity and virtue that transcends all other forms of prayer by demonstrating self-less care for others.

Is your life a life of prayer fully committed to praying as the Holy Spirit leads? Spending time in prayer on the behalf of others satisfies your soul. Let us be found faithful instead of "sleeping" spiritually, "for the eyes of the LORD range throughout the earth to strengthen those whose hearts are fully committed to him" (2 Chron. 16:9).

Love is a choice of the will and Jesus demonstrated this perfectly. Setting prayer as a priority is making a choice to love. To be intentional and plan to pray is being committed to loving others and yourself. The more you pray, the more your love increases for God and others. Camaraderie among those you intercede for becomes stronger through prayer.

If Jesus lives to pray for us, then truly he is thinking of us, always pouring out his heart of love talking to God about us. If we examine our prayer lives, what we tend to think and pray about pertains to our own circumstances, or deliverance from our problems. Continually praying for others is a sure way to get our mind from being preoccupied with ourselves and focus on the needs of others. The unseen work of prayer is a labor of love. Our joy is made complete as we follow Jesus and give of our lives by praying for others.

Journal Entry June 12, 2000

LORD, I've come to realize after tension in my relationship with my husband, getting short with my daughter, resisting to see my neighbors or calling my friends, that I am not loving anyone!

What am I saved for if I am not loving others? Just eternal life—for myself?! How selfish! I really am in a pit right now—I feel like I'm going through the motions, but not with real genuine love.

"Be imitators of God, therefore, as dearly loved children and live a life of love, just as Christ loved us and gave himself up for us as a fragrant offering and sacrifice to God" (Eph. 5:1–2).

> Help me, LORD, to have a deep genuine love for people, overflowing love that is a fragrance to you and to them of Christ Jesus in me!
>
> Numbers 14:18 God's love—"abounding and forgiving sin"
>
> "Love your neighbor as yourself" (Matt. 22:39). If I did that—that would be great!
>
> God's love—the source, not withholding, endures forever, merciful, tender, unfailing, reaches the heavens, priceless!

Jesus labors in love, praying for his disciples. He shares with them his glory. He prays for their protection from evil and for their unity of being one mind, spirit, and purpose. He prays for the full measure of their joy. This joy is found in self-abandonment as they lay down their lives, in praying for and serving others. He prays for their sanctification, blessing, and perfection accomplished through exposure to his truth. He prays for their reception into the world (John 17:6–19).

Jesus labors in love, praying for all believers. He prays for us to believe in him, to be completely unified as the Father and the Son to let the world know God sent him. Jesus shares with us his glory and declares he lives in us who believe, that he has loved us since before the creation of the world. Jesus prays that this love God has for Jesus, this same love be in us. Remember Jesus prayed for us at his most crucial moment in life, at the height of his suffering, at his death on the cross. As he offered himself as the final sacrifice, physically and spiritually, he cried out in agony yet with authority and prayed for us, "Father, forgive them, for they do not know what they are doing" (Luke 23:34).

Jesus knows the spiritual battle looming around us. What hope we can possess knowing Jesus is praying on our behalf while we are naive about the eternal ramifications. As we see when Jesus prayed for Peter, he said, "Simon, Simon, Satan has asked to sift you as wheat. But I have prayed for you, Simon, that your faith may not fail. And when you have turned back, strengthen your brothers" (Luke 22:31–32). What reassurance and comfort to know Jesus is constantly praying for us!

Are you investing in your decisions with a selfless heart in the work of prayer? Sometimes Jesus denies himself much needed rest to pray. When he needed to make a decision, Luke says, "Jesus went out to a mountainside to pray, and spent the night praying to God. When morning came, he called his disciples to him and chose twelve of them, whom he also designated apostles" (Luke 6:12–13). Our decision-making skills can be affected by the pressures of life, often resulting in the negligence of prioritizing rest. Let us follow Jesus' example to discern of our need to rest and pray over our decisions that will have eternal influence and impact others.

Job left us another wonderful example of a selfless, sacrificial prayer for his friends who encouraged Job to turn his back against God. God said, "My servant Job will pray for you, and I will accept his prayer and not deal with you according to your folly. You have not spoken of me what is right, as my servant Job has" (Job 42:8).

From a wounded and hurt soul, Job in his suffering, after losing all that he loved and owned, prayed for his spiritually blind friends. He did not only pray for himself, but lifted up his face in obedience while extending forgiveness. God honored his prayer of sacrifice along with his burnt offering. After Job prayed with a sacrificial heart of love for his friends, the LORD made him prosperous again and doubled his blessings.

Leave a Legacy of Love

DO YOU WANT to know God intimately? Do you truly believe God loves you and wants to communicate with you? Then take a step through the door of faith and spend time with him in a quiet place. He has profound thoughts to share with you. Is God's message to you important enough for you to write it down so you will remember? God actually says, "Keep my commands and you will live; guard my teaching as the apple of your eye. Bind them on your fingers; write them on the tablet of your heart" (Prov. 7:2–3). Journal so that God's Word is more effectively written on the tablet of your heart. Journal in order to pass on a godly legacy to the next generation.

Spending time in prayer and reading God's Word is vital to experience intimacy; journaling helps us in that process. As in the same reference to prayer, I want to reemphasize in the aspect of journaling, honestly expressing who you are before God and what you are thinking or feeling brings liberation, healing, and growth. When you pray humbly, believe you can obtain a depth of relationship that grows beyond your expectation. Believe that you are fully known and fully loved by God!

Are you comfortable expressing to God that you love him? Do you trust him with the concerns of your heart? Write out a prayer in your journal and honestly tell God your thoughts about him. Dare to ask him to reveal more of himself to you.

If we are not comfortable telling God we love him then we need to spend more time getting to know him and his immense love for us through prayer, his Word, and journaling. I wasn't always comfortable telling God, "I love you."

One of my dear friends has unknowingly impressed upon me the importance of expressing my love to God in my prayer life. My friend, of fourteen years, has had a degenerative eye disease since birth. She has persevered through many trials of daily living, activities that you and I take for granted like driving a car, reading recipes, watching TV, and going to the grocery store. She has tried several treatments that resulted in little improvement of her eyesight. I look at her life and I am inspired by the fact that I have never seen nor heard words of complaint or grumbling.

There are several new technologies which enable her to read, study her Bible, and listen to her e-mails (and my book), and I still gaze in amazement of her grateful attitude. With two teen-age boys, maintaining her home, cooking, teaching visually disabled adults, and recently going on her first mission trip, her purpose and confidence does not wane. She always ends her prayers in the sweet words, "We love you, LORD."

How does she do that? My friend lives by grace—surrendering to God. Hearing her pronounce her love for God each time we prayed, drove me to examine my heart, to search the reason I felt uncomfortable saying the same sentiments, much less out loud. The realization came to me that my humble friend knew the great depth of the love of God in her suffering. She was thrust into a place of complete dependence, and she found God faithful.

Please understand that this love takes time. How can you love someone you do not know? Seek to know him and his extravagant love will woo your heart. To love the LORD our God with all our heart, soul, mind, and strength—that is our goal and glory. There is no better way to show our love than when we obey the greatest and first commandment. We should strive to know and believe God through his Word, communicate with him through prayer, respond in obedience to his will and purpose, and remember his commands and his work in our lives by journaling. "The LORD confides in those who fear him; he makes his covenant known to them" (Ps. 25:14).

Do you want to know the mysteries and blessings of God? Seek him.

As we journal, we leave a labor of love in order to pass on a godly legacy to the next generation. Journaling is a great opportunity to record all the LORD has done for us! The generations following may see and know our faith is real and they can at least learn from our mistakes!

As I trained for a half marathon, I learned that I can accomplish more than I ever believed. Change is possible with God's help. While training for a half marathon, I learned many aspects about the physical body. I always worried about dehydration, but I never knew about hyponatremia, low blood sodium levels due to over hydration. This occurs when too much water is taken into the body too quickly and the body is not shedding the excess water. The runner can begin to feel dizzy and disoriented, often unable to finish the race.

When people are training for a long run, it is easy to think we need more water because we are sweating profusely, but "14–27 ounces are recommended per hour, with the higher end of the range applying to faster, heavier individuals competing in warm environments and the lower rates for the slower, lighter persons competing in cooler environments."[6]

This proves the right amount of water is needed to remain strong and healthy. Again, the same analogy applies to the amount we take in spiritually from the water of the Word. I truly believe the LORD teaches us truths that are to be shared. We have many opportunities to give direction and encouragement overflowing into the lives of others.

Spiritually, we become "over hydrated" when we focus only on what we are learning, saturated with so much truth and knowledge, but fail to spill over into the lives of others. Like a good sponge that can only soak up so much water—a good 'squeeze' will pour it out so we can soak up (truth) again. The reverse is also true. When we don't spend time in God's Word and prayer, we easily become dehydrated, empty, and not able to give of ourselves.

Throughout the Bible we can see God's emphasis on recording his work for the generations to come. "One generation will commend your works to another; they will tell of your mighty acts. They will tell of the glory of your kingdom and speak of your might" (Ps. 145:4, 11).

Moses reminded the Israelites how to love the LORD God with all their hearts and with all their souls and with all their strength—by impressing these commandments upon their hearts and the hearts of their children.

His instructions were clear on how to accomplish the task. The Israelites were commanded to talk about the scriptures at home and when they walked along the road, when they laid down, and when they got up. They tied the scriptures as symbols on their hands and bound them on their foreheads. They were to write them on the doorframes of their houses and gates (Deut. 6:4–10).

What is God's purpose for us in discussing and writing the Words of the LORD? God wants us to remember him! He wants us to see all that the hand of the Lord has done and to tell our children for the future generations to build their faith. Just as he delivered the Israelites, he delivers us into the "promised land" out of our own deserts into a "land of abundance." Everything comes from him! All that we have, all that we are comes from his hand. "And he is not served by human hands, as if he needed anything, because he himself gives all men life and breath and everything else" (Acts 17:25). We are to be careful and not forget the LORD.

If God is confident, then why would he be so concerned that we remember him? God wants us to know he is with us. Why? He loves us. He desires our companionship, the whole purpose for our existence. He does not want us to forget his love and presence, Emmanuel—God with us.

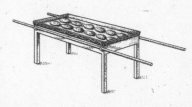

The LORD commanded the Israelites to take a physical symbol, an omer of manna, and keep it for the generations to come, so they could see the bread God gave them to eat in the desert when he brought the

Israelites out of Egypt (Exod. 16:32). Elizabeth Elliot in *Passion and Purity* encourages keeping an "omer of manna" by means of journaling.[7] Journal so that God's faithfulness is written, giving life to your soul, and an inheritance of faith for generations.

As in the tabernacle at the table of the bread of Presence, the priests refurbished the twelve loaves of bread continuously before the LORD each Sabbath. The priests were allowed to eat the bread in a holy place. The bread was burnt as an offering on the altar for a pleasing aroma to the LORD. In the new covenant, Jesus welcomes us to fellowship with the invitation to freely partake as he declares, "I am the bread of life. He who comes to me will never go hungry . . . I am the living bread that came down from heaven. If anyone eats of this bread, he will live forever. This bread is my flesh, which I will give for the life of the world" (John 6:35, 51). Jesus, the bread of heaven, sustains your heart.

The Israelites gathered manna enough for each day. As we seek our daily bread, it is each day's grace for the journey. Receiving his Word brings life and light to guide our path in righteousness. Meeting with God daily, we "see to it that we do not miss the grace of God" (Heb. 12:15).

Can you imagine the impact, the hope, and the generational blessing that can be passed down through the records of your journals? "Let this be written for a future generation, that a people not yet created may praise the Lord" (Ps. 102:18). "Go now, write it on a tablet for them, inscribe it on a scroll, that for the days to come it may be an everlasting witness" (Isa. 30:8).

Today's Prayer Journal Task

- Look at your life, past and present. How often have you been gathering your "daily bread?"
- How are you storing your "daily bread" as a visible witness for future generations?
- What is one intentional way you can share the depth of your relationship with God to the next generation?
- Pray with all your heart and tell God you love him!

Overcoming Unbelief

Our own insecurities and lack of faith can be obstacles to prayer. At the age of 36, I entered what is commonly called a mid-life crisis. I began to wonder and tried to discern: What was my purpose? Who I was created to be? What were my roles, other than those of a wife and mother? I felt discouraged and deflated.

We are all called to pray, and I had long considered my personal gifts to be mercy and encouragement for others communicated through my prayers. But my self-concept was cast into doubt after taking a spiritual gift test and discovering prayer was not qualified as a gift of the spirit. Could it be that I had failed to discern or properly interpret my spiritual gifts? Or was I being misled? This confused me further and forced me to reexamine my purpose and God's call on my life.

In the midst of searching for my identity, I was struggling inside by comparing myself to a friend. She "had it all" in the outwardly gifted department: beauty, hospitality, teaching, artistic expression, and ability. In my eyes my gifts were not outwardly apparent. I did not like what the potter had given me. In my darkness, I was convicted that it is not wise to compare. Can the pot say to the potter, why did you make me this way? (Isa. 45:9).

To accept myself as God created me is like saying to him, "I love you. Thank you. I trust you with the purposes for which you have created me." To be dissatisfied in how and who he made me to be is a form of disrespect. Could I have designed or created any better than he? Better to learn to love myself, forgive my mistakes, and accept who I am. Being true to oneself can bring real freedom.

Many times I have prayed a similar prayer like the father who prayed and begged Jesus to come heal his sick son. When the father made his request that "if" Jesus could heal, Jesus immediately responded with a rhetorical question, "If you can?" said Jesus. "Everything is possible for him who believes." Immediately the boy's father exclaimed, "I do believe; help me overcome my unbelief!" (Mark 9:14–24).

We are encouraged to keep building our faith by praying. "But you, dear friends, build yourselves up in your most holy faith and pray in the Holy Spirit. Keep yourselves in God's love as you wait for the mercy of our Lord Jesus Christ to bring you to eternal life" (Jude 20–21). Every request made to God should be tucked in an envelope of faith—believing "He can." And each request stamped with thanksgiving.

The more we yield our lives in prayer, building a relationship with God by coming and remaining in his presence, the more our faith grows. "Just as you received Christ Jesus as Lord, continue to live in him, rooted and built up in him, strengthened in the faith . . ." (Col. 2:6–7). It is biblical to pray, "that out of his glorious riches he may strengthen (us) with power through his Spirit in our inner being, so that Christ may dwell in our hearts through faith" (Eph. 3:16). Faith in Christ is the only means to approach the throne. "In him and through faith in him we may approach God with freedom and confidence" (Eph. 3:12).

In the Psalms, after seeing the success of the ungodly and feeling life was unfair, David took his doubts into the sanctuary of God. His heart became envious towards the success of the wicked. As David came before God in the temple, he regained perspective, faith, and hope of his own eternal destination. "When I tried to understand all this, it was oppressive to me till I entered the sanctuary of God; then I understood their final destiny" (Ps. 73:16–17).

Jesus gives us a vision of faith when our faith seems to dwindle. We are to come before him with a simple, childlike faith. Jesus said, "Let the little children come to me, and do not hinder them, for the kingdom of heaven belongs to such as these" (Matt. 19:14).

Oh, how much grace we can receive when we have faith! The mustard seed is only slightly larger than the period at the end of this sentence. As a reminder of the promise of faith given to us, I keep a tiny mustard seed in a little bag on my desk with this verse. Jesus meant this tiny seed (so little faith), which was hardly any faith at all, could do incredible things. With his help the impossible can be accomplished. "Because you have so little faith, I'll tell you the truth, if you have faith as small as a mustard seed, you can say to this mountain, 'Move from here to there' and it will move. Nothing will be impossible for you" (Matt. 17:20).

One of the most fascinating stories in the Bible of overcoming unbelief is the story of Peter walking on the water toward Jesus. During the night, Jesus walked on the lake toward the boat. When the disciples saw him they were terrified and cried out in fear. But Jesus immediately said to them: "Take courage! It is I. Do not be afraid."

"Lord, if it's you,' Peter replied, 'tell me to come to you on the water.'

"'Come,' he said. Then Peter got down out of the boat, walked on the water and came toward Jesus. But when he saw the wind, he was afraid and, beginning to sink, cried out, 'Lord, save me!' Immediately Jesus reached out his hand and caught him. 'You of little faith,' he said, 'why did you doubt?'" (Matt. 14:25–31).

Peter reminds me of myself. One minute I am walking on water, stepping out of my boat of security like Peter, and the next, I take one step and find myself sinking in doubt. Admiringly, Peter eagerly asks to be called by Jesus to come to him. He wanted to be where Jesus was, doing the amazing, unthinkable thing of walking on water. Jesus invites him to "Come."

Peter willingly obeys. The moment he looks at the waves, he panics. He takes his glance off the One who sustains him, and he begins to sink. Peter's miracle moment quickly became a moment of unbelief. But not a second passed before the hand of grace was reaching out to catch him.

Jesus' hand is also stretched out for you and me. Through grace, I survived my identity crisis and renewed my purpose. It was six months before my friend and I were able to talk about why I had been distant, comparing and choosing to withdraw from our friendship. Amazingly, she confessed having similar thoughts toward me, envying my gifts.

I also considered that maybe God used my mid-life crisis to prepare me for change. Two years later, our family needed to move. The discontent with myself and my surroundings may have been preparing me to embrace all new things in my life; home, church, school, and neighborhood. As we settled into a new church, my husband and I were able to take a new spiritual gift test. My gifts clearly came through with shining colors.

Now, six years later, I am over my crisis, slowly transforming into who God wants me to be and accepting it. Through much prayer and seeking God, I rediscovered anew that I am how God has created me to be—a passionate person with an unseen, somewhat hidden gift of prayer. Yes, we are all commanded to pray, but in some of us God cultivates a heart for prayer that exceeds all other gifts we possess.

The crucible of a mid-life crisis can be a good thing when we choose faith to believe God is using it to help us seek his will and purpose for our lives. Losing who we perceive ourselves to be can be the beginning of a whole new discovery of our true selves. Being lost showed me my true identity slowly emerging as a writer and speaker who is passionate about prayer. I was double-minded in my faith to become a writer and God gently gave me correction, "Stop doubting and believe" (John 20:27).

As we respond to God with a surrendered heart, he cultivates a heart for prayer in us. The life of prayer is a work produced by faith that believes the promises of God's Word and prays them; believes God listens to our hearts and overcomes unbelief by choosing faith—not fear—as we enter beyond the veil that was torn. A person designed for a life of prayer believes our prayers are heard and not forgotten.

CHAPTER 6

ENTER HIS COURTS
WITH PRAISE & HIS GATES
WITH THANKSGIVING

S TAND ON YOUR feet—Applaud GOD! "Bring a gift of laughter, sing yourselves into his presence. . . . Enter his courts with praise!" (Ps. 100:1–2 MSG). Is there any other that deserves our unending applause and song as much as God? Does the measure of our praise depend on how we feel or on our circumstances? God commands us to praise him, regardless of how we are feeling at the moment. The fact is we gain a renewed perspective of who he is and what he has done when we offer sincere praise. God receives all the glory that is due his name for no other reason than the fact that he is God alone. Praise is the most precious perfume!

God inhabits the praises of his people. With the assurance that God is with us, our praise should be all the fuller, no matter what kinds of trials we are facing. In the recent movie, *Facing the Giants*, a new head football coach has the challenge to improve a team with a history of defeat. In a desperate attempt to motivate the team and reverse their hopeless efforts, the coach encouraged the team to choose a positive attitude by saying, "Praise him when we're up and praise him when we're down." The team's transformation of heart began with praise. Praise led them to victory on and off the field.

We are a "people (he) I formed for (himself) myself that (we) they may proclaim (his) my praise" (Isa. 43:21). Throughout the Bible spiritually strong men like Moses, Abraham, King David, and Daniel succeeded because the LORD's presence was with them. They were men who praised God despite their circumstances. God promises he is with us—so let's praise him! "Praise be to the LORD . . . Not one word has failed of all the good promises he gave . . ." (1 Kings 8:56). The power of praise is evident in that God ordained that even children and infants silence the enemy by giving God praise. Know what a privilege we have to be able to come into his presence and sing praise as we reflect on the words of David in Psalm 84.

> How lovely is your dwelling place, O LORD, Almighty! My soul yearns, even faints, for the courts of the LORD; my heart and my flesh cry out for the living God. Even the sparrow has found a home, and the swallow a nest for herself, where she may have her young—a place near your altar, O LORD Almighty, my King and my God. Blessed are those who dwell in your house; they are ever praising you. Better is one day in your courts than a thousand elsewhere; I would rather be a doorkeeper in the house of my God than dwell in the tents of the wicked.
>
> —Psalm 84:1–4, 10

My grandmother and mother have passed down to me a love for birds. Maybe as we begin to slow down in life, we notice and appreciate the beauty they bring into the world with their variety of color, form, and song. In Psalm 84 above, I wonder if King David wrote these words while he was worshipping in the temple. He may have observed the bird nest near the ceiling of the tabernacle, or up in the tree top against the heavenly blue sky, close to God Most High. In either place, what a beautiful picture of the sweet innocent presence of a mother bird in her nest singing praises to Almighty God; they are always praising him. How much does he long for us to come into his presence and sing eternal praise?

Even the least of these is not cast from his presence. This we do know . . . we were created to love, worship, and honor God. When you wake early in the morning, sing praise!

> One thing I ask of the LORD, this is what I seek: that I may dwell in the house of the LORD all the days of my life, to gaze upon the beauty of the LORD and to seek him

in his temple. For in the day of trouble he will keep me safe in his dwelling; he will hide me in the shelter of his tabernacle and set me high upon a rock. Then my head will be exalted above the enemies who surround me; at his tabernacle will I sacrifice with shouts of joy; I will sing and make music to the LORD. Hear my voice when I call, O LORD; be merciful to me and answer me. My heart says of you, 'Seek his face!' Your face, LORD, I will seek. The LORD will receive me.

—Psalm 27:4–8, 10b

Journal Entry November 16, 1997 . . . Traveling in Israel

Luke 19:40

Mt. of Olives—Beginning of descent to death

They missed God's coming—as we miss God's visitation. Beware of the things of God as you are walking with him. Jesus wept over Jerusalem. This is the largest Jewish cemetery at the Mt. of Olives. Gethsemane sits below.

v.40 "If the disciples keep quiet the stones will cry out." Many, many, stones and rocks are all over this country! The wall, the city, the terrain, the roads—all are made of stones! The rocks cry out his glory!

Now I see . . . Your people everywhere! You give us whole hearts; you put a new Spirit in us. You remove our hearts of stone . . . and give us tender hearts to worship you.

—Ezek. 11:19

My prayer I placed on the Wailing Wall:

Dear Father in Heaven, here this day, Nov. 16, 1997, in Jerusalem, I dedicate and surrender to you my marriage; that you would keep us strong and together. For my children; to have you in their hearts and serve you all the days of their lives.

—1 Chron. 28:9–10, 20

God works in mysterious ways when we offer a sacrifice of praise in our trials. An amazing story from the Old Testament validates the principle of praising God in the battle. Several armies came to declare war against Israel. Jehoshaphat, the king, was warned that an immeasurable army was coming against him. Alarmed, Jehoshaphat did the right thing; he immediately inquired of the LORD and decreed a fast for all the people to come together to seek assistance from the LORD. Jehoshaphat was reminiscent in prayer as he stood before the people and acknowledged to God that God was and is the God who rules with power over the enemy, "Power and might are in your hand, and no one can withstand you." Jehoshaphat cried out, "For we have no power to face this vast army that is attacking us. We do not know what to do, but our eyes are upon you" (2 Chron. 20:6, 12).

King Jehoshaphat and all the people fell prostrate with their faces to the ground in worship before the LORD. Then some stood up and shouted praise. Jehoshaphat encouraged them to have faith in their God and they would be defended and triumphant. Jehoshaphat appointed men to sing praises of thanksgiving to the LORD for his great love as they led the marching troops.

Can you see the enemy perplexed, hearing the revelry of the army in the distance singing their battle songs of joy? The Israelites on the front lines sang praise before they caught sight of the enemy. They believed (God's) his promise and sang his praise (Ps. 106:12). The LORD set a surprise attack against the enemy. In the enemy's confusion they turned against each other; destroyed and annihilated themselves!

All the men of Judah returned joyfully to Jerusalem, entered the temple celebrating and blowing their trumpets with thanksgiving, "The LORD had done this!" God had kept his promises to fight for them and be with them. The under-dog victory was heard all over the country; the fear of God spread throughout the region. Jehoshaphat and his kingdom were able to live in peace after his obedient leadership.

Remember the singers in the front lines of battle? These soldiers led them to victory! Within our churches and fellowship groups, God has called and gifted certain people to lead us in praise. Our worship teams and choirs are on the front lines of warfare. Each week in your companion journal, let's remember to pray for our worship leaders as they reverently lead us into God's presence.

Let us be confident as we engage in prayer, praising Almighty God as we enter into the invisible battle. Let us sing before we see the victory. Praise shifts our eyes off of our hopeless circumstances onto God, who is our only hope. Trust the unconquerable

LORD whose Word stands unmovable. He is worthy of our praise. Only believe! The simple obedience of praise brought the enemy down. There's no limit to God's power when we praise.

Today's Prayer Journal Task

- How often do you spend time alone singing praise to the LORD? Start today and make it part of your prayer time.
- The next time you are fighting doubt and discouragement play some Baroque or praise music. Pay attention to what happens in your spirit.

Rest in God's Sovereignty

Many books have been written addressing the question, "If God is sovereign, then why pray?" We pray because out of his sovereignty; God actually commands it. He knows it is best for us. We pray because God loves us. We are created as eternal beings. God wants us to communicate and fellowship with him along life's journey forever. He wants us to share in the joy of participating in his work through ministry and prayer.

Our prayer lives are hindered when we are easily deceived by our false perceptions of God, his view of us, and how we view ourselves. We often choose to believe the lies Satan—the deceiver, the father of lies—tells us; lies about God and ourselves. If Satan can break down how we think God views us and the way we view God, it can create a wide chasm of separation by false perception. When we believe the lies, we act on these lies, pulling away from God and truth. Satan attempts to thwart our relationship with God by lying to us and telling us we are not doing enough for God's Kingdom and we get too busy to pray.

It takes intentionality and work to protect our intimacy with God and our subsequent life of prayer. Let us be on guard—"Guard your heart above all else, for it determines the course of your life" (Prov. 4:23 NLT). Satan lies and tells us God does not hear, or sadly God does not care nor respond. He will tell us our prayers are not effective. Satan will twist the truth of who we are and tell us we are not seeing answers to our prayers; we are not righteous enough or worthy. We may not see answers in the physical realm, but our prayers influence the spiritual realm. If you have heard these lies or experienced these thoughts and feelings, my prayer for you is this: may God remove your veil of unbelief. We have every resource to combat the lies through prayer and keeping our minds on his truth—that God loves us, he hears us, and he answers us.

To combat the enemy and to gain a right perspective on our view of God and how we view ourselves, we must study the Word of God. As we study the scriptures, learn them, and walk in the truth we can use scripture as a weapon and tool for prayer. You are designed for this spiritual work produced by faith, capable of trusting in God's sovereignty.

God's sovereignty compels us to pray. "Is anything too hard for me (God)?" (Jer. 32:27). "Do I (does he) lack the strength to rescue you?" (Isa. 50:2). Sovereignty is defined as the exercise of his supremacy. God does as he pleases. He is God, there is no other. God's purpose will stand. He cannot be thwarted or hindered. Nothing is impossible for him.

The Christian view affirms God created the universe, together with all its properties and powers, and that he is preserving all that he has created. As a holy, loving, wise, and powerful being, he also exercises sovereign control. This means God's continuous activity makes all events of the physical, spiritual, mental, and moral phenomena work out for his purposes; and that this purpose is nothing short of the original design of God in creation. Evil has entered the universe, but it is not allowed to thwart God's original, compassionate, wise, and holy purpose.

God is sovereign over evil and sin. He has used the fall of Adam and Eve to reveal his attributes more completely against the backdrop of evil. We see more fully God's light in the darkness: his goodness triumphs over evil, his love covers a multitude of sin, his freedom releases the prisoner, his salvation delivers the lost, and his life conquers death.

The Father is listening and wants to answer us. God welcomes us into his holy presence. As we believe and receive this incredible love, we respond with a willing heart of prayer desiring to communicate with him. The more we rest in God's sovereignty and presence, the love grows fonder and the passion for prayer grows deeper. The invitation remains. Won't you come?

Intended for God's Pleasure

THE KING IS thrilled when his distinguished guests arrive! And the attendants with him, the (angels) rejoice when one wanderer who has rejected his invitation in the past, returns to the banquet. Let the rejoicing begin! But even when the faithful show up for the feast, the King is delighted.

We learn from history that God desires sincere worship. God spoke of the Israelites, "These people come near to me with their mouth and honor me with their lips, but their hearts are far from me. Their worship of me is made up only of rules taught by men" (Isa. 29:13). God wants us to live in freedom, beyond the heaviness of dos and don'ts attempting to keep the entire law, but instead to live by the new covenant of grace. By the merits of Jesus alone, he invites us to come near to him with our hearts.

My husband expressed to me once how he wished our twelve-year-old son, at the time, would merely come and ask him to go shopping for a video game. Our son is amazingly skilled with quick eye-hand coordination and thoroughly enjoys playing his games. But this particular day, he seemed hesitant to ask, being unsure of the answer. My husband knew what my son wanted by his non-verbal behavior. But as a father, my husband wanted our son to initiate and communicate in his own words by simply asking, "Dad, can we go to Game Stop today?"

When there is open communication our home seems to flow with unity and peace. Our communication with God is the same way. He already knows what we need even before we ask (Matt. 6:8). So why would God want us to ask? He desires for us to ask because we are his children and he loves us. He longs for us to willingly share our hearts and concerns. Usually, whatever we are asking of God is what is important to us at the moment—and to him.

Embrace the mindset of conducting a running dialogue with God all day long. Have a conversation with the One who knows you best and loves you most. Talk to him throughout the day about decisions that need to be made, people you speak with, or the concerns that come to your mind.

Prayer keeps us in close communion with God and acknowledging our dependence on him. God wants us to ask and he uses prayer to bless us. God is generous! "The LORD longs to be gracious to you; he rises to show you compassion . . . Blessed are all who wait for him! . . . How gracious he will be when you cry for help! As soon as he hears, he will answer you whether you turn to the right or to the left . . . Your ears will hear a voice behind you, saying, 'This is the way; walk in it'" (Isa. 30:18–19, 21).

If I am not running, I walk frequently with a friend at a park nearby. Our walks and talks are catch up, stay-connected days. One particular morning as we walked, we noticed my name was written on the path in big bold letters, over the top was drawn a big heart. We continued to walk along; there it was again, my name written on the ground in the dirt. Sometimes, I wish following God's will was always that clear, but what a great word picture. God promises to lead us on straight paths. There is an element of faith when we walk with him. We have to take the steps to follow him and trust in his perfect love. This experience brought to life a verse that I had memorized, "For your love is ever before me, I will walk continually in your truth" (Ps. 26:3). The truth of knowing this perfect love goes before me like the hearts drawn on the path. In the routines of our busy lives do we take time to pray and notice where God is leading?

Our walking with God, communicating with him through prayer brings him enjoyment, gladness, and pleasure. He says in his Word, "The prayer of the upright pleases him, the prayer of the upright is his delight" (Prov. 15:8 NIV, KJV). God finds your relationship irresistible!

What do we pray about so that God is pleased? Timothy says, "I urge, then, first of all, that requests, prayers, intercession, and thanksgiving be made for everyone—for kings and all those in authority, that we may live peaceful and quiet lives in all godliness and holiness. This is good, and pleases God our Savior" (1 Tim. 2:1–3). God enjoys it when we pray about everything. God appreciates our giving thanks about everything. The thankfulness coming from our lips overflows from trust in our hearts for his love for us—his provision, care, and sovereignty.

ENTER HIS COURTS WITH PRAISE & HIS GATES WITH THANKSGIVING

Thanking and talking to God about everyone in our sphere of influence is a matter of importance. "First of all," he says. To put thanksgiving and prayer first in our day and first in our associations with others would please him. We have an opportunity to join Jesus in interceding for the salvation and God's will of everyone we encounter. Our reward is peace by yielding to interruptions and inconveniences with an open heart as we face the day knowing God's presence is with us. I encourage you to make a daily commitment to pray over your activities and encounters for the day. Jesus did; so should we—with thanks.

Journal Entry March 14, 2008

Thank you, LORD. So often when I am lost in scripture looking for one passage, I am found—finding a new lesson or truth.

Luke 18:35–42 A blind man was sitting by the roadside begging as Jesus was walking to Jericho. It did not say how long he'd been blind, but I would assume since birth. He was probably an expert at begging by now. When he heard the crowd going by, he asked what was going on. They told him, Jesus was passing by. The blind man did not stay small and unnoticed, this beggar begs for Jesus despite the rebuke from the shushing crowd. Two times the blind man cries out, "Son of David, have mercy on me!" Mercy—God's unmerited favor.

Amidst the noise of the crowd and clamor of people— Jesus heard him crying out. Jesus hears us! Jesus stopped and ordered the man be brought near to him.

When the blind man came near, Jesus asked, "What do you want me to do for you?"

"Lord, I want to see," he said. Jesus replied, "Receive your sight. Your faith has healed you."

People everywhere are crying out but to the wrong god.

Jesus asks us, *"What do you want me to do for you?"* He wants to "do" for us!

> If Jesus asks what he can do for us, then he wants us to
> pray. He wants us to ask. He wants us to cry out to him
> for what we need, day in and day out.

Jesus knew the blind man's need or else he would cease to be God in the flesh. So why did Jesus ask the question, "What do you want me to do for you?" He preferred for the man to communicate the desires of his heart.

What do you want the King who owns the cattle on a thousand hills to do for you? God delights in blessing you . . . Come to his table of grace! Remember to give thanks before and when he answers!

Proclaim God's Holy Name

DO YOU KNOW the King who invites you to his banqueting table? Do you know to whom you pray? Prayer is worship. In prayer, first take time to adore and praise the LORD. Praise is an act of expression in reverence to an Almighty God for all of his attributes.

Focus on who God is, The great "I AM"! Think about his character. Praise him for his faithfulness, holiness, sovereignty, strength, and might. Praise him for his justice, presence, power, tender mercies, and unfailing love; for his goodness, kindness, wisdom, grace, and compassion. Ask God to reveal himself personally to you. God wants to be known by you. God promises to be totally accessible to you.

In prayer we often address God as our "Father." The word "Father" is used to describe God only fourteen times in the entire Old Testament. In each of those instances, it refers to God as the father of the Israelite nation. The word "Father" occurs seventeen times in Jesus' Sermon on the Mount. Clearly, Jesus' coming has opened a beautiful and wonderful way of approaching God. The apostle Paul wrote about this: "Because you are sons, God sent the Spirit of his son into our hearts, the Spirit who calls out, 'Abba Father.' So you are no longer a slave, but a son; and since you are a son, God has made you also an heir" (Gal. 4:6–7). God desires to reveal himself in relationship as father, a provider, to his children who come. He wants to give to those who ask . . . more of himself, more of his Spirit. Ask God to show you the truth of *who* he is.

Your earthly father can often shape your view of your heavenly Father, but no matter your relationship with your earthy father in our human frailty, it is not beyond God's healing of inaccurate perceptions.

As we grow to know God's character we can stand on God's attributes and pray with confidence reaching beyond our human limitations. "An attribute of God is not just a part of God; it is who God is and how he is. Love, for example, is not something God has, but what he is. All the attributes of God are truths about him, and they are as infinitely interrelated as he is infinite. God is self-existent, therefore his love has no beginning; he is eternal, his love has no end; he is infinite, his love has no limit; he is holy, his love is the essence of all spotless purity. He is immense; his love is as deep and wide as a bottomless, shoreless sea. When God loves us, he is being himself."[1]

We are so quick to forget who God is—The great I AM! All of his attributes are who he is and how he responds. He is holy! His love is holy. His justice is holy. His mercy is holy. All that he is and does is holy, perfect, right, and true.

A beautiful picture expressing the holiness of God was recorded for us in the book of Isaiah. Isaiah saw a glorious vision of God seated on his throne. His robe filled the entire temple. Above him were angels, each with six wings: The glory was so brilliant the angels had to cover their faces with two wings, in honor and humility, with two wings they covered their feet, and with two they were flying. They were calling to one another: "Holy, holy, holy is the LORD Almighty; the whole earth is full of his glory" (Isa. 6:1–3).

The majestic voices shook the temple's foundations and completely filled it with smoke. At that moment, in awe of God's holiness and acknowledging the weight of his depravity, Isaiah could do nothing but fall before the LORD's throne crying "I am done! For I am a sinner, a man of unclean lips, . . . and my eyes have seen the King, the LORD Almighty." After taking a live coal from the bronze altar with tongs, one of the angels flew over to Isaiah, the angel touched his mouth and said, "See, this has touched your lips; your guilt is taken away and your sin atoned for" (Isa. 6:7). The blood-stained coal taken from under the sacrificed offering on the altar touched the very part of Isaiah that represented his heart and ministry. God's holy cleansing power anointed Isaiah's mouth for the ministry of reconciliation.

After God's sign of approval, Isaiah heard the voice of the LORD saying, "Whom shall I send? And who will go for us?" And Isaiah, now prepared to be God's prophet, was to proclaim the message of a suffering servant who was coming to bring salvation. Isaiah responded with a surrendered and ready heart, "Here am I. Send me!" (Isa. 6:8).

Until we grasp God's holiness, we will never see the depth of our depravity and understand the seriousness of our sin, that we are sinners in need of a Savior. In his great mercy, he provides a way of deliverance. We truly come to a throne of grace and do not need to fear death in his glorious presence. Remember what God said in the old covenant that "No one can see my face and live" (Exod. 33:20). We rejoice in the grace of the new covenant ". . . for his mercy is very great" (1 Chron. 21:13).

Do you understand the boldness for which we can now come into his presence? *Because of his great love we are not consumed!* (Lam. 3:22). *But now in Christ Jesus you who once were far away have been brought near through the blood of Christ* (Eph. 2:13). We freely enter into his company without fear of death and we find life!

All of creation is designed to give God praise and glory. The Psalms proclaim that everything from the heavens to the depths of the sea is to praise the name of the LORD. I was told years ago in a Bible study that there were rainbows at the depth of the ocean, so deep that humans would rarely go. So who, but for God's enjoyment alone would these rainbows be created? "Praise him (the LORD) from the heavens, from the earth and . . . all ocean depths" (Ps. 148:1–7).

How much more should we praise him, we, who are created in his image with a spirit, soul, mind, and body? Ask God to reveal himself to you. He is gracious to gradually unveil himself because we could not comprehend him all at once. "What mighty praise, O God belongs to you . . . What joy for those you chose to bring near, those who live in your holy courts. What festivities await us inside your holy Temple. You faithfully answer our prayers with awesome deeds. You are the hope of everyone on earth" (Ps. 65:1, 4–5 NLT). The Hebrew names below are given to help us in our prayer life to focus on who he is and how he reveals himself.

Reflect on The Hebrew Names of (

JEHOVAH
The Self-Existent One Who Reveals Himself
Revelation 1:8, Romans 1:17–20, Psalm 103

JEHOVAH ROPHE
The LORD Heals
Exodus 15:22–27, 2 Chronicles 7:14, Psalm 147:3, Isaiah 19:22
Isaiah 53:5, Matthew 8:16, 17, Luke 4:18, 1 Peter 2:24, 25

JEHOVAH ROHI
The LORD Our Shepherd
Psalm 100:3, Psalm 23, Isaiah 53:6, Jeremiah 23:16
John 10:1–17, John 10:26–33, John 21:17

JEHOVAH-M'KADDESH
The LORD Who Sanctifies
Exodus 1:13, Exodus 19:2–6, John 17:15, 19
1 Thessalonians 4:3–8, 5:23, Hebrews 10:10–14, 1 Peter 2:9

JEHOVAH-SHALOM
The LORD Our Peace
Numbers 6:22–27, Isaiah 9:6, Jeremiah 29:11, John 14:27
Romans 5:1, Philippians 4:4–9

JEHOVAH-SHAMMAH
LORD is Present
Deuteronomy 12:7, 2 Chronicles 6:19, Psalm 16:11
Psalm1:6, Psalm 31:20, 89:15
Proverbs 18:16, Ezekiel 48:35, John 16:7
Hebrews 13:5, Revelation 21:3

JEHOVAH-JIREH
The LORD Our Provider
Genesis 22:1–19, Job 3:16, Matthew 6:7, 8, Acts 8:32
Romans 8:32, Philippians 4:19

THE INVITATION

JEHOVAH-TSIDKENU
The LORD our Righteousness
Matthew 5:6, John 1:12, John 1:29,
Romans 3:22, 6:18, 2 Corinthians 5:21

JEHOVAH-NISSI
The LORD our Banner and Victory
Exodus 14:13, Deuteronomy 20:3–4
Romans 8:17, 2 Corinthians 2:14
Ephesians 3:20–21, Ephesians 6:10, 2 Timothy 4:7

EL SHADDAI
The LORD our Sufficiency and Caregiver
Exodus 15:2, 13, 2 Samuel 22:33, 1 Chronicles 16:27
Psalm 18:32, 2 Corinthians 12:9, 1 Peter 5:7

EL ELYON
The Most High God
Numbers 24:16, Deuteronomy 32:8, 2 Samuel 22:14
Psalm 7:8, 10, Psalm 1:1, 9, Psalm 9:2
Psalm 21:7, Psalm 47:2, Psalm 57:2
Psalm 78:35, Psalm 83:13, Daniel 4:2

Today's Prayer Journal Task

- Is there a circumstance in your life that you need to trust in God's sovereignty?
- Pick one of the Hebrew Names of God and read the corresponding scripture.
- Write down a prayer of praise for God's revelation of himself in that attribute.
- "Dog ear" the corner of this page. Come back later and read more names of God!

Enter His Gates with Thanksgiving

God's invitation for the Israelites was to come worship his presence in the tabernacle. There was only one way to enter—on the eastern side. The sun rose in the east every morning and shone on the entrance to the temple gate with all its brilliance—a symbol of faithful invitation, welcoming God and us daily. The priests prayed and cried, "O you gates; be lifted up, you ancient doors, that the King of glory may come in" (Ps. 24:7).

In the New Testament, Jesus was the fulfillment of this welcoming sight, affirming through his life as being the one and only way to God. Jesus proclaimed, "I am the gate; whoever enters through me will be saved. He will come in and go out, and find pasture" (John 10:9). Jesus often used simple analogies to teach spiritual principles. He refers to finding life by entering a narrow gate.

When we choose to enter the narrow gate companions may be few. God's Word, will and standards are the fence of love and protection. His boundaries result in freedom. When we take the time to dwell in the safe pasture of his presence, he guides us on fragrant paths. The wide gate is the way of the temporal pleasures of this world. Those who enter the wide gate are mislead and misplaced without hope.

Have you ever thought of prayer as God throwing open the doors of communication between us? Jesus says, "Knock and the door will be opened to you . . ." (Matt. 7:7). Once we knock, the LORD promises to open the way to his heart and be near us whenever we pray to him. When we receive the invitation by God's Holy Spirit, an inner witness, a knowing or sense of peace; we take a step of faith and come into his presence with our whole heart, mind, soul, and body. Paul writes of Lydia's conversion in Philippi after gathering in prayer. "The Lord opened her heart to respond to Paul's message" (Acts 16:14). Acknowledging belief in Jesus through prayer is the method God has given us to respond and receive his Son by faith. Through belief in God's Word, believing in Jesus and the power of his death and resurrection, the invitation remains.

Give thanks with all your heart! Give thanks to God's gracious provision! The veil was torn so that we may enter into his Holy

Presence! He has "placed before us an open door that no one can shut" (Rev. 3:8). As we remember God's character and his wonderful works, "enter his gates with thanksgiving and his courts with praise; give thanks to him and praise his name, come before him with joyful songs" (Ps. 100:4, 2), for he blesses those who come in his name, those who seek his face with thankful hearts.

God does not need our words of thanksgiving, but he values them. When God commands us to give thanks it is because he knows it does a greater work in us. A thankful heart changes our perspective and attitude. "Give thanks in all circumstances . . . (1 Thess. 5:18). An attitude of gratitude will help you persevere in the race of life.

Thankfulness involves two responses from us—remembering and valuing. Pray, remembering all the good things the LORD has done and your heart will overflow with thanksgiving. Pray, thanking him first for knowing what you need before it is even on your tongue. When your heart is welling up with gratitude, give thanks! When you are not feeling gratified, look for something good and choose to be thankful. Making a list of what I am thankful for gives me a renewed perspective and makes me feel better.

Remember the great lengths God has taken to extend his invitation of his presence. Let us pray with King David, "Open for me the gates of righteousness; I will enter and give thanks to the LORD. This is the gate of the LORD through which the righteous may enter. I will give you thanks, for you answered me; you have become my salvation" (Ps. 118:19–21). Thanksgiving comes from valuing Jesus.

In prayer, offering a sacrifice of thanksgiving honors God. We may not always feel like giving thanks . . . so it is somewhat of a sacrifice made out of obedience. It is God's will for us that we ". . . be cheerful no matter what; pray all the time; thank God no matter what happens. This is the way God wants you who belong to Christ Jesus to live" (1 Thess. 5:16–18 MSG). Our constant prayer can obviously be accomplished, or otherwise God would not have commanded us to do it. Our lives can overflow with joy and thankfulness as we trust God's love and provision for us. So much so, that we should not worry about one single thing, but instead be in prayer over everything, every thought, and every concern that comes to our minds. We may not always feel cheerful, but we can possess an underlying sense of joy as we entrust every care to God with thanks because he is the great I AM—the giver and maker of everything. Everything belongs to him that we could ever need according to his redemptive grace.

The story of the one thankful leper in the New Testament reinforces the importance of not so much the healing, but the reaction itself, giving thanks to God for what he has done. Jesus was on his way to Jerusalem and ten men with leprosy, labeled as outcasts, had met him and stood at a distance. They called out with awareness of Jesus' authority in a loud voice, "Jesus, Master, have pity on us!" When Jesus saw them, he did not reach out and touch them as he often did in most healings, but he spoke from a distance, "Go, show yourselves to the priests." This command took a step of faith for the lepers to leave and go, not yet having experienced healing. It was a custom of the day for the priest to approve them cleansed of leprosy. And as they departed, they were healed.

In the moment of jubilee, ten men started jumping and shouting, "Look! We are healed!" But in their excitement or in their excuses only one of them remembered to turn back and look for Jesus, praising him in a loud voice throwing himself at Jesus' feet. "Thank you! Thank you!" The words rang loud and sincere—as he had formerly been doubly rejected as a leprous Samaritan. Jesus asked, "Were not all ten cleansed? Where are the other nine? Was no one found to return and give praise to God except this foreigner?" (Luke 17:11–18).

God's mercy should yield thanksgiving in our lives with heartfelt shouts of appreciation. Often on a beautiful day I roll down the window of my car, turn up the volume and sing a song at the top of my lungs, praising him and giving thanks!

Each Christmas my husband and I try to give gifts equally to our children. On paper, the gift amounts look the same. But one Christmas in the eyes of a nine-year-old, my youngest daughter didn't seem to see eye to eye that the gifts were equal because of their physical size or abundance. However, she was the first to show appreciation by making my husband and I a little thank you card out of her new stationery gift box. My heart was touched by her gratitude. There are times when those who "appear" to receive the least are the most thankful. Our thankfulness comes from a mature heart bearing fruit.

Let us trust God that the gifts he gives us are the best ones for us, no matter the appearance or our preconceived value. Trust God's judgment and plan for the use of his gifts in your life and be thankful. Often God's ways are not our ways and his gifts are not what we perceive as gifts. The gifts, although possibly a suffering, are being used by God to transform your heart into his image, for his purpose, and for his kingdom. Let us give thanks for all things.

A heart of gratitude is cultivated from a surrendered heart that desires to give God recognition and glory. God commands that we give thanks for everything. Make it a thought pattern to give thanks for who God is and for his provision even before we present our requests and see his response. The thankful heart understands all we are and all that we have received comes from the Sovereign hand of God.

Today's Prayer Journal Task

- Write a prayer of thanksgiving for all the provisions God has made for you to enter his presence.
- What is one area in your life where you need to change your attitude to gratitude in order to persevere in the race of life?
- Make a list of all the things you are thankful for and know you are blessed.

PART III

YOU ARE A SACRED TEMPLE

AT MY CHURCH, we had a missionary pastor from Uganda speak. He discussed three types of prayers common to us, especially in the United States. Casual prayers said flippantly, being "all about me" lasting only for a few minutes (wanting a car space or a win for our favorite team). Second, there are crisis prayers cried out in emergencies; for example when tragedy struck on 9/11. When the disaster has passed we often forget God and return to a routine of living without him. And there are prayers of commitment; yielding ourselves to him, prayers that are sincere and consistent day after day. Of the three types of prayer, the pastor exhorted us to pray prayers of commitment.

"Did you know that your body is a temple of the Holy Spirit, who is in you, whom you have received from God? You are not your own you were bought at a price. Therefore honor God with your body" (1 Cor. 19–22). As you devote your life to prayer, start daily committing your heart, soul, mind, and strength to God—surrendering your whole life to him to be used for his purposes. I find this kind of prayer needs to be done throughout the day.

Just like running, we need to pray even when we don't feel like praying. "Our prayers offered when we do not feel like it are more acceptable than those offered when we do."[1] We sacrifice ourselves, our feelings, and our time to come talk to God with a disciplined spirit. "Evening, morning, and noon I cry out in distress, and he hears my voice" (Ps. 55:17). We not only need to develop a habit of praying throughout the day, but it is necessary to have times set aside for longer periods of prayer. Our lives are dependent on times when we pull away from all the distractions and sit at his feet.

Do we treat God with the same courtesy we do with people? If we have an appointment with someone, we keep it, even though we may not feel like it. We persist in meeting together because we value the relationship. And more often than not, we walk away from the time together refreshed. Do we demonstrate that we honor people, prize them, and esteem them worthy of their presence? So it is in keeping our appointments with God.

If you lack the desire to pray, ask for it. Pray for the desire and it will come. Tell God how you feel about prayer. Ask him for the discipline, the focus, and most importantly, for the mind of Christ. Let your "yes" be "yes" and be committed to the discipline even though you might not feel like praying. God will give us the desires of our hearts as we enjoy him (Ps. 37:4). Enjoying him is the basis to all prayer.

Think of your commitment to God as cool or tepid water. Have you ever taken a drink of lukewarm water? I have on my runs and it is not pleasant, is it? God uses the same analogy when he describes our hearts and minds. We are to be either hot or cold or else he will spit us out of his mouth. Paul, the apostle, lays it on the line concerning wholehearted devotion. It sounds harsh, but God is a jealous God. We cannot drink the cup of joy at the LORD's banqueting table one day and then meditate and mingle with evil intentions the next. He wants us—all or nothing (1 Cor. 10:21).

Daily pray and surrender your life to the LORD. Habitually pray, "Into your hands I commit my spirit; redeem me, O LORD, the God of truth" (Ps. 31:5). Even in the confusion or uncertainty of our lives know that "those who suffer according to God's will should commit themselves to their faithful Creator and continue to do good" (1 Pet. 4:19). Hand over everything in your day to him. Remind God saying, "I know whom I have believed" and that he promised ". . . he is able to guard what I have entrusted to him for that day" (2 Tim. 1:12).

For years the LORD kept putting on my heart to write this book. I started by putting a notebook together for my own prayer journal. I also began keeping quotes and ideas about prayer and journaling. The impression to write was a continual prompting God gently placed on my heart. It just would not go away no matter how busy my life became with three children.

Several years ago, I began writing in the quiet of my home. Little by little, I kept committing it to the LORD repeatedly. "Commit to the LORD whatever you do, and your plans will succeed" (Prov. 16:3). God gave me the idea, it became a desire, and then he put wings on my dream. Commit your time, talents, and treasures to the LORD in daily prayer, allowing God's purposes to be accomplished. Commit your desires, your dreams, your ways. You are his sacred temple where he longs to dwell and share his glory.

CHAPTER 7

OFFER YOUR BODY AS
A LIVING SACRIFICE

A RE YOU making excuses not to attend the royal banquet? Jesus shares through a parable that the kingdom of heaven is like a man preparing a wedding banquet for his son. In Jesus' day, invitations in advance were hand delivered to guests by servants, with a reminder given the day of the wedding. "Come, everything is ready." But sadly the guests in the parable make excuses. The first one was worried about a field he just bought and needed to go see. The second one wanted to try out his five new oxen. The third guest had just gotten married and he had other activities on his mind. The father asked the servant to go out into the streets and invite everyone so his house would be full.

During this time, it would have been an insult to decline an invitation to a royal wedding, to make an excuse on the day of the celebration would have been even worse. Not having proper clothing was no excuse either. During Jesus' day, wedding garments may have been provided for the guests by the king.

God invites us all to come and celebrate the wedding feast of the Lamb. Someday we will join him in celebration of our perfect union with him forever. Scripture promises that God "raises the poor from the dust and lifts the needy from the ash heap, he seats them with princes and has them inherit a throne of honor" (1 Sam. 2:8). Can you lay aside excuses to attend and let God clothe you with Christ's righteousness? Throw off the excuses that hinder your prayer life and wake up to reality. Wholehearted devotion ushers us into his presence.

Journal Entry January 13, 2007

> Distractions are rampant. I experienced them today. After getting the kids off to school, I turned on some soothing Baroque music, lit a fragrant candle, and sat down to journal. After a few moments of peace, it all broke loose! The phone rang, my cell phone rang, a garbage truck arrived, and the dog barked relentlessly. This went on for several minutes. I even turned up the music in an attempt to focus, but my agitation grew. This was not a peaceful atmosphere to listen and reflect. So, I took some deep breaths, blew out the candle, and turned off the music. I wrote, "I am done."

Sometimes we have to fight to focus and remain committed to prayer and journaling! Choose to pray and write in your journal as a daily priority. It is okay to disengage the world for thirty minutes and turn all things electric to the off position. I give you permission! I struggle when my cell phone battery dies or I leave my phone at home. I feel like my connection to the world has been severed and I cannot be reached by anyone who might need me, especially my children. What did we ever do before the age of cellular phones?

One secret for dodging distractions which always works for me, as I mentioned before, is to rise early when no one else is awake, not even the dog. The day begins free of responsibilities pounding on your heart's door and activities beckoning you away from the quiet.

Be intentional. Expect success! Protect your quiet time to be still, pray, read, and journal. The discipline will nourish your soul and spill over into other areas.

"Therefore, when Christ came into the world, he said: 'Sacrifice and offering you did not desire, but a body you prepared for me; with burnt offerings and sin offerings you were not pleased.' Then I said, 'Here I am—it is written about me in the scroll—I have come to do your will, O God'" (Heb. 10:5–7). God recorded his will for Jesus' life purpose, death, and resurrection. God longs to fulfill his will, promises, and purposes through you. Do you know "a scroll of remembrance was written in his presence concerning those who feared the LORD and honored his name" (Mal. 3:16)? Your name is honored. Take time to honor God's as you seek his will for your life.

As you offer your bodies as a living sacrifice, holy and pleasing to God—that is your spiritual act of worship. Do not conform any longer to the thought patterns of this world, but be changed by renewing your mind, praying and meditating on scripture. Then you will be able to know what God's will is—his good, pleasing and perfect will (Rom. 12:1–2). God's will for sure . . . we were created to intercede.

In Isaiah's discourse on sin, confession, and redemption, he states "And he (God) saw that there was no man, and wondered that there was no intercessor" (Isa. 59:16 KJV). God is looking for those who intercede. What a high and holy calling we possess in Christ. We may miss the opportunity to know God and to help others when we are not listening to God, living in disobedience, therefore not fulfilling our purpose. Remember Noah, Abraham, Moses, in their defining moments all prayed and obeyed. Their obedience has brought us Life. "In him we were also chosen, having been predestined according to the plan of him who works out everything in conformity with the purpose of his will . . . for the praise of his glory" (Eph. 1:11–12).

A beautiful story is found in Luke 7:36–50, when Jesus visits the Pharisee's house for dinner. Jesus made himself at home reclining at the table. But this day was different. A woman, possibly Mary Magdalene, ignored cultural tradition, which did not allow women to eat with men or engage in philosophical discussion. Mary Magdalene in her disgrace, having lived a life of a prostitute (the text does not specifically say this but alludes to the possibility) was invited to fellowship among men in the home of the Pharisee. These men could not tolerate her offenses to see her broken heart.

Mary Magdalene had observed Jesus in the crowd long enough to know he was different. He had not passed harsh judgment on the outcast. He was a friend to sinners.

At the Pharisee's home, I can just see Jesus reclining at the table, glancing up from all the commotion, to see at the door a woman's face full of apprehension and holding nervously in her hand a small stone jar—a small gift of faith. Jesus' eyes full of compassion and his hand beckoning her to come closer, draws her in with all her fears, insecurities, and shame. His mannerism clearly said, "You are of value, my daughter. You are welcome here."

Mary responded to the invitation given only by Jesus. She boldly approached and humbly stood behind him at his feet. I can see her drawing closer to Jesus, overcome with the sorrow of her sin, yet flooded with the overwhelming acceptance and love displayed by Jesus alone.

In her defining moment, she "crashed the party" and poured her most valuable possession of highly expensive perfume on Jesus' feet. Who did she pour out her love to? Jesus. The fragrance permeated the room, Jesus' body, Mary's hair, and the home of the Pharisee. The fragrance was a physical reminder through the sense of smell—the true condition of her heart. Love is wonderfully extravagant when given sacrificially. Love was given and love was received; love was reciprocal.

Jesus says, "Give, and it will be given to you. A good measure, pressed down, shaken together, and running over, will be poured into your lap. For with the measure you use, it will be measured to you" (Luke 6:38). Mary poured out her offering of worship—all she had, all she owned, with all her heart—and Jesus gave her all she needed . . . acceptance, forgiveness, a fresh start, and a new life. Just as the house was filled with the permeating fragrance, Mary's costly sacrifice affected the hearts of others. The greater the sacrifice—the far reaching effect of its influence.

What drew this sinful woman forward to perform her loving act of adoration upon Jesus' feet? In our fleshly nature, at least I am this way when I am hiding anger or sin, I feel like avoiding people whose very presence will confront my wrong behaviors and attitudes. Even though I know that is exactly where I need to be. But Mary found courage to seek Jesus.

Being touched in her heart by Jesus' presence, Mary began weeping—*for his kindness leads to repentance.* She humbly and spontaneously began to wipe his feet with her hair, kissed them, and poured her very expensive perfume on them. From the time she entered his presence, she did not stop kissing his feet with adoration. Jesus expressed disapproval to the judgmental Pharisee who had failed to welcome him according to social customs by washing his feet, greeting him with a holy kiss, and anointing him with oil. But Mary had honored and anointed him with all her heart. Jesus honored her faith and saved her by grace. Jesus announced, "Her many sins have been forgiven—for she loved much" (Luke 7:47).

To physically kneel behind Jesus, at his feet, pouring out her most prized possession, showed her humility and reverence. The perfume she used was costly, almost a year's worth of wages. Such anointing was practiced for the purifying of the priests in the tabernacle. Mary poured out her whole heart. Her generosity did not save her, but it was her willing response to be welcomed into Jesus' presence and receive his forgiveness. She left the Pharisee's house changed into a new woman full of grace and freedom, absolutely beautiful after risking her heart in Jesus' presence.

So what will be our response to Jesus? Why should we respond to him? Allow him the throne of your heart. God wants us to see our need of him in our sin and to draw near, for our hearts to be reconciled and free. Jesus welcomes the association with sinners with open arms of mercy. For the sinner, the realization of bountiful forgiveness by God's grace results in the potential for great love. Our sacrifices of obedience have a great effect on others—a ripple of devout influence bringing others near to Jesus.

It costs us something to offer God adoration. The Psalms contain some of the most passionate prayers in existence. There are many prayers concerning the confession of sin and of adoration. Prayers of adoration are healthy and holy. We must deny ourselves before we can give honor and praise to him. Once our focus turns from our circumstances, trials, and needs to his holy character and limitless love, we are given a fresh perspective that nothing is impossible with God and he alone is worthy of all glory.

"Through Jesus, therefore, let us continually offer to God a sacrifice of praise—the fruit of lips that confess his name" (Heb. 13:15). I cannot emphasize enough that our prayers are a sweet fragrance to God. In Song of Songs, a book written about love, some scholars view it as a picture of Christ's love for his people. The more common view is that it is a collection of love poems between a lover and his bride. Throughout the book, fragrance and perfume are mentioned as an enticing romantic aspect of love. Pleasing was the fragrance of the bride's perfumes; her name was like perfume poured out. The bride said her lover was like a sachet of myrrh resting between her breasts. Her thoughts were so consumed with him. So much so, that her fragrance exudes this man of grace. The groom likes knowing that he's being thought about and responds with an invitation,

"Arise, come, my darling; my beautiful one, come with me" (Song of Sol. 2:13).

As we come to God, surrendering our will for his, he cultivates our hearts through prayer into hearts that search for sin, commit to him, and obey his will. Our hearts learn to listen and appreciate his gifts. Through prayer, we exude his fragrance as we spend time in his presence humbly giving adoration. We pour out our praises like perfume.

When we respond to God with a surrendered heart, in prayer and daily reading the Bible, we learn to identify and eliminate the things that hinder our prayer life. As we walk with God, he teaches us his ways. He established his law so we would learn to follow and keep him first in our lives. In prayer taking the time to intentionally examine our priorities is a labor prompted by love.

Each day we are given 24 hours to spend however we choose. Do these activities satisfy you deep within? We can easily lose our thirst for the Living Water and try to satisfy our needs with the temporary things of this world. Taking time to examine the condition of our hearts can help remove the barriers to prayer. We often lack honesty within ourselves.

Honesty requires the courage to admit my attachments that occupy my thoughts and dictate my behavior. My perfectionist mindset causes me to be obsessed with people pleasing; how people view my weight or my spiritual life, my house, and my opinion.

We all commit idolatry everyday when we give precedence to anything other than God. Many idols have no personhood, but sometimes our greatest idol can be ourselves. We hide behind an idol of self-protection. We fear having our hearts exposed and then rejected. We gloss over the fact that eliminating idols isn't just giving up our sinful habits and dependencies, but of doing something far more difficult—giving up our right to ourselves.

Bow to God Alone

After teaching on honesty, Jesus confronts the sneering Pharisees with their wealth and says, "You are the ones who justify yourselves in the eyes of men, but God knows your hearts. What is highly valued among men is detestable in God's sight" (Luke 16:15).

God is not insecure, but he is a jealous God. He is wise and all knowing. He knows our hearts can easily be swayed to serve, worship and love other temporary, gratifying created things. From the beginning he has commanded us to love him and worship him alone. Ralph Waldo Emerson once said, "A person will worship something, have no doubt about that. We may think our tribute is paid in secret in the dark recesses of our hearts, but it will out. That which dominates our imaginations and our thoughts will determine our lives, and our character. Therefore, it behooves us to be careful what we worship, for what we are worshipping we are becoming."

Do you remember Exodus 24, when Moses went on top of the mountain to be with the LORD? While he was receiving the Ten Commandments, the Israelites at the foot of the mountain chose to worship another god. Calloused  and cold, their hearts had turned away from worshiping the true God. They had forgotten the promises and presence of the great I AM. They created their own idol of gold, a calf.

Moses returned and discovered the Israelites' foolishness. Standing in the gap on their behalf, he offered an animal sacrifice and prayers as penitence for their sin. Moses pleads desperately for God's forgiveness and that his presence would not abandon them as they journeyed toward the Promised Land.

In Moses' moments of insecurity in leading God's disloyal people, he asks who would help him. God promises the provision of himself, again, "My Presence will go with you . . . because I am pleased with you and I know you by name" (Exod. 33:14, 17). Moses responded to God, asking what would distinguish him and his people from all others. In desperation, Moses asks for proof to see God's glory. In God's mercy, his goodness passes by, affirming his promise and covenant to be with his chosen ones. Due to the Israelites' rebellion and to purify his people, God allowed the Israelites to wander in the desert for forty years. God disciplines those he loves, allowing consequences to their rebellion. "These things happened to them as examples and were written down as warnings for us" (1 Cor. 10:11).

Moses reminds the Israelites of the mighty deeds God had performed. What other nation had heard the voice of God speaking out of fire or had seen deliverance by his mighty hand and an outstretched arm with miraculous signs and wonders? These things were done before their eyes so that they might know that the LORD is God.

As we look at the Ten Commandments in Exodus, God's first command addresses idols. "You shall have no other gods before me. You shall not make for yourself an idol in the form of anything in heaven above or on the earth beneath or in the waters below. You shall not bow down to them or worship them; for I, the LORD your God, am a jealous God, punishing the children for the sin of the fathers to the third and fourth generation of those who hate me, but showing love to a thousand generations of those who love me and keep my commandments" (Exod. 20:3–6). God, who knows our tendencies and our weaknesses, established these boundaries because he knew we would search for things of this world, things we can see and touch, to satisfy and fill our void. But we are designed so that only God can fill our empty longing to be loved.

Throughout Israel's rebellion God sent prophets to warn them to stop worshipping other gods. Jeremiah tells them they have provoked the LORD's anger by burning incense, (the incense representing our prayers) offered to other gods. The LORD actually calls it "detestable" this "thing that (he) hates!" (Jer. 44:4). But the Israelites did not listen nor humble themselves by showing God reverence. The LORD compares their idols to a scarecrow in a melon patch unable to talk or walk, calling them a fraud without a breath in them.

God is honored when we live with integrity. Putting God first, praying about everything, and choosing not to spend consuming amounts of time worrying over the ideals of the world frees us to worship God more fully. Pray and ask God to establish your convictions and for his strength to help you stick to them.

In contrast to the Israelites, another story providing a superior response to the worship of idols of gold was written about Shadrach, Meshach, and Abednego—young men who refused to bow down to worship the golden god. Consequently, they were thrown in a blazing fire. With such courage and confidence they replied to the King, "We do not need to defend ourselves before you . . . the God we serve is able to save us, and he will rescue us from your hand. But even if he does not, we want you to know that we will not serve your gods or worship the image of gold you have set up" (Dan. 3:16–18).

How could these young men say these words with such conviction in the face of death? They knew their God and had determined in their hearts to be loyal. King Nebchadnezzar stood in amazement, recognizing these men were willing to give up their lives rather than worship any other god.

The fire had not harmed their bodies, singed their hair or left any hint of odor. A fourth was seen walking in the fire . . . God among them. God received the glory from their test of dedication. ". . . no other God can save in this way" (Dan. 3:28–29).

Do you have idols in your life? Money, sex, material possessions, work, relationships, sports, popularity, religion, ministry, praise of man, and the list continues.

As we have seen in the current recession, the root of our problem is greed. Greed in any area is a form of idolatry and can rob your spiritual growth (Col. 3:5). Scripture teaches, "No servant can serve two masters. Either he will hate the one and love the other, or he will be devoted to the one and despise the other. You cannot serve both God and Money" (Luke 16:13). What do you need to change or to eliminate to put God first and serve him with wholehearted devotion? What a powerful testimony we declare when we do not give allegiance to our idols.

God commands ". . . those who are rich in this present world not to be arrogant nor to put their hope in wealth, which is so uncertain, but to put their hope in God (him), who richly provides us with everything for our enjoyment. (He) commands us (them) to do good, to be rich in good deeds, and to be generous and willing to share. In this way (you) they will lay up treasure for yourselves (themselves) as a firm foundation for the coming age, so that they may take hold of the life that is truly life" (1 Tim. 6:17–19).

God promises we will receive blessing when we do not offer our heart to any other.

We all worship something. Pray today and ask God, "Give me the grace today to see what creeps in and pushes you out of my life." In God's grace he will gently expose the other dependencies in your heart. There is hope. Despite our other loves, he knows our wayward hearts and still loves us. This kind of love and grace is amazing.

God declares of himself, "I am the first and I am the last; apart from me there is no God" (Isa. 44:6). God has designed us to be in an intimate relationship with him and he knows the needs of our hearts better than we know ourselves. Only God promises to refresh the weary and satisfy the faint when we come to him. He wants us to come and ask for help in our weakness so he can fill us with himself, with his power, love, and strength.

Acknowledge and take to heart this day that the Lord is God in heaven above and on the earth below. There is no other GOD. Throughout scripture there are inferences to our intimate relationship with God as compared to the same intimacy within marriage. God is referred to as our Maker—our Husband. In the Old Testament Israel was called an adulterous nation. In our human independence we all need to know we can return to our first love and ask him for the grace to remain close (Rev. 2:3–5).

Today's Prayer Journal Task

- Embrace God's teaching as your treasure by writing down scripture, memorizing them to renew your mind. What scripture has God impressed on your heart?
- Be intentional, taking time to pray and to ask God to show you if any area of idolatry has crept into your life. Write down the idol and find a verse to help you overcome it.
- Pray for obedience to live by God's ways and pray through your temptations. We are easily deceived into thinking our hearts line up with the priorities and values that we speak. What priority in your life do your intentions need to match your actions?

Empty of Self

ONE OF GOD'S purposes accomplished through prayer is that we come to him with an attitude of surrender, yielding our lives to his Holy Spirit's work through prayers of emptying, committing, and obeying, with wholehearted devotion. Before we were saved by grace we were separated from God, lacking the faith to see our self-centered, sinful desires. Remembering our position in our fallen humanity . . . remembering the gospel of grace produces humility. We are created from dust, cursed with sin, and in great need of a Savior. As we pray, the Holy Spirit enables us to empty our hearts of selfish pride, vain ambition, and independence apart from God. Emptying prayers surrender the fleshly, carnal nature so God can fill us with his Spirit of love, peace, and all the fullness of himself. God can fill us in every way, for every need when we acknowledge our dependency on him.

Empty your heart of self dependence, "Arise, cry out in the night, as the watches of the night begin; pour out your heart like water in the presence of the LORD" (Lam. 2:19). The most significant function of emptying prayers is the acknowledgement of complete dependence on the faithfulness of God and his deliverance from any pride of the flesh.

When we are emptied of the need to achieve perfection in our own strength, or pay penance for the wrong we have done, the cultivation of a Christ-like heart may begin. It comes from being still and knowing he is God. The more time we spend with God, the more we see the behaviors in our lives that obscure his reflection. If we faithfully allow God to point out, prune, and purge the areas that bear no resemblance, God will accomplish his highest purpose in conforming us to the likeness of Jesus.

Another journal entry I'd like to share is a picture principle about emptying the debris in our lives so god can fill them with his goodness; more importantly my realization that on my own I can do nothing "right" without God's help.

Journal Entry April 3, 2002

I can't sleep. All this praying for unity and being slow to speak just flew out the window in a moment's time. I humbly see my lack of spiritual maturity because of how quickly I reacted with my emotions and let my mouth speak!

Oh, I was upset yesterday! Through the woods about fifty yards away, my backdoor neighbor had been cited by the city to clean up his yard. He owned three to four outdoor storage buildings and an old barn. All the buildings were run down, and no telling how many years of trash had accumulated. The owner was 90 years old.

The neighbors to my right also have a view of the man's backyard. Together, we offered to help remove the untidiness. But the elderly man's son refused our offer and said his dad had someone scheduled to clean it up. I was so excited when the trucks arrived. They started piling up mountains of trash and debris from the barn. It was looking good!

The next day, however, as I gazed out my window, a front loader was digging a huge hole. To my shock, the driver of the front loader was burying the debris! My heart raced, my legs trembled, and I called my neighbor next door. We could not believe it! Both of our yards were going to back up to a landfill. My neighbor asked me if I wanted to go speak with them. Immediately, I said, "Yes! We've got to stop them!" By that time I called the city and every sanitation manager's phone number I could get my hands on, it was 4:30 on a Friday afternoon. No one answered!

Highly emotional about this situation, I went out and projected my opinion, "This is not right!" I strongly disapproved! It seemed I was raising my voice, which I was, to talk over the running equipment. The man stopped the front loader and said he was just doing what the old man asked. His son denied knowing anything about what was happening. The older man said it was cheaper to bury his junk. Did he even ask how much it was for the city to haul it away?

My next door neighbor and I offered to help pay some of the bill or to take up a collection from our neighborhood. I felt somewhat responsible. I had made the complaint which caused the man to be cited by the city.

The city supervisor did receive my voice mail and came over right away to tell the men to stop working until they got a permit. I felt better that we'd stopped the burial landfill before it was too late, but on the other hand, I felt badly that I let my emotions and mouth take over.

I should have let my neighbor speak. She was much calmer than I! *But* I had to stand up for what was right. The landfill would be right at the top of our property line. I know from cleaning our woods before, due to erosion, the trash would move down through the years, shifting into our yard where the kids play. It was not just wood from the barn, but included corroded wagons, broken glass, large metal barrels, busted window frames, farm equipment, beat up bicycles, old rusty paint cans—the list continues—a mountain that needed to be moved! I say to that mountain of trash, "MOVE"! But I needed to have love for my neighbor and I was only a clanging symbol.

My gift of mercy was buried as well. Here I claim to be a Christian and invited my neighbor to our church, and then I go lose my cool with my backdoor neighbor! Great witness, Sarah! I did apologize for getting so upset.

Jesus had anger of righteous indignation in the temple when the people were being cheated out of money. I feel comfort in that I too was standing up for what is right for the environment, my children's health, and the property value of our homes. I created tension between us as neighbors, for the son of the man verbally complained about my dog being on their property. Fortunately, God can redeem our issues.

LORD, *thank you for your forgiveness. I have offended you and my neighbor. I have been a poor witness, and I confess that I need you desperately to help me be slow to speak, slow to anger, and quick to listen* (James 1:19). Why didn't that come to mind earlier? Because I failed to stop, pray, and listen; to respond in a calm way, choosing to trust God with his own land!

I was reacting to the situation instead of responding to their issues of the heart which seemed to be the fear of financial burden. But if I had done nothing—how disappointed in myself I would have been. Next time, I need to calm down and let my friend do the talking! Unbelievable! That's all I could say!

Satan does crouch at the door waiting to devour and steal our joy. I love this house, this city, and my yard, especially when the dogwoods are blooming. Now I get to look at garbage and wonder, "How long, Oh LORD, must I call for help?" (Hab. 1:2). Will my neighbor and his son get a permit to bury the trash? What can I do to stop that? Show up at city hall with my documented pictures? Oh, LORD, this should not be! I didn't buy this beautiful home to back up to a landfill! God, help my neighbor and his son to do what is right. Help us do what is right. Show us how to help them. LORD, into your Almighty, Powerful, and Cleansing Hands I commit all this.

This story is a great word picture of what our fleshly nature wants to do in our lives concerning the sin, hurts, pain, and bitterness. We allow a negative attitude or sin to build up; when it is ignored or we simply do not take the time to examine our conscience to realize it is there festering, escalating over time. Piece by piece, sin accumulates in our overcrowded landfill. When God comes prodding to remove the debris of our soul, to bring the issue or attitude into the open, we tend to suppress and bury the truth. As an alternative, we should make every effort to prevent harmful debris from accumulating. Keep short accounts with God—examining your conscience daily. To be set free, let God take the deepest rubble away; always remembering the gospel that can heal our hurting hearts and remove our fears. The sin will eventually sift back to the surface if it is not properly handed over to Jesus to clean up and carry away through his forgiveness. "As far as the east is from the west, so far has he removed our transgressions from us" (Ps. 103:12).

Remember the work of the priests in the tabernacle? Their work was to be wholesome. Pure gold was overlaid on many of the tabernacle furnishings. They also made the sacred anointing oil and the pure, fragrant incense. When we desire to come before God with honest prayers he promises to show himself to the pure in heart. "Blessed are the pure in heart for they shall see God" (Matt. 5:8). Ask God to create in you a pure heart. He wants to give us new hearts. He takes our cold hearts and makes them tender, responsive to his Spirit (Ezek. 36:26). Those who believe and receive his invitation into his salvation are pure in heart. The righteousness of Christ is now ours. Spontaneously at any moment, at any time, we are free to "call on the LORD out of a pure heart" (2 Tim. 2:22). Offering gracious words and a pure heart you are promised to have the King for a friend. Friends talk honestly and Jesus calls you his friend.

Hearts that empty of self and ask for his Spirit in prayer are a sweet fragrance of humility. Embrace self-abandonment in your prayer life. "Whoever finds his life will lose it, and whoever loses his life for my sake will find it" (Matt. 10:39). Let go of all the things you cling to for meaning, success, security, and validation. Let Jesus be all of those for you. Compared to Jesus all else is of lesser value. Trust Jesus to intercede for you through the process of transformation. "Humble yourselves before the LORD (in prayer), and he will lift you up (James 4:10).

One of my daily prayers was spoken from Jesus as he addressed the crowds and his disciples: "If anyone would come after me, he must deny himself and take up his cross daily and follow me" (Luke 9:23). This is not an easy calling to obey when our fleshly nature and the world clamors, "me, myself, and I, come first." We can choose whether to pick up our cross of self-denial. In obedience, denial is something voluntarily sacrificed or offered for the sake of Jesus.

Are you willing to give up a little sleep, skip a lunch break, turn the music off in your car, or say "no" to another night of television to spend time in prayer? Do you consider the cost to not lay down your life for another in prayer? "Greater love has no one than this, that he lay down his life for his friends" (John 15:13). Set a goal of transformation—to grow more loving everyday . . . pray!

A simple prayer of emptying of our desires to follow God's will begins with a humble heart acknowledging his provision of everything we need. In Luke 14, Jesus was in the home of a well-known Pharisee and surrounded by religious people. He exposed their hypocrisy of pride by telling a parable.

> When someone invites you to a wedding feast, do not take the place of honor, for a person more distinguished than you may have been invited. If so, the host who invited both of you will come and say to you 'Give this man your seat.' Then, humiliated, you will have to take the least important place. But when you are invited, take the lowest place, so that when your host comes, he will say to you, 'Friend, move up to a better place.' Then you will be honored in the presence of all your fellow guests. For everyone who exalts himself will be humbled, and he who humbles himself will be exalted.

We are called to respond with humility to the invitation. Through the process of emptying, our prayers help us let go of self and consider others more important. Invite others to the throne of grace who cannot repay you. Aren't we all in a position of never being able to repay the debt that was paid for us? Bring others through intercession into the King's presence for a lifetime of communion.

As we sift through our "debris," remember Jesus willingly took the sin upon himself; therefore we can trade in our ashes for his beauty. As we empty ourselves, he fills us up with his fullness. We empty the fleshly nature, so he can fill us with the fruit of his spirit, revealing more of his character.

Thankfully, my neighbors were not allowed to bury their mountain of trash in their backyard because of city regulations. Several weeks later, the city came and took away eight truck loads of garbage weighing six tons each. What is amazing to me is that in our city we have a bulky pick up once a year that freely takes away any non-toxic item that we place by the curb. A reminder is even sent in the mail to let us know the dates for pick up. Unfortunately, our neighbor never used this free service and refused the help we offered to take it to the curb for them. The junk became so overwhelmingly massive that it required heavy machinery to be removed.

Let us pay close attention to the sin we've buried and not wait years before we examine our hearts. Take time to empty daily and appreciate the free gift of grace: God taking your debris away and placing it on Jesus for your liberty. Emptying yourself, exhale, praying, "God, help me to empty my heart and mind of all fear, anxiety, and any doubt of your security" and inhale deeply saying, "Fill every cell of me with more of you. Fill me with your fullness—faith, power, hope and love."

Find Balance

God brings about more in a believer's heart through a life of prayer than we will ever comprehend. Approaching his throne is a gracious, generous gift. In his rest we can find balance for our busy lives that nothing else on earth can offer.

To truly love others, we need to seek our direction, rest, and regain our strength through time in the Word and in prayer. In his presence we find the grace we need to minister to others. Remember, Jesus often went off by himself to pray. Jesus received direction from God so he could minister to the needy people along the way wherever he traveled.

Jesus took care of his own heart and those of the disciples. During their ministry so many people were coming and going that they did not even have a chance to eat. Once Jesus said to them, "Come with me by yourselves to a quiet place and get some rest" (Mark 6:31). Jesus prayed for perfect balance for us to be in the world, but not of it. When we fail to feed our spirits, we lose strength for living faithfully. "Let your moderation be known unto all men. The LORD is at hand" (Phil. 4:5 KJV).

Journal Entry Sept., 20, 2005

Speak LORD, for your servant is listening (1 Sam. 3:10). I am trying to quiet my heart and mind from my petitions and really listen . . . I think as a woman I tend to either dominate and control or withdraw and hide—to keep from vulnerability. I can be all of these . . . a longing is still there . . . so I indulge in "little affairs of the heart."[1] Indulging is a less subtle form of taking matters into my own hands. What are ways I indulge my heart? Food, ice cream, movies, a cleaning frenzy . . .

These aren't in and of themselves bad, but crutches at times instead of running to you.

I heard over and over, "Bring your heart to me, Sarah."

LORD, *help me realize these tendencies during the day that are subtle, especially hiding my truest self and offering only what I think is wanted.*

He satisfies the thirsty and fills the hungry with good things.

—Psalm 107:9

We have a responsibility to maintain a healthy balance to provide the best possible care for our body, soul, and spirit as each part is inseparable from the other. "May your whole spirit, soul, and body be kept blameless at the coming of our Lord Jesus Christ" (1 Thess. 5:23). "Don't you know that you yourselves are God's temple and that God's Spirit lives in you?" (1 Cor. 3:16). Pay attention to your heart "for we are the temple of the living God" (2 Cor. 6:16).

Find rest in the act of praying. Find rest in the discipline of being still and quiet. The Greek word for rest is *hesychia*[2], a term meaning silence, to settle down in quietness. A similar Word came to mean quietness of work. Resting puts us in a place of dependency and trust. Take time to still yourself—yes, in the Word, but maybe watching the stars at night on a blanket, painting, taking a walk, playing, or watching children at the park.

God invites us to converse where listening and waiting on his profound thoughts are vital aspects of prayer. As you wait, you will discover rest is a holy work. "The LORD your God is with you, he is mighty to save. He will take great delight in you, he will quiet you with his love. He will rejoice over you with singing" (Zeph. 3:17). When my life feels out of control I have to ask myself, how can I be overwhelmed when the great I AM is with me?

My daily commitment to feed myself spiritually has helped my diligence and commitment to remain physically healthy. I have experienced when discipline in one area of my life spills over into other areas. "No discipline seems pleasant at the time, but painful. Later on, however, it produces a harvest of righteousness and peace for those who have been trained by it" (Heb. 12:11). The fruit of discipline and balance parallel in the physical and spiritual realms. As we persevere in our physical workouts, let us not give up doing our spiritual reps! Pray, LORD *help us to finish strong in spiritual discipline for "everyone who competes in the games goes into strict training. They do it to get a crown that will not last; but we do it to get a crown that will last forever"* (1 Cor. 9:25).

Today's Prayer Journal Task

- What are some ways you can better love yourself and find balance by taking care of yourself so you can love others better?
- What is one discipline you can start today to improve your spiritual or physical well being?
- Examine your life for "red flags" that you run to as minor indulgences instead of to God.

Obey with a Willing Heart

An imperative purpose of prayer which God desires as we come before him is that we simply listen and obey. There is nothing more in life that gives us peace and confidence within our hearts as when we are walking in obedience to God's moral will and following his plan for our life. Jesus said, "If you want to enter life, obey . . ." (Matt. 19:17).

When we are obedient, God promises to hear our prayers, bless us, and extend mercy, grace, and life to us. Once we understand and live this truth we reflect his love. "And this is love: that we walk in obedience to his commands. As you have heard from the beginning, his command is that you walk in love" (2 John 1:6).

God is using this book to impress on my heart the very lessons I have written pertaining to listening, obedience, trust, and perseverance. It is not easy to obey when God asks you to go outside your comfort zone into unknown territory. But the responsibility seems lighter as I remember what a dear friend once told me, "Simply obey and leave the results up to God."

At the beginning of my decision to become a writer, I began exploring the publishing arena. Many books and people were helpful, giving me insight especially on the marketing side. With excitement, I realized my increased desire to write and teach were God's seeds of preparation for me to build a speaking platform about prayer and journaling.

On a cool fall morning when the kids were at school, after discovering this new revelation to celebrate and confirm, I picked up a mocha frappuccino, my Bible and journal, and headed outside to the swing—my sanctuary. I asked the LORD, "Is *this* where you're taking me?" Outside my comfort zone for sure! This calling had never occurred to me before, but deep down it lined up with my passion for prayer; writing and speaking opened a doorway for me to share this passion with others. Although unsure of my abilities, my desire was to do his will, his way, and to be whatever he wants me to do and be, even if it calls me to be uncomfortable.

Step by step pursuing what God has planned, my heart has come alive with the possibility of ministering the message of reconciliation. By helping people understand that the Creator of the universe loves them and wants a relationship with them—restoring hearts through prayer and journaling and that God would entrust me with such a privilege—has thrilled my heart!

History proves the call to obedience takes sacrificing our security and comfort. Writing has been the most difficult thing I have ever attempted to do. Running a half marathon comes in a close second, along with birthing three children! There is a choice, a decision we must make to obey God. Be on guard making decisions; the easy way is often the least difficult, most popular, the most tempting, but the most unfruitful route we should take.

It feels backward, but choosing to deny yourself actually brings life. Look at the word obedience. What do you see in the middle of the word? "Die." In the middle of the act of obedience is the price we pay, to give of ourselves for others as Jesus did on the cross. "'My food,' (his sustenance, his life) said Jesus, 'is to do the will of him who sent me and to finish his work'" (John 4:34).

Jesus was not immune to the difficulty of obedience during his brief time in human form. His experience in submitting to God is another example of how Jesus is able to sympathize with our struggles of obedience. "During the days of Jesus' life on earth, he offered up prayers and petitions with loud cries and tears to the one who could save him from death, and he was heard because of his reverent submission" (Heb. 5:7). Our attitude in coming into his presence should be in humility in reference to the position of our hearts and posture. "Your attitude should be the same as that of Christ Jesus" in submission, yielding your will to his divine will (Phil. 2:5).

Ask God for the strength to obey. "LORD, who may dwell in your sanctuary? . . . he whose walk is blameless and who does what is righteous, who speaks the truth from his heart, who does his neighbor no wrong, . . . who keeps his oath even when it hurts" (Ps. 15:1–2,4). Those who obey and do what is right, dwell with him.

Frequently we are confronted by the Holy Spirit to pray for someone who has hurt us or disappointed us. Obedience is tested when we meet something head-on that we really do not want to do. I am learning that with obedience comes freedom to pray however the Holy Spirit leads me, and through that process comes transformation in my heart. We can obey because the Sovereign LORD helps us. He promises we will not be disgraced when we make a decision of commitment to obedience with resolve to do what pleases God.

Not only did Jesus learn obedience from what he suffered, but Daniel was a man strong in faith who was determined to honor God through obedience in prayer. Through prayer and obedience God will provide. In Daniel's case, he provided protection and life. Daniel had favor in the eyes of King Darius, yet during his reign, King Darius' administrators plotted to have Daniel trapped because of their envy. Hoping to please the King, these jealous men established an edict that no man could pray to anyone except the king.

Daniel learned that the decree had been published; however, without fear he *set his face like flint* toward obeying God rather than man. Risking his life, he decided to pray anyway. Three times a day in his upstairs room he threw open the windows facing Jerusalem. Looking over the city, he knelt to pray just as he had done before, giving thanks to his God (and maybe asking for a little help). The men reported Daniel's violation to the king. They seized Daniel and threw him into the lions' den. The king said to Daniel, "May your God, whom you serve continually, rescue you!" (Dan. 6:16).

The next morning, Daniel, alive and well, honored the king and his God. He answered, "O king, live forever! My God sent his angel and he shut the mouths of the lions. They have not hurt me, because I was found innocent in his sight. Nor have I ever done any wrong before you, O king" (Dan. 6:21–22). Because of Daniel's obedience God brought deliverance . . . to many. Daniel prospered and was rewarded for his commitment to God and his faithful obedience.

Prayer is a matter of obedience. How do we obey if we are not listening? "Does the LORD delight in burnt offerings and sacrifices as much as in obeying the voice of the LORD? To obey is better than sacrifice and to heed is better than the fat of rams" (1 Sam. 15:22). Jesus alluded to this same insightful verse from Samuel in the gospels. To follow him was no longer about the "work" of salvation, keeping all the laws that occurred in the old covenant and offering sacrifices, but we are invited to come to love him. Out of our love we will listen and obey his voice—this is better than all the sacrifices! Surrender your insecurities and believe his promise that he opens our ears, not to hear ourselves talk, but to hear his words of love, encouragement, comfort, guidance, and hope.

It is inspiring to see God work in response to our obedience. One morning a lady came to our prayer room to receive prayer for her recent separation from her husband. My husband and I knew the issues taking place that burdened her heart. But another lady present was unacquainted and uninformed of the situation with our hurting friend who came for prayer. As she began to pray, the prayers were sent from above by the Holy Spirit addressing exactly what this hurting woman needed to hear, perfect words of affirmation for her troubled soul.

Prayer comes with diligent and purposeful intention of dying to ourselves and obeying God's command to pray continually. The discipline of prayer and the study of God's Word help to nurture our obedience. As you choose to daily intercede for others, you will find life. As we obey and pray, and pray and obey, in our obedience he will answer. "(We) may ask for anything in (his) name, and (he) will do it" (John 14:14).

Put your faith into action, planting seeds by serving others through prayer. If we sow the things of the Spirit, we will reap the things of the Spirit. Proverbs 21:13 declares, if we shut our ears to the cry of the poor—physically and spiritually, we will not be heard. There are so many needs and we are encouraged not to give up praying (Gal. 6:8). We may not see the harvest of our obedience in our life time, but according to God's promise, it will come. Obedience results from our love for God.

CHAPTER 8

CLEANSE WITH THE LIVING WATER

T HE MORE WE spend time in God's Word and in prayer, we become quickly aware of our sin. Sin hinders our ability to boldly approach the throne. If we fear anything, we should fear sin. Sin hinders our relationship with God. Sin, at its core, can be summed up as pride, focusing on ourselves. In our humanity there is a need to overcome self-centeredness. When we put ourselves first, pride and selfishness are at the root of what keeps us from praying, being effective, and seeing answers.

My journal entry may fix a picture principle in your mind of God's perspective of sin. The verses listed below came flooding to my mind as I recorded my experience.

Journal Entry, June 12, 2001

Be sure your sins will find you out.

—Numbers 32:23

Somewhere in some version of the Bible I think it says that sin is a stench to the LORD. Yesterday, I experienced one of the worst, grossest, sickening things—cleaning out our broken down 4 foot by 8 foot freezer in the garage after who knows how many days or maybe weeks it went unnoticed!

It was summertime and our family kept noticing an odd smell in the garage. We even wondered if an animal had died under the foundation. Then it hit me; the smell came from the freezer. The longer it sat, the stronger it reeked. Thankfully, there was little food being stored, but it stank to the point where, when I was cleaning it out I had to run out the back garage door and gag.

My son, age seven at the time, was so helpful. He kept spraying Lysol so I could breathe and bug spray to keep the hundreds of flies away as I cleaned. The food and juice had fermented terribly. I was thankful I had not eaten.

Once I cleaned out the food, I was able to use the shop vacuum to suck up the juice. I tried paper towels. It was disgusting and hard. There was too much to soak up.

Of course as a mother, I wanted to make this a teaching moment and I began comparing the stench to sin. The stench must be what sin is to a holy God who cannot even look upon it. I could hardly look in the freezer!

"Hate what is evil. Cling to what is good."
—Romans 12:9b

The LORD was grieved over evil in men's hearts.
—Genesis 6:5–6

"You have loved righteousness and hated wickedness."
—Hebrews 1:9a

"The wages of sin is death."
—Romans 6:23

"They parade their sin like Sodom. They do not hide it . . . In that day the LORD will snatch away their perfume bottles . . . Instead of fragrance there will be a stench."
—Isaiah 3:9, 24

I share this story as a word picture to impress on your heart how important it is to confess our sins daily, moment by moment, as the Holy Spirit, his Word, and others convict us. This discipline needs to be a continual part of daily prayer. If we deal with the sin immediately we are not burdened by its compounding tendency to overwhelm and weigh us down, creating a chasm between us and God. Each of us is designed with a conscience. If we took each conviction to heart, realized the offense that sin is to God and the barrier it builds between us, then we would spend more time in prayer confessing.

Our wrongdoing separates us from God and hinders our communication. The scriptures and our conscience make us aware of our sin. If we are doing something in secret and we fear being caught or if we are ashamed of what we have done, then it's probably wrong. When sin tarries, it ferments, it reeks, it ripples over to hurt others, and it grieves God. It builds a stronghold in our lives unless we choke sin out by persevering in prayer, soaking up God's Word, seeking counsel and accountability, and removing ourselves from the temptations.

The curse of original sin leads to death and a permanent severed relationship with God, but for believers, sin has no everlasting hold. We can have victory over sin. For this reason Jesus died and set us free. He conquered death so that we might have hope and victory, bridging the chasm between God and mankind.

Do you daily examine your words, attitudes, and actions? Do you pray about them when you sense you have not loved others, been kind or living for God's glory? Or do you wait in desperation until you are miserable, burdened by the weight of guilt? As you pray and read the scriptures, trust that God's Word brings conviction of our sinfulness, a gratitude for Jesus' sacrifice, and a love for him which brings obedience. When we make mistakes and chose our own way, the Spirit extends an invitation "to cleanse you by the washing with water of the word" (Eph. 5:26).

Search and Confess

Let searching and confessing be first priority in your prayers, after praise and thanksgiving. Take time to ask the Holy Spirit to search your heart and reveal any wrong or ways that you have wandered from or disobeyed God. Pray, "Search me, O God, and know my heart; test me and know my anxious thoughts. See if there is any offensive way in me, and lead me in the way everlasting" (Ps. 139:23–24). As you search for sin, ask if there is anything that stands between you and your relationship with God first, then with others. He is faithful to gently confront your sin. Keeping your heart tender to his prodding and his gentle correction will bring you life.

There may be a spirit of heaviness or a repeated action that keeps coming to mind that bothers you and brings an uneasiness or lack of peace. Immediately, after the Holy Spirit brings the offense to your attention, willingly admit and acknowledge your sin to God. Confess each sin individually that the Spirit confronts specifically. Confession is agreeing with God about your sin. Remember the Sacrifice; accept the final offering for your sin. Atonement is God's solution to restoration. Repentance is our response to God's solution.

James Dobson once said on his radio show, "Forgiveness is worth asking for." It sets the heart free. King David in the Psalms attests that if we cherish sin in our heart the LORD would not listen; but when we have acknowledged our sin and his forgiveness God has surely listened and heard our voice in prayer. "Let us draw near to God with a sincere heart in full assurance of faith, having our hearts sprinkled to cleanse us from a guilty conscience and having our bodies washed with pure water."

God is glorified when we are reconciled, extending forgiveness to one another, especially when it is not in our strength to forgive. When we are deeply hurt we can choose to respond by the surrender of our will, asking for help to forgive by his grace. As we keep in prayer giving the offender back to God and claiming his forgiveness, our heart will heal over time until the sting in our heart has ceased.

How can we live out God's message of reconciliation and forgiveness to the world if we cannot accept it for ourselves and live out reconciliation in our relationships? To restore a relationship or to bring healing, confess to others when it is beneficial for you and for them. "Therefore, confess your sins to each other and pray for each other so that you may be healed" (1 John 1:9). Make restitution when possible or as the Holy Spirit leads you. It may be necessary to make restitution with others to bring restoration.

Once we have asked for forgiveness and come into fellowship with Jesus, we must believe that we have received it. "As far as the east is from the west, so far has he removed our transgressions from us" (Ps. 103:12). Often the enemy will continue to bring your sin to mind—the sin which you have previously confessed—and lie about the fact that you have been forgiven. But you must claim that ". . . there is now no condemnation for those in Christ . . ." (Rom. 8:1), and walk in freedom and joy for the grace and mercy you have been given.

Sinking Sin

Every summer our family vacation is spent on a rented houseboat at Lake Norris, Tennessee. The whole week is filled with water-skiing, tubing, and having all swims—when everybody puts on a life jacket and jumps in for a dip. This year toward the end of the week, my youngest daughter asked me if I'd seen her glasses. After hearing those words my stomach sank.

The only time the family had seen her glasses was earlier that day when she had them on her precious, freckled face. The whole family searched the houseboat. We looked through her suitcase, through the games, and through the towels. Leave it up to mom; I even went through the trash can. As we backtracked through the day's events and discussed the last time she had worn them, we couldn't exactly remember.

After an "Ah ha" moment, we decided the answer was in the camera. Earlier that afternoon the kids had jumped 20 feet off the top of the houseboat while the parents were in their ski boats taking pictures below. As we reviewed the digital photos, the first shot taken was of all the kids lined up at the top of the boat ready to jump together. There was my daughter, pretty as can be in her baby blue life vest, her pearly smile and her brown wire-rimmed glasses. We had found her glasses all right! They were at the bottom of the lake. There was no fetching her specs that were now 60 feet deep.

As soon as we made this observation and showed my daughter the proof, tears came flowing from her eyes like a faucet. Many words were offered to bring her comfort. I myself had been reminded that same day to remove my hat and sunglasses before going skiing! Encouraging my daughter that we had experienced a safe week and no one had been hurt brought a slightly new perspective and gratitude—being thankful that she didn't have to drive us home brought a little giggle.

I was reminded that the Bible says, "(God) You will have compassion on us . . . and hurl all our iniquities into the depths of the sea" (Mic. 7:19). The deepest depth of the ocean is approximately 36,000 feet. There is no fetching our sins from the bottom of the sea. What God says he will do, he will do!

Leaving the glasses at the bottom of the lake was such a great picture of what God does with our sin. My daughter's loss was an accident, but God's Words are intentional. How freeing is that? I need to work on believing that my mess-ups, angry responses toward my kids, and lack of patience with the process of my book, can all be forgiven. When I am stirred in my heart to confess these things, then I need to believe God takes them and hurls the sin no longer to be seen. . . . Our sin sinks!!

I'd be a whole lot better off if I'd just leave my sin down in the depths, but I am the one who tends to go deep sea fishing. I drag it all back up, practically drowning in the meantime, forgetting that God hurled my sin there into the deep, not me. Just like my daughter, I often need a new perspective, seeing with eyes of faith. Embracing the truth of our sinful remedy sets our hearts free—to breathe, laugh, and go on living—by faith.

When our heart is examined, our sins are confessed and relationships are made right, believe God's promise that "the prayer of a righteous man is powerful and effective" (James 5:16).

In the Old Testament, God even provided a visual example as the priests made their offerings in the tabernacle. Aaron was to cast lots for the two goats that were brought into the tabernacle. One goat was to be sacrificed for a sin offering. The other offering was to be presented alive before God to be used by sending it into the desert as a scapegoat (Lev. 16:8–10). Jesus again fulfilled the symbolism of the tabernacle regulations. Jesus is our scapegoat for our guilt and shame. He takes it away to be seen no more.

Remember the priests in the Old Testament entering the tabernacle; after they passed the bronze altar, they washed their hands and feet in the bronze basin. In the prophecy of Jesus' death, David proclaimed in the Psalms that Jesus would be poured out like a drink offering. His sacrifice proclaims, "I cleanse you from all your sins . . ." (Ezek. 36:33).

The rich symbolism in this truth is fulfilled as Jesus said to his disciple Peter, "Unless I wash you, you have no part *with* me. A person who has had a bath needs only to wash his feet; his whole body is clean . . ." (John 13:8, 10). In the culture of that day as a courtesy extended to the guest, feet were washed as they entered the home to remove the dirt from their sandaled feet. Feet seem to symbolize where the body has been and the person's future destination. I think feet are the least desirable part of the human body and the funniest looking, yet they bring such stability and performance. Jesus said of himself, Follow me ". . . I am the way . . . No one comes to the Father except through me" (John 14:6).

The cleansing water is also the water of Life, as Jesus proclaims; "Whoever believes in me, as the Scripture has said, streams of living water will flow from within him" (John 7:38). The cleansing is a necessary step to prepare your heart to come humbly before a holy God to receive his filling and fullness, then to let love flow.

Remember, we must come before God on his terms and by his standards. In the Old Testament, a young man, Uzziah, was placed in position as King over Jerusalem. As a righteous leader, he sought the LORD and had success. Uzziah was excellent at being commander and chief. He assembled a well-trained army and provided every artillery weapon; including shields, spears, helmets, coats of armor, bows, and slingshots for the entire army. Uzziah ordered skilled men to design machines and catapults for Jerusalem's protection. But "pride goes before destruction, and a haughty spirit before a fall" (Prov. 16:18). Uzziah became powerful and he dishonored God's laws ignoring the fact that only priests were to serve in the temple.

Uzziah entered the temple to burn incense on the altar. Eighty other courageous priests rushed in to rescue him. They warned Uzziah that it was not right for him to burn incense and strongly encouraged him to leave. Uzziah did not listen and become enraged at the priests in front of the altar. Immediately, leprosy broke out on his forehead. He willingly was swiftly escorted out of the temple. Uzziah had leprosy for the rest of his life—never to enter the temple or rule from the palace again.

God must be approached in a holy way. The beauty of the new covenant of grace is that he can be approached in a holy way when we reverently acknowledge our sin and believe our sin has gone to the depths of the sea. The invitation from God says, "Come now, let us reason together. Though your sins are like scarlet, they shall be as white as snow; though they are red as crimson, they shall be like wool" (Isa. 1:18). Accept his forgiveness and walk in the freedom of being clothed in the righteousness of Jesus. You are his bride dressed in white. We are free to enter his presence and find rest.

By the way, my daughter loved her new glasses! Her optometrist told her, "Some little fishy needed new specs!"

Today's Prayer Journal Task

Confessional Sin Passages: Mark 7:20–23, Colossians 3:5, 8, 9, Galatians 5:19–21, 2 Corinthians 6:9–10, Revelations 21:8

- Read the confessional sin passages regularly.
- Examine your heart and write in your journal the ones you need God's assistance to conquer.

Face Fear

Responding to God's invitation—focusing on his immense love for us—conquers our fears. Knowing and trusting all God's love has planned for me, and accepting those things that come into my life as filtered through his hands, keeps me walking step by step as each day unfolds. I find his love irresistible.

Fear is a peculiar apprehension that strikes within us at any time. Fear manifests itself in different ways; many paralyze us and we become ineffective and unfruitful. We face fear of failure, fear of what others might think of us, fear of the unseen world, and fear of the future. We fear anything—you name it. So many phobias exist today which consume our thoughts. I am not addressing psychological fear in its vastness, but briefly touching on the fear of praying. Because there are risks involved we have a choice to make. We can choose not to pray and obstruct our very lifeline, freezing in fear by focusing on the object or circumstance. Or we can choose to pray by faith, think truth, and conquer fear. Abiding in his love is the key to overcoming fear.

In my life, I had a fear of running. I always hated running and never wanted to run any farther than my high school coaches asked me. When I became engaged to my husband, he also encouraged me to run, but my response was the same. At the age of forty, I started running with a younger, persistent friend of mine who can outpace me by minutes!

Once I heard someone say, "The more you run, the more you can run. The more you run, the more you desire to run." The euphoria experienced from running can become an addiction. I think the same case is true for prayer. The more you pray, the more you can pray, and the more you desire to pray.

Life hands us little analogies to help us along in our faith. I began to consider taking a running 101 class with this very persuasive friend. I will confess doubts arose in my mind. Fear of failure lurked behind the questions . . . "Will I be able to run a 5K? Will I run and not fall flat on my face? Will I be able to finish?" The fear of not knowing the future or my capabilities almost kept me from even trying to learn.

Fear threatened to hold me in its grip and paralyze me in a rut. My friend encouraged me, "I'll do it with you. You can do this." These comforting words kept giving me the reassurance I was not alone in this adventure. We made it together. I was gently pushed beyond what I thought I could do by myself.

Looking back, I realized I needed to commit to the race, pay the money, take one step at a time, and begin training with my friend. Some training days were more successful than others. Some days I made three miles without stopping. Other days my body ached and I cramped. I often had to stop and walk a few minutes and take some deep breaths. On difficult days I threw in the towel after a shorter distance and ran again the next day. My friend never left my side through difficult training days nor during the race.

To miss the opportunity to change and to grow because I chose fear would have been a mistake. I have gained a marvelous running buddy, a new circle of friends, a stronger marriage, and a new interest beyond my expectations.

Running is much like prayer; we are uncomfortable with the unknown. We fear getting involved, being vulnerable, and the uncertainty of change. But the good news concerning our fear of praying, we have been given a friend, a "Helper"—the Holy Spirit who aids us in our prayers when we don't even have the words to speak. As I look at both workouts, running and prayer, we can choose fear or faith, life or death. "Now choose life" and the activities that promote it and receive blessings (Deut. 30:19). Simply embrace what the spirit is doing in you!

Some days prayer is like running; it is a struggle to get started, but worth every attempt to condition your heart. Often the outcome is based on my feelings. But despite how I feel, the fact that I show up and make an effort is good. I listen to the need of my body and spirit. It is always worth it. I know it is still beneficial for my heart even though every run is not perfect. It is the same with my prayer time. To be faithful with what he has given me, I have a fuller life and a heart that received some conditioning because I made the choice to meet with him.

Into Me You See

My idol of self-protection keeps God and people out of my heart. I fear they won't like what they find. I fear the pain of rejection I might see in their eyes or actions. But God is teaching me the wound or weakness in our lives is the very thing that he uses—the hurts can create vulnerability. God desires to rescue us! "Praise be to the LORD, the God of Israel, because he has come and has redeemed his people. He has raised a horn of salvation for us in the house of his servant David . . . to show mercy to our fathers and to remember his holy covenant, the oath he swore to our father, Abraham: . . . *to enable us to serve without fear* in holiness and righteousness before him all of our days" (Luke 1:68–69, 72–75). As we cry out for mercy, intimate prayer necessitates vulnerability. We all struggle with being vulnerable, but vulnerability creates intimacy. I have heard intimacy defined—into me you see.

When I was dating my husband, I finally realized after much wooing on his part that he was the one for me. God and I talked about that decision often. I sought God's direction as I read the scriptures to guide and encourage me in my decision (Rom. 15:4). As I was praying, I read Proverbs 21:1, which says, "A king's heart is in the hand of the LORD; he directs it like a watercourse wherever he pleases." Most importantly, I *knew* Eric loved me. He loved my weaknesses unconditionally. In particular, he was drawn to me in my coke bottle glasses! My vision is off the charts at -16.

When I was growing up the hurtful and careless words of others penetrated my heart regarding my thick glasses. But God in his goodness sent me this man who cared for me in my weakness. Every evening he intentionally went to get my coke bottle wide rimmed glasses and my contact case so I could rest my eyes. There is no greater gift than to receive the unconditional acceptance of love. Through that very act, unaware to him, he brought healing. Without that former pain of rejection, I am not sure I could grasp and totally appreciate the immensity of my husband's acceptance and love.

What a valuable lesson this has taught me in life. God loved me (and you) first too, unconditionally accepting me; he knows me completely, including my weaknesses. Understanding that great and immutable love of God brings hope of our true security and identity. He wants us to come to him offering our weaknesses and insecurities so he can take those things in our lives and transform them for his glory.

Being human and conditional, this is hard to grasp, but I am clinging to the truth by faith and committing to focus on his perfect love, "Perfect love casts (drives) out fear" (1 John 4:18). Understanding the truth of all that comes into my life is permeated with his love, helps me to overcome fear and gives me a sense of security.

Henri J. M. Nouwen said, "I wonder if fear is not our main obstacle to prayer. When we enter into the presence of God and start to sense the huge reservoir of fear inside us, we want to run away into the many distractions which our busy world offers so abundantly. But we shouldn't be afraid of our fears. We can confront them, give words to them and lead them into the presence of the One who says, 'Be not afraid. It is I.'" Ask God to "enable us to serve him without fear" in our prayer life (Luke 1:74).

Think of our prayer life as being entrusted with some money and ask, "How will I invest it?" The parable was given by Jesus in the New Testament, "Again, it will be like a man going on a journey, who called his servants and entrusted his property to them. To one he gave five talents of money, to another two talents, and to another one talent, each according to his ability. Then he went on his journey. The man who had received the five talents went at once and put his money to work and gained five more. So also, the one with the two talents gained two more. But the man who had received the one talent went off, dug a hole in the ground and hid his master's money" (Matt. 25:14–18).

Who was commended by the master? The men that invested their talent wisely were told, "Well done, good and faithful servant! You have been faithful with a few things; I will put you in charge of many things. Come and share your master's happiness!" (Matt. 25:23). The man with the one talent was afraid to disappoint his master by taking risks. He was afraid to fail. His talent was taken from him.

I sure want to be found faithful and responsible with the gifts God has given me, don't you? The gift of intercession is often buried as a forgotten commodity. The greatest responsibility we have is to pray for the lives of those we love and encounter. Let us not fall short of using the resources we have been entrusted and sin against God by failing to pray for one another (1 Sam. 12:23).

Training to run so I could participate in a 5K has led me to some interesting encounters. During my run, I have finally managed to get to the point where I can think about other things besides breathing and actually have a short conversation. When I run alone, I pray as often as I can stay focused. I often run a route near my neighborhood. At the end of one very long hill there is a magnificent magnolia tree. One of my running buddies said one day, "If we can just get to the magnolia tree it's all downhill from there."

"That certainly is my goal," I thought to myself. Then I proceeded to tell her between gasps for breath that a magnolia tree is my Christian metaphor. I grew up with gorgeous strong magnolia trees in my front yard. Their fragrant scent is a wonderful reminder of my childhood memories. Initially, magnolias are the most scraggly looking of trees, but after years and years of growth they become mighty and magnificent trees, bearing pure white flowers with a pure soothing fragrance. Like the Christian life, it is not always a pretty process, it takes time, but strength and beauty await us all.

One particular day, my running buddy cancelled and I was on my own. Getting out there to run is 80% of the battle—just get started! I was tempted not to go, but I was dressed and felt the need to exercise. After about a mile into the run, instead of focusing on each step I was taking, I happened to glance up. To my right I saw a man in his driveway on his knees with a cane. I kept running and looked down at my steps as I was thinking to myself, *That man was on his knees?*

I heard him yell, "Hey, could you help me?"

I turned and looked again and slowed down my jog at this point. Then I actually realized, "This man is on his knees!?"

"Could you help me up?" he yelled again.

He was an elderly man, but with a very large frame. My heart began to fear the unfamiliar situation, a normal response in our society. There was risk involved to jog over and help him up. I gradually crossed the road to the other side. In my action I made a decision to help. I grabbed his arm underneath his elbow. He grabbed my entire arm; he put his weight on his cane as we both worked his way off the ground. I smelt an odor thinking it might be alcohol on his breath, but it was only mid-morning. He said he was going to pick up his newspaper. He had fallen about six feet away from it.

"Let me get it for you," I said.

I made sure he was okay, and as he returned inside his home, he thanked me.

"Thank you, I needed the break."

On the rest of my run that morning, I thought about the encounter with the elderly man. I was saddened I did not respond sooner to seeing the sight of him kneeling. I regretted fearing what he might do to me. I prayed for him a while, thanking God that he could use me in a simple way to help a man in need. But conviction came as I prayed; I realized I can be that way in life. I get so busy attempting to get it all done, to keep up with it all, rushing, focused on me and my problems, that I miss noticing people who need help. Fear keeps me from risking love.

On my route back by the man's house, I realized his yard was the yard with the magnolia tree. I wept a little on that run as I prayed for the elderly man. Have you ever cried and tried to breathe while running at the same time? It is not easily done. Now, whenever I pass the elderly man's house by car or on foot, I say a prayer for him. I don't know what he is going through, but the encounter has led me to pray for him, for his health, and salvation. The yard with the magnolia is a reminder. I may not ever know how my prayers have touched his life until I reach heaven.

God will show us what and for whom to pray. Start praying for whomever enters your path or is put on your heart. We are commanded to pray "on all occasions" (Eph. 6:18), "in every circumstance" (Phil. 4:6 AMP), "continually," and "without ceasing" (1 Thess. 5:17 NASB). Never stop! We are told to "always keep on praying for all the saints" (Eph. 6:18).

Prayer is our lifeline to God. As I mentioned before, a great correlation I discovered in my runs would be that prayer become as essential and frequent as breathing. It's most definitely necessary for life. Breathing is natural and prayer is natural once we have trained our minds to conduct a dialogue with God throughout the day. But when you run, it is so important to get into a rhythm and pace, to enter the "zone" my friend calls it. At that point in the run the miles seem to merge and the breathing becomes less laborious. I am no longer dying to breathe and struggling with each step. Prayer is much the same. Step by step, little by little, you gain endurance as you practice praying. It takes getting past the wall and entering into the zone. Surrender yourself, let go of control, commit, and banish fear even when it's hard.

"We can't let our fear that God may not affirmatively answer our prayers keep us from praying."[1] Jesus Christ did not get everything he asked for in prayer. Jesus pleaded for deliverance from the eminent suffering on the cross, bearing all of our sins, and the heartwrenching separation from his Father. Jesus fell on his face, praying, "My Father, if there is any way, get me out of this. But please, not what I want. You, what do you want?" (Matt. 26:39 MSG) Jesus yielded to God's will and for that we need to be thankful. The cup of suffering and sacrifice of death was never omitted by God from Jesus' purpose here on earth.

Many other biblical figures incredibly used by God did not get everything they asked. Moses never got to cross the Jordan River into the Promised Land. King David never built God's earthly temple. Looking back through our own lives we can often say . . . "Thank goodness . . . God didn't answer that prayer the way I wanted!"

Believing and receiving God's love can set us free from the barrier of fear in prayer. Taking small steps in prayer toward God will bring you to a new place in a month from now and more growth in a year from now. Invest your time wisely, in a labor of love, offering prayer for others. In heaven you will hear, "Well done, good and faithful servant! Come and share your master's happiness."

Face the Fear of Journaling

How do I convince you that journaling is a safe place to record your experiences and feelings without an intimidating fear that what you have written will be read by someone else? First, build an atmosphere of trust. I journaled for years before my children were born. When my children were toddlers, I would use every golden opportunity to write; I never tried to hide it. Really, there is little to hide. My journals are my story of who I am and who I am becoming.

Feel free to discuss with others the virtue of respect for your writings as personal belongings. Be aware though, especially with children, the more you act possessive and protective, conveying suspicion, the more curious others may become and be tempted to read your journal without an invitation.

Journals are a collection of recorded moments in time. Many of my moments are not perfectly handled and my responses in life are far from loving, but they are my real feelings and reactions all the same. If indeed someone peruses the pages of my journal, I hope the entries would not be read judgmentally, but with grace; gaining an understanding that God is still at work in my heart. I hope they would see the process of transformation through the pages written about my life. Not one part or one entry, but the whole, would need to be taken into consideration to recognize that God is not finished with me yet.

Hopefully through my writings people would see Jesus living, working, and moving in my life. This life is not really about me anyway, it's about him. With his grace, God always brings me around in my journaling to see the need for him in the situation—forgiveness, repentance, restoration, and redemption are fully extended to me and others. None of us is perfect. We fail ourselves and each other time and again. We are better to release our mistakes and remember what Christ has done for us. When we do not forgive others we limit Jesus' work on the cross. Choose to quickly forgive and move forward to the new things God has for you.

The benefits of journaling are numerous. Do not forego journaling because of the possibility others might read it. What is the worst that could happen? A significant person reads your journal entry and is possibly hurt by your frankness, perception or truthfulness. It boils down to trust. Trust God with the possibility that what you have written might be found. There may be a purpose for further discussion or reconciliation between you and the inquirer. Nowhere in the Bible does it say, hide the truth, but rather it says, "Speak the truth in love" (Eph. 4:15).

Confidently, I can say those who have been close to me in proximity—my parents, my roommates from college and my single adult years, my husband, and my children—have never read my journals without my willingness to share them. Trust God to protect your words because they are your written words brought to him. All things belong to him—even our words.

Without God's help I find my words and my heart are like a heap of unfolded clothes on the floor. When I start my day praying before I speak, my thoughts become organized and I am prepared for the day ahead. God is pleased as we offer up our prayers, and our lives, orally and written, as a sweet aroma rising up to him. As I spiritually mature in self-control over my mouth, I desire that my words be like Samuel. Samuel was the first in a great line of prophets. When he was young, it was recorded in scripture that Samuel was lying down in the temple and he did not know the LORD; after three attempts he finally recognized God calling, "Samuel, Samuel."

Samuel readily replied, "Speak LORD, for your servant is listening."

The LORD instructed Samuel that he was going to do something in Israel that would make everyone's ears tingle. God had in mind that Samuel would be an instrument in establishing Israel as a nation. Amazingly, after God speaks, Samuel lies back down and falls asleep in front of the altar. What a foreshadowing of the new covenant of grace! Remember, no one but the priests were to enter into the Holy of Holies and that was once a year! It's such a great picture of where we need to find rest!

In the morning, Samuel opened the doors to the house of the LORD. "Here I am," Samuel replied to the priest, Eli. Here we find those same three words of surrender, "Here I am." These three words said humbly, yielding to God, can lead you to fascinating destinations. It was here in the temple, asking God to speak to him, that Samuel discovered God, his purpose, and calling. The LORD continued to reveal himself to Samuel through messages in the tabernacle. The LORD was with Samuel as he grew up and he became a prophetic figure, priest, and judge. Samuel would help institute Israel's first king, Saul, and later announce his withdrawal of divine favor, and then his successor as King David. These kings sought out Samuel's godly counsel. Scripture says, "He let none of his words fall to the ground" (1 Sam. 3:19).

What an honor for Samuel, to have God record in scripture his thoughts regarding Samuel's words. How could this honorable account be fulfilled? Samuel became a priest of reliability who knew God's Word. In Samuel's authority he spoke blessing and prayers over his people. He was a man of prayer. His words from prayers of blessing, wise counsel, and honor went up to the throne as a fragrance to the LORD. Samuel's speech reflected his heart, and his ability to pray reflected his knowledge of God. As we can see in Samuel's humble reply to God, his daily prayer life did not consist of only talking to God; he listened. He heard wisdom from God to be able to speak hope and give direction to the Israelites.

Samuel grasped the amazing truth that our great Intercessor is never silent. In an intense time of leadership before preparing for battle, Samuel said, "Assemble all of Israel . . . and I will intercede *with* the LORD for you" (1 Sam. 7:5). To keep his prayers from being an empty shadow, Samuel offered the burnt sacrifice of a lamb while crying out to the LORD on Israel's behalf. He prayed with God and God was pleased. Israel was victorious as God thundered against the enemy and overthrew them. Samuel honored God by setting up a stone of remembrance. "He named it, 'Ebenezer,' saying, 'Thus far has the LORD helped us'" (1 Sam. 7:12). Your journals can be like an Ebenezer for you, a ready reminder of all that God has done to help you on your journey in life.

Not only do we fumble over our words that come out of our mouths, but we also fear our thoughts. Have you ever heard of cognophobia? It is a legitimate fear of facing our own thoughts.[2] Maybe this is the cause of our addiction to busyness and noise. There is a sense of awkwardness when we are alone. We fear discovering our true selves and not liking what we find. But all this is good to see ourselves as we really are—desperately in need of a Savior. In prayer ask God to see yourself as he sees you—not how you perceive yourself. Believe me, from my own experience, you will want to write this down.

To journal your journey is truly a gift from God. Think back in time when only the spoken language existed. Later, symbols were created and used to communicate and record history. Letters for languages were established so the language of communication could be written and be precise. Through God's preservation of his Word and after years of interpretation, when you hold God's sacred Word in your hand, thank him for the blessing. It is a treasure like gold to have it recorded and available freely at our finger tips.

Do you ever ponder that we may lose our freedom of reading God's Word during the end times under the one world government of the antichrist? With the efforts in the past few years to remove the words "Under God" from the Pledge of Allegiance, I have wondered if in our lifetime or that of our children, we will lose the freedom of having God's Word accessible in our homes.

When I was traveling in Israel, I had a vivid experience that has fostered such thoughts. Our tour group was entering the Islamic Temple grounds, the location of the Dome of the Rock. Soldiers stood at the entrance and by their governing laws no Bibles were to be taken into the Temple area. As I walked through the entrance, my Bible was taken out of my hands. I was whisked through the gate; my heart sank and tears began to flow.

My Bible is very sentimental to me, not only because it is God's Word, but because it contains years of history during my life's journey. My parents had given me a thin, black Bible my freshman year of college. I had worn it out during twelve spiritually vibrant and growing years of my life; traveling overseas, finding my career, jobs, moves, getting married, and having my children. Even in Europe traveling, I actually locked my Bible in a safe in our room. It was priceless to me.

My heavy heart did not even attempt to guide my feet into the Temple to see inside the Dome of the Rock. As we exited the temple grounds that morning, my Bible was returned to me, but it has left an eternal impact of valuing the freedom to have God's Word, accessible daily, and the importance of having it hidden in my heart.

Scripture proclaims, "They overcame him (the enemy) by the blood of the Lamb and by the word of their testimony" (Rev. 12:11). We have the privilege and responsibility to write down the story of our lives and capture significant moments to pass to the next generation. There is power in sharing our testimony; our lives demonstrating the power of the gospel.

As we reflect on our journals, we will begin to see a transformation taking place in our surrendered hearts bound in God's Word, living for his purposes and empowered in prayer. "Bind them (God's Word) upon your heart forever; fasten them around your neck. When you walk, they will guide you; when you sleep, they will watch over you; when you awake, they will speak to you. For these commands are a lamp, this teaching is a light, and the corrections of discipline are the way to life" (Prov. 6:21–23). Do you see God's protection and provision for all that we need in life is hidden in his living Word? We not only need to hear the Word preached at church on Sundays, but we need to search for it ourselves, dig in and hide it in our hearts . . . so it's accessible in time of need.

Remember as the priests experienced in the tabernacle, the only light given from the lampstand must be kept burning day and night. Jesus is our light. "He is like the light of morning at sunrise on a cloudless morning, like the brightness after rain . . ." (2 Sam. 23:4). He is the light that breaks through into our dark uncertain paths of life or even into our seasons of rebellion. His Word brings us back to righteous living. How desperately we need to read it every day. Our reward is not only protection and clarity in our paths, but promised blessings and victory for those who have learned to walk by faith in the light of his presence, daily letting him filter our life with his truth.

The Holy Spirit is the fire living in us that empowers us to live in victory over sin. We can change so that we might not sin against him. Through prayer—fan into flame the ember in your heart and do not allow the enemy to snuff out your light like a burning wick of a candle. Then we can proclaim God's name by shining and by simply being different in the ways we treat people; maybe just by caring and sharing the word of truth, giving hope to others. Daily as we walk and talk with God, the Lamp shines certainty of his love into our hearts day and night.

As Jesus dwells within you, you reflect and magnify his light. May the cry of our heart be, "O Lord keep my lamp burning" (Ps. 18:28). In the new covenant of grace when his spirit lives in you, "you are the light of the world" and you are blessed (Matt. 5:14). Reflecting on God's Word through your journals can often be a light to your path. "Your journal is your history with God."[3] The testimony you have recorded is a lasting witness.

Today's Prayer Journal Task

- Do you fear others reading your journal? Why or why not? If so, what steps can you take to experience freedom in your writing?
- What would God say about your words?
- Make your journal an Ebenezer that reminds you, "thus far has the Lord helped us."
- Write down a time when God's Word was a light for your path, giving you direction.

CHAPTER 9

MEET WITH GOD
BEYOND THE VEIL

T HE WORK OF prayer believes that God invites us to come, seek him, and pour out our hearts to him with a promise that he will listen. God is mighty to save, to redeem our lives and our mistakes. He is the great *I AM* and can handle what we bring to him. There is no sin, no failure, no hurt, that one drop of Christ's atoning blood cannot cover. Let us not limit the blood by failing to take our every request, concern, and heartache to him and wait patiently for his reply, his salvation. "How gracious he will be when you cry for help! As soon as he hears, he will answer you" (Isa. 30:19). We have direct access to the King's listening ear.

Picture your heart as a sheet of smoked glass. Do you know God sees through all the facades and the false self we use to cover up our sinful hearts? (Ps. 44:21). God sees through our smoke screen. We must be truthful when we come to Jesus. Jesus is approachable, accessible, and responsive. Our prayers should be raw, gut level, and honest. He knows our thoughts and the words on our tongues before we even speak them. Only truth can dwell in heaven, all else is perishable. We can receive refreshment from God when we choose to be honest and tell him our sin. We each have a conscience. When our unspoken thoughts and behaviors are not in love and disturb our hearts, we can acknowledge them before God or suppress and hide them. But God sees and knows, "for there is no one who does not sin" (1 Kings 8:46).

One of my favorite passages that God uses to confront my busy lifestyle is the story of Mary and Martha found in Luke 10. Jesus and some disciples, possibly seventy men, were invited by Martha into her home. Martha was anxiously hosting Jesus. She was bustling about getting things perfect. Martha noticed and resented that her sister, Mary, was not helping in the kitchen, but relaxing and enjoying some quality time with Jesus. In the heat of the moment, in Martha's hastiness and distraction, she forgot *who* Jesus was—God's Son. Jesus had just recently provided food to feed five thousand men from five loaves of bread and two fish.

I respect the fact that Martha poured out her complaint to Jesus, instead of literally continuing to stew in the kitchen when she realized she was doing all the work by herself while Mary sat at Jesus' feet.

"Lord, don't you care?" was at the depth of Martha's cry for help. Jesus listens and responds with a gentle correction, reminding Martha that being in his presence and getting her heart right must come first. Jesus penetrates beyond her words of frustration and addresses the issues in her heart. Martha's honesty begins her journey of humble transformation.

Pour out your heart to Jesus. "Cast all your anxiety on him because he cares for you" (1 Pet. 5:7). Jesus asks us to come and he listens with intention to respond to your heart. "Jesus never interrupts."[1] His love is patient and kind. He is gentle so his correction is gentle. As we remain teachable, applying his Word, drawing near in prayer, transformation begins. It is to our benefit to remain humble and willing to receive correction. God says, "If you had responded to my rebuke, I would have poured out my heart to you and made my thoughts known to you" (Prov. 1:23). Our pride can cut off our communication with God to the wonderful things he has to say.

Pray when your heart is disappointed or broken. King David strengthened himself in spending time with God by pouring out his complaints, his failures, and heart aches. David wrote that in the evening, morning, or at noon he cried out in distress, and God heard his voice. David wrote some psalms of thanksgiving, some of wisdom, but many were psalms of heartwrenching complaint. God invites and encourages us over and over to pour out our hearts to him. "In my anguish I cried to the LORD, and he answered by setting me free" (Ps. 118:5). Surrender your hearts to him. Some days all you can cry is "Help!" His ears are attentive. He replies, ". . . I Myself will help you" (Isa. 41:14). Of course, God cares! God delights in blessing our lives with his very presence.

Remember Mary and Martha, *only one thing is needed*—abide and remain, the result will be the abundant fruit from attentive listening. "Prayer is sitting at the feet of Jesus rather than working through a list of requests."[2]

Come before him in worship while you wait, through praise and thanksgiving. These two vital aspects of prayer may very well be represented by the two golden cherubim that were over the ark of the Testimony, where God de-clares, "There . . . I will meet with you" (Exod. 25:22). An important part of prayer is waiting as long as it takes, listening expectantly for him to respond to our prayers and to guide us. In the silence, he is there. He never leaves us.

God longs for us to communicate with him. He is pleased, he is delighted when we respond to his invitation and share the desires of our heart. God is excited for us to receive his love and be in his presence. By bringing him our every encounter and concern he is included in our journey. Our communicating with him is his pleasure; the very reason that we were designed for a life of prayer; the very reason the veil was torn.

Today's Prayer Journal Task

- Do you ever feel like Martha, wanting to ask, "Lord, don't you care?" Ask him and wait for his response.
- What do you want God to do for you?
- Do you know what you have to say is important to God? Write a specific prayer and invite God to act.

We Listen

MOST OF US WOULD agree that listening is the key to a good quality conversation. Without attentiveness to the words of another we do not know how to properly respond. In any relationship there is a time to share and a time to be quiet and listen. Often the greatest gift you can give to another is to listen, to listen with your whole heart. Do you listen attentively with your eyes, ears, mind—with your whole being?

As we enter beyond the veil and comprehend that prayer is a two-way line of communication with God, let us approach his throne with reverence, intentionally spending more time listening to what God might say to us than bringing our lists of needs to him. We will come to realize prayer is more than sharing our requests and desires with him. It is vital that we listen, offering thanks in the meantime, as we wait to hear God's thoughts toward us. He is God and we are not. This humble attitude accomplishes an essential part of praying—that we value God's Word, will, and thoughts.

How can we serve God by fulfilling what he has said if we have not first taken the time to listen? "The key to a successful ministry is hearing from God."[3] God wants to communicate with us even more than we want to listen. As he has already demonstrated through the gift of giving us his Son, he continues to communicate his presence in our lives through the encouragement of the Holy Spirit, revealing himself through his Word and through others.

What a wonderful way to show God we love him by listening and recording his voice. "The words I have spoken to you are spirit and they are life" (John 6:63). Friends share secrets—and Jesus, who calls you friend, longs to share the secrets of his heart with you as you pray, read his Word, and journal. Be free to communicate with God unreservedly, but be intentional about listening. God has a message for you.

So often we speak, and God listens. But do we listen with reverence when God speaks? Repeatedly, God will encourage me through a verse I need and shed light into my heart's concerns. God's Word is timely, perfect, and brings contentment even when it's confronting my sin. "When your words came, I ate them; they were my joy and my heart's delight . . ." (Jer. 15:16). Pray and ask God to help you listen with his heart—a heart of perfect trust and love.

King Solomon, in his wisdom, wrote the Proverbs, stating, "Just as lotions and fragrance give sensual delight, a sweet friendship refreshes the soul" (Prov. 27:9 MSG). The LORD wants to speak with us, as a man speaks with his friend. "Prayer is essential because it puts us in a posture to hear from God."[4] Listen, listen, listen to his voice with a Bible open to receive from him. He wants to make his thoughts known to you. When he leads you to a verse or promise write it down. "He wakens me morning by morning, wakens my ear to listen like one being taught. The Sovereign LORD has opened my ears, and I have not been rebellious. I have not drawn back" (Isa. 50:4b–5). John Bunyan simply states, "In prayer it is better to have a heart without words than words without a heart."

As we consider the realm of prayer, everyone should be quick to listen. "Let the wise listen and add to their learning, and let the discerning get guidance" (Prov. 1:5). There is no other way than God's way—to listen and obey. God reprimanded the Israelites and called them wicked for plugging their ears and living independently from him. "'While you were doing all these things' (worshipping idols), declares the LORD, 'I spoke to you again and again, but you did not listen; I called you, but you did not answer.' They did not listen or pay attention; instead, they followed the stubborn inclinations of their evil hearts. They went backward and not forward" (Jer. 7:13, 24). I don't think I want my life to be digressing backward. The lesson? Listen and follow him.

"God has spoken from his sanctuary" (Ps. 108:7a). God speaks in a variety of ways. There are traditional ways he speaks to us and others we may not easily perceive. We know that God speaks through his eternal Word and Spirit, but he may communicate his message through dreams, through the comfort of a friend, through music, the gentle arrival of a butterfly or the beauty in the song of a bird.

Listening is a mark of a believer. Jesus declares, "My sheep listen to my voice; I know them, and they follow me" (John 10:27). Listening in prayer often leads to supernatural direction. ". . . At your feet they all bow down, and from you receive instruction . . ." (Deut. 33:3b). The Holy Spirit counsels our thoughts through the teaching and guidance of God's Word. He prompts us in practical ways to love and serve him by demonstrating love as we serve others.

THE INVITATION

God emphasizes the importance of listening to Jesus in the story of Jesus' transfiguration. When Jesus took Peter, James, and John up a high mountain by themselves, Jesus was transfigured before them. "His face shone like the sun, and his clothes became as white as the light. Just then there appeared before them Moses and Elijah, talking with Jesus. Peter said to Jesus, 'Lord, it is good for us to be here. If you wish, I will put up three shelters—one for you, one for Moses, and one for Elijah.'" Peter's words make me laugh because in a moment like this I know I would be fumbling over my words too, and scrambling to figure out what to "do" instead of just simply being still in awe.

"While (Peter) was still speaking, a bright cloud enveloped them, and a voice from the cloud said, 'This is my Son, whom I love; with him I am well pleased. *Listen to him!*'" Almighty God declares his immense love and approval for his Son. God commands them to listen to Jesus. "When the disciples heard this, they fell facedown to the ground, terrified. But Jesus came and gently touched them. 'Get up,' he said. 'Don't be afraid.' When they looked up, they saw no one except Jesus" (Matt. 17:1–8). I am sure Peter, James, and John were convicted to listen to Jesus like never before. I would think Peter learned to listen twice as much as he spoke.

May we all have willing teachable hearts that pray, "Speak, LORD, for your servant is listening" (1 Sam. 3:9). Listen, surrender, and accept the answer . . . "Yes," "No" or "Wait." Many times we are *made* to accept the answer by circumstances out of our control, but learning to yield to God's will and way with a good attitude helps, instead of fighting against it. In response to our prayers, rooted in God's love for us, we may or may not receive the answer we wanted. Our attitude in response to any of these answers should be with a heart of surrender, "Yes, LORD" and give thanks, even when it is difficult. Know God is seated on his throne.

It takes time to develop the spiritual discipline of being still and quiet. Start with a small amount of time like five or ten minutes. Gradually, your length of time will increase as you learn to concentrate and wait on God. I keep a notepad or use the top of my journal page to write down the interrupting thoughts of the things I need to do that can come to invade or distract my time of worship. The seemingly interrupting to dos and ideas that the Holy Spirit may place on my heart—*Call Peggy, send a card to—*

In my own experience, I have never heard an audible, thundering voice of God speak. But I have experienced a verse found or given to encourage, counsel, or give me direction at just the right moment—a gentle calling of my name, a conviction impressed upon me, a rapid heartbeat, and quickening by the Holy Spirit. The Holy Spirit instructs us in purposeful, persistent, and practical ways. "But when he, the Spirit of truth, comes, he will guide you into all truth. He will not speak on his own; he will speak only what he hears, and he will tell you what is yet to come" (John 16:13). We have been given a Counselor who is a Guide to navigate us through life if we will listen and follow.

In the new covenant of grace, the Holy Spirit preserves God's living Word on the tablets of our hearts. "But the Counselor, the Holy Spirit, whom the Father will send in my name, will teach you all things and will remind you of everything I have said to you" (John 14:26). Most of the time, there is no supernatural encounter, but just a calm assurance that God is present and we have spent time together.

Listening takes a patient heart that is willing to wait in the quiet, willing to risk not hearing something of great monumental significance or that which gives an emotional high. Our true motive for prayer should be simply a longing to be in God's presence.

As one woman described her prayer life, "'Most of the time, my prayer consists in experiencing the absence of God in the hope of communion.' She is not richly endowed with mystical experiences. That is fine because it reflects the truth of her impoverished humanity. Yet the experience of absence does not mean the absence of experience. For example, the soldier in combat who, during a lull in battle, steals a glance at his wife's picture tucked in his helmet, is more present to her at that moment in her absence than he is to the rifle that is present in his hands. Likewise, the poor in spirit perceive that religious experience and mystical 'highs' are not the goal of authentic prayer; rather, the goal is communion with God."[5] Make it your goal to "be" with God daily. Not to necessarily receive something, but we come *just to love* him.

Today's Prayer Journal Task

- How much time do you take each day to examine and listen to the condition of your own heart?

- Recall a time when the Holy Spirit was faithful to bring you a truth in a time of need.
- What has the Holy Spirit purposely, persistently, and practically put on your heart to do?
- Are you content building your faith in the absence of mystical highs?

God Listens

I love the hymns and one of my favorite is *What A Friend We Have in Jesus*. The author, Joseph Scriven, had more than his fair share of prayers that went unanswered according to our human perception. After losing two fiancées, one to drowning and another to illness, he could have been bitter. In addition, he suffered ill-health throughout his life. As Joseph poured out his pain, he left us with inspired words of comfort found only in Jesus.

What a Friend We Have in Jesus

What a Friend we have in Jesus
All our sins and griefs to bear!
What a privilege to carry
Everything to God in prayer!
O what peace we often forfeit,
O what needless pain we bear,
All because we do not carry
Everything to God in prayer!

Have we trials and temptations?
Is there trouble anywhere?
We should never be discouraged:
Take it to the LORD in prayer.
Can we find a friend so faithful,
Who will all our sorrows share?
Jesus knows our every weakness:
Take it to the LORD in prayer.

Are we weak and heavy-laden,
Cumbered with a load of care?
Jesus only is our refuge;
Take it to the LORD in prayer.
Do thy friends despise, forsake thee?
Take it to the LORD in prayer,
In his arms he'll take and shield thee;
Thou wilt find a solace there.[6]

Like Joseph Scriven, we all have sorrow in our lives; problems that drive us to God, and when we choose not to respond in fear it is a reflection of our faith. We are wiser to press through the pain with prayer, looking for God and trusting in his sovereignty.

Some of the trials in our lives may be in response to our fleshly, faulty tainted perception alone, but other situations may be justified. No matter how I am treated, I am responsible for my response. I am learning about freedom in the Holy Spirit as I listen to him, and in particular, as to whether I should contribute or refrain from any conversation.

Do you ever feel unheard? Do you sometimes feel invisible? I am working on sharpening my listening skills by listening intently to others with my ears and my eyes. Repeatedly throughout my life there have been circumstances when I was speaking with individuals who did not even acknowledge my comments or ideas. I have learned that sometimes people do not engage in conversation to listen. I have come to realize my own kids have selective hearing too! As I consider the situations, perhaps my voice was too gentle or I was not assertive enough. Yet the non-verbal message was sent. Deep within me my not being heard communicated a lack of value—my perception of not being important enough.

In our fast-paced society, I wonder if people are too busy or their minds are too stressed to be sensitive to others. Maybe people are not taught relational skills, the value of considering others by listening, and the appropriate skills to effectively communicate. In addition, our current forms of communication within our society appear to hinder—more than help—our listening skills.

Statistics say that ninety five percent of people really do not mean to hurt your feelings. After praying through this concern, it has actually gotten quite funny to me. I need to accept that it is not necessary to always be heard to validate my identity. I share this to tell you what Jesus impressed on my heart one day in the quiet as I wrestled with this issue of security and being heard.

Several years ago, I was able to get away for a weekend with a friend at her mountain home in Boone, North Carolina. The hush of the mountains and the rushing water from a stream by her cabin calmed my soul. I was sitting in a rocking chair praying through this recurring wound, asking God *why is it that no one hears me?*

A soft, gentle impression came to me. "I want to listen to you, Sarah." I sensed this gentle voice was from the Holy Spirit. At first I wondered, *What did you say*? It lined up with scripture, so I received it as so. Jeremiah 29:12 says, "You will call upon me and come and pray to me, and I will listen to you." The King of the Universe wants to listen to me?! At that moment I was in awe, clinging to the tender words that brought healing, validation, and transformation to my soul.

We have access anytime, day or night, to talk to the King of the Universe. He promises to listen, primarily when we have been listening to him. I choose to believe the truth. It certainty heals a wound that continues to open, restoring my confidence. I walked away changed that day by a personal encounter knowing . . . *Jesus wants to listen to me.*

Now I hold on to the truth that he is listening to me. I am learning how to discern the lies when situations repeatedly communicate that I lack value. Instead of withdrawing in fear, I pray through my moments of insecurity. I choose to remember this promise that God listens to me. This truth gives me great value.

There are times in life when we do not sense if God hears us. That is our perception of what we see as inactivity in the physical realm. God is working whether we perceive it or not. This is one of the hardest works produced by faith, to simply trust him when we cannot see that God is listening or answering our prayers.

As we acknowledge in all areas of our lives where we need his help and begin to see our need for obedience in prayer, God reveals his heart and Word to us. The fact that God Almighty not only listens to us, but reveals his truth to us, should draw us to come reverently in expectation to meet with him. "Anyone who wants to approach God must believe both that he exists and that he cares enough to respond to those who seek him" (Heb. 11:6 MSG). God acts on what is earnestly brought before him. "We need to be the kind of intercessor that invites God to act."[7]

We are all called to pray. If God is sovereign and he commands us to pray, we need to trust there is valuable purpose. Do you believe the King of the Universe wants to listen to you? Jeremiah 33:3 says he will answer with an advantageous promise, "Call to me and I will answer you and tell you great and unsearchable things you do not know." God is God and he can do anything he wills whether we pray or not, but in the mystery of prayer, he wants us to come and participate in his work.

We know God is listening when after we pray specifically, we will recognize God's hand is working in response to our prayers. We see answers. Otherwise, we would fail to acknowledge him as God and give him the glory. When we do not see answers according to our expectation or by our perception as being "good," we must choose to trust by faith that God is sovereign and he is seated on his throne. To this end, for his glory, we labor in prayer, struggling with all his energy, which so powerfully works in us (Col. 1:29).

Keep Asking, Seeking, Knocking

Perseverance in prayer produces character. With God's unending invitation extended to us by the provision of his grace and mercy, we come, we come, we come again to the throne of grace, pouring out our hearts and waiting to listen for his. We cannot wear out our welcome!

One morning I had a conversation with a lady at church who is a golf widow. Her husband does not attend church with her and her two small children; instead he plays golf on Sundays. My eyes have witnessed the transformation of my dad's passion changed from holding a golf club to a Bible on Sunday mornings. So with great hope it has been a continual prayer of ours that my friend's husband would someday come to church with her and become a believer.

My friend shared with me that she was very disturbed when she had heard on the radio, "You can pray for something once, twice, and three times, but after that you don't need to pray for it anymore." My mouth dropped open and my heart sank. The truth is we are to "pray without ceasing" (1 Thess. 5:17 NASB). Ask and keep asking, seek and keep seeking, knock and keep knocking in prayer until we have assurance from God that he has answered or removed the burden to pray for a particular person or situation. Such hope, comfort, and peace come to us from participating in prayer with God; seeing him work in the hearts of those we love.

There is a parable, a story Jesus told to explain to the disciples they should always pray and not give up. It is found in Luke 18:1–8 about a persistent widow. The widow in a certain town kept coming to plead her case to a care-less judge. After repeated visits the judge concedes and finally says, "This widow keeps on bothering me, I will see that she gets justice, so that she won't eventually wear me out with her coming!"

In this parable, Jesus associates our perseverance in prayer with our possessing faith. As Jesus wraps up his point he says, "And will not God bring about justice for those who cry out to him day and night? He will see that they get justice, and quickly." The widow tirelessly approached the judge. With humility and boldness we too may approach the throne persistently.

Before I ran my 5K, my husband shared Isaiah 40:28–31 (AMP) with me. He called it the runner's prayer.

> Have you not known? Have you not heard? The everlasting God, the LORD, the Creator of the ends of the earth, does not faint or grow weary . . . He gives power to the faint and weary, and to him who has no might He increases strength . . . Even youths shall faint and be weary, and young men shall feebly stumble and fall exhausted; But those who wait for the LORD [who expect, look for, and hope in Him] shall change and renew their strength and power; they shall lift their wings and mount up [close to God] as eagles [mount up to the sun]; they shall run and not be weary, they shall walk and not faint or become tired.

The words in this passage were to encourage me to remember that my strength comes from God, but the words "the everlasting God, the LORD, the Creator of the ends of the earth does not faint or grow weary" pierced my heart. As I pondered this verse a revelation struck me that God *does not grow weary* of our coming to him in prayer. He just wants us to come! I was able to share this insight with my perplexed friend in hope that it would bring her comfort.

Prayers of perseverance keep our eyes on him as we wait for his answer. When we know God hears us, we fix our eyes in expectation to God's response to our prayer, and there is hope.

Persevering prayers are the prayers of the mature in heart. We may not see answers, results, or circumstances turning out with our understanding or perspective in mind, but faithful prayer warriors see with the eyes fixed on eternity, "sure of what they hope for and certain of what they do not see" (Heb. 11:1).

Be strong and do not give up, for your work in prayer will be rewarded. John Calvin once said, "If we must repeat the same supplications not twice or three times only, but as often as we have a need, a hundred, a thousand times . . . We must never be weary in waiting for God's help."[8] Endurance inspired by hope is patient when we do not see or get the answer we want.

Another analogy came to my mind not long after I finished running my first 5K. Unsure whether I'd continue to run as a form of exercise, there were many days when I started out the door to walk and the urge to run amazingly overcame me. I actually missed running. I continued to run three miles several times a week. The thought occurred to me that I would commit to running as long as I was writing this book. *Surely* that would keep me motivated so I would finish the book more promptly. The same is true of prayer. We begin to miss the time in prayer when we allow less important priorities and the tyranny of the urgent to interfere.

My husband has been running half marathons for the past few years. He knows that setting a goal for himself and committing to a race keeps him motivated to exercise on a regular basis. He has asked me several times to consider running a half marathon with him.

Since I was enjoying my runs at this point, I contemplated this huge decision knowing it would take lots of work and time to train. But 13.1 miles was crazy in my mind! I did pray about it because if it concerns me, it concerns God. That same week in my devotions I was reading in Galatians and found affirmation. "You were running a good race. Who cut in on you and kept you from obeying the truth?" (Gal. 5:7). I applied this verse to my physical training, but more importantly, to the spiritual decision to obey God with a good attitude and not quit writing because someone cut in front of me (someone wrote with more elegance than me); I chose (with

God's help) to push myself to a higher level of spiritual and physical discipline. By setting goals, I was able to lengthen my runs to achieve my objective of completing the half marathon, as well as short term attainable goals to be met in my writing.

Allow me to encourage you to set spiritual goals to spend more time with God. If this month you spend 10 minutes in daily prayer, next month commit to 15 minutes. Continue to lengthen your amount of time spent with God until you have reached your goal. . . . *If only I may finish the race and complete the task the Lord Jesus has given me—the task of testifying to the gospel of God's grace* (Acts 20:24) through my writing and through my life.

Several times while writing this book, my husband challenged me to finish when I felt weary. I needed spiritual endurance to finish the book and physical endurance to train for the race. At this point, I wanted to quit both running and writing this book! Writing became a daunting, overwhelming process. Days of discouragement came in waves when I had to go back through several wordy manuscripts. But it all came down to obedience and perseverance and someone to run alongside to keep my eye on the goal; God's purpose, and God's glory.

God had placed the idea for this book on my heart nearly fourteen years ago. I have been seriously working on it for five years. I cannot quit now. I kept my commitment; as long as I was writing this book I would continue to run physically. I will "run" spiritually with a passion for prayer. I will finish strong. Prayer will set the pace. Prayer is the fuel for my energy. "Let us not become weary in (prayer) doing good, for at the proper time we will reap a harvest if we do not give up" (Gal. 6:9).

In a morning of discouragement as I wrote out my concerns, God met me there.

Journal Entry August 28, 2006

Good morning LORD! Thank you for the many prayers I sensed yesterday—for you surely lifted my head! You picked me up and put my feet on solid ground. You spoke to me—the words jumped off the page of Matthew 9:22 "Take heart, daughter."—as if you were saying, "Be strong, hold on, this is not over yet."

Let's move our hearts into action by praying. Do not give up praying! We need to persevere so that when we have done the will of God, we will receive what he has promised . . . *carried on eagle's wings* and brought close to his heart (Exod. 19:4).

We can persevere and obey through today, when in prayer we take time to focus on the provision of God's grace—our daily bread; his ever present help in time of need (Ps. 46:1). When I am struggling, I say out loud, "I can do all things through him who strengthens me" (Phil. 4:13 NASB). What a great promise! The God who has no end, who raises the dead, will provide energy and strength for whatever life has for you.

One way he does this is by directing your heart into his love and Christ's perseverance (2 Thess. 3:5). Grasping the strength he has provided for us will enable us to pray until his Spirit releases the burden. Pray through the suffering. Pray through the pain. Pray through the wait. Pray through the longings until your restless heart is settled and at peace in him. Press through life with prayer. (In the companion journal available space is provided for special concerns on each Daily Prayer page and on Saturday's Weekday Prayer pages).

CHAPTER 10

BE TRANSFORMED

The goal of prayer is consistent intimacy with the Father; as a result, bringing him glory. As we spend time in God's presence a transformation occurs inadvertently. We begin to reflect God's likeness and mirror his reflection. The Holy Spirit makes this transference supernatural. Spending time with God means we more readily recognize the sinful desires of ourselves and how desperately we need his help for change. Often God uses our trials to draw us back into his presence. Through these daily encounters, a change occurs and we begin to display more and more of his countenance and glory.

The gradual alteration within our hearts from our daily time together with God reminds me of a story that a friend of mine gave me out of a little book called *Learning of God* by Amy Carmichael.

> "Sometimes in Dohnavur we, who dearly love the little children about us (and the older ones too), have looked up from some engrossing work to see a child beside us, waiting quietly. And when, with a welcoming hand held out, to the Tamil 'I have come'; we have asked 'For what?' thinking, perhaps, of something to be confessed, or wanted, the answer has come back, 'Just to love you.' So do we come, LORD Jesus; we have no service to offer

now; we do not come to ask for anything, not even for guidance. We come just to love Thee."[1]

Wouldn't our Father just love for us to come . . . just because we love to spend time with him? It's also good when we seek his help to change, for only he can change the heart. The more time we spend with him, the greater our desire is to change—for our good and his glory.

For those who belong to him, there is no place we can be cast from his presence. There is nothing—not one thing able to separate us from his love. There are times when life gets difficult, and I think to myself—*this is a strange kind of love*. I desire to escape and many times have said to myself, "If I had wings of a dove I would fly away and be at rest" (Ps. 55:6). I gripe, and imagine I can get away from it all, but God allows the chaos, the trials that direct my heart and make me run to him once again.

Scripture invokes the truth by asking us a question . . . *Where can we go to hide from his presence*? I mentioned earlier that when trials arrive at my doorstep and life gets difficult, I'd like to *fly away*. Honestly, where would I go? God promises to be with us if we climb to the highest mountain peak; if we plummet to the depths of hell, he is there. Even to the sea's far horizon, even there his hand will guide us, his right hand will hold on to us (Ps. 139:7–10). He will never let go of us. By faith we believe God is with us everywhere.

It seems kind of silly to think we can escape his presence; running away when he is the very remedy of our problems. His goodness and light permeate our darkness. God promises, "I will lead the blind by ways they have not known, along unfamiliar paths I will guide them; I will turn the darkness into light before them and make the rough places smooth. These things I will do; I will not forsake them" (Isa. 42:16).

Let's not shrink back so quickly from our trials. As we persevere and hope in him during our trials there are treasures in the dark to be found, riches stored in secret places, so that we may *know* that he is the great I AM, the LORD (Isa. 45:3–5). Knowing that God allows the darkness and suffering to come into our lives we can seek treasures; an unlimited supply of compassion and comfort, and as a result we can comfort others. God's treasures are like diamonds, multifaceted. We can crush or cloud our treasures with worry and fret. Instead when we look to God and *fly away* to him, he blesses us with the grace to receive with open hands the "gifts" of suffering with glad and thankful hearts. The richness of peace and joy can be found in the midst of suffering. God allows the heartache and draws us to his side to provide us with more of himself, which results in lasting change.

In our trials, or dark nights of the soul, great blessings of transformation await those who surrender to God's work and will in their lives. In the height of our suffering, God is glorified when we receive it with grace. We have access to this grace to stand firm with faith and patience while we are waiting for God's holy work to be accomplished through suffering; and then to inherit what has been promised.

Founding our hope on the love of God we can find strength to face our trials as opportunities for growth and change. "We rejoice in the hope of the glory of God. Not only so, but we also rejoice in our sufferings, because we know that suffering produces perseverance; perseverance, character; and character, hope. And hope does not disappoint us, because God has poured out his love into our hearts by the Holy Spirit, whom he has given us" (Rom. 5:2–5). This love that we see and experience is only a small glimpse of the love we will know completely in heaven. God's love is limitless and extravagant. God is a God of change and love is the key. No door is too difficult for love to unlock. To choose to love others and ourselves, it changes us from the inside-out. We can change as we grasp God's love for us, respect ourselves as his sacred temple, and then always think to extend love to others.

"Those who look to him are radiant; their faces are never covered with shame" (Ps. 34:5). Remember when Moses came down from Mount Sinai with the Ten Commandments in his hands? Because Moses had spoken with the LORD, Moses was not even aware that his face was radiating God's glory. Being in God's presence we cannot help but be changed; he loves us to wholeness. We may not see the transformation ourselves. Our eyes may be veiled to the true spiritual condition of our hearts to keep us humble and in need of him . . . thank goodness! Now and then God will let you see growth.

A transformation occurred in me concerning an area of trust in my life. I finally learned to trust God in how he was leading my husband, after repeatedly facing the uncertain future of another possible job change and the prospect of moving again. I kept praying, "LORD, you promise to surround us with your favor as with a shield" (Ps. 5:12). This time around God *made* me trust in him.

Journal Entry March 5, 2004

Psalm 34—The man poor in spirit called and the LORD heard him and saved him out of all his troubles . . . those who seek the LORD lack no good thing. v.15 The eyes of the LORD are on the righteous and his ears are attentive to their cry.

LORD, I pray Psalm 51—Cleanse me, forgive me for my lack of belief, my anxiety and fear because I chose to forget WHO you are!! Grant me a willing spirit to sustain me.

Last night I even dreamed there were rainbows all around me everywhere—large ones and small ones! Thank you, LORD—that you are up to something! You are seated on your throne and you are working.

If I remain . . . then I will know.
                                    —John 8:31–32, 15:4

Looking back through my journal entries, I discovered that I had changed after the repeated circumstances and training—of waiting in the unknown. What a blessing my journal pages were to me. During my wait, I continued to read my journals and recalled to myself, *God was faithful in the past. He will be faithful in the future.* Seeing how God was transforming me over time, I was able to respond with less fear and more faith. Thankfully, the "knowing" and peace came after trusting God's ways and being able to yield to his answers. We were able to stay and not relocate.

The hope of the rainbow dream permeated my heart with peace. I was right where I was supposed to be, finally growing in my response to life's uncertainties.

Choose to believe God is working and do not doubt, as you wait to hear from him in the uncertainties of life. He who invited you and called you by name, he who began a good work in you will finish it and it will be glorious! God's goal of transformation is to conform us to the image of Christ, "to become like him in his death" (Phil. 3:10) by giving up our lives to serve and bring salvation to others—in fervent prayer. "Did not the Christ have to suffer these things (betrayal, spit on, beaten, hung on a cross, suffer the wrath of all sin poured upon him, separated from God's presence), and then enter his glory?" (Luke 24:26). Jesus, being completely sinless, suffered. Peter wrote that Jesus left us an example . . . Christ suffering for us. To this we are called: suffering. Why are we so surprised when it comes? It is a mystery, but "as heirs of God and co-heirs with Christ, if indeed we share in his sufferings in order that we may also share in his glory. I consider that our present sufferings are not worth comparing with the glory that will be revealed in us" (Rom. 8:17).

God wants us to come whether we are happily running into his presence because we just want to love him or whether we are crawling to him, weary of our suffering. As we respond to his invitation in prayer God uses our time together to accomplish his purpose— his glory in us! God's purpose is accomplished when we offer our bodies as a living sacrifice and meet with him in our hearts—his sanctuary. As a result, his glory is revealed through a transformed life.

Spiritual Confidence

Through prayer God develops strong and confident hearts. "Spiritual strength comes into our lives by spending time in prayer."[2] As you step into a more committed prayer life, "Do not throw away your confidence; it will be richly rewarded. You need to persevere so that when you have done the will of God, you will receive what he has promised. For in just a very little while, he who is coming will come and will not delay. But my righteous one will live by faith. And if he shrinks back, I will not be pleased with him. But we are not of those who shrink back and are destroyed (by fear), but of those who believe (we are loved) and are saved" (Heb. 10:35–39). It is a battle of the mind at times, but choose to believe that God enables us to do what we perceive as the seemingly impossible. We are saved from negative thoughts by grace in Christ Jesus. As we step out by faith, these truths apply to our prayer lives.

The word confidence means *with faith or belief one will act in a right, proper or effective way*. Prayer is a manifestation of an inward faith. We pray by faith, moving into the unseen realm. I want to emphasize that as uniquely designed as God created you, so is your individual prayer life. Who is to say you are or are not praying correctly? "In the freedom of the Spirit there are as many ways of praying as there are individual believers."[3] When I think my words, prayers or actions have not been adequate I find strength in quoting God's Word. "Such confidence as this is ours through Christ before God. Not that we are competent in ourselves to claim anything for ourselves, but our competence comes from God" (2 Cor. 3:4–5). Accept the fact that it all comes from God: the faith, the competence, the love, the ability, and the saving grace.

Everything is provided for us to respond to God's invitation through the means of prayer. People can have an idea that prayer is hard or difficult, or that we can't pray very well, so we chose to not pray at all.

Who is the judge of a sincere prayer? If a prayer is prayed with wholehearted devotion, whether liturgical or offered with cries and groans, is it not acceptable? God is concerned about the heart. What is your heart motive when you pray? He is more concerned with your intent than your style. When we say, "Oh, I do not want to pray, I am not very good at it," or "I do not feel like it," we are thinking about ourselves and what we might sound like. Instead, trust the Holy Spirit; focus on Jesus, who offers each prayer perfumed with the incense of atoning blood. Focus on the encouragement and need of another person.

Do you believe with confidence that your prayers matter? We miss opportunities to work with God, to love and encourage others when we choose to believe that our prayers do not matter. We cannot believe Satan, the father of lies, who desperately wants to keep us from praying earnestly and confidently. We must throw out the lies and set our minds on things above, seeking God's will for his glory in any matter and attitude.

Prayer must come from a sincere heart, whether full of faith or with faith as tiny as a mustard seed. Our faith is not in our capacity to pray, but in God's character, his name, and his ability to act. In faithfulness Jesus said, "And I will do whatever you ask in my name, so that the Son may bring glory to the Father. You may ask me for anything in my name, and I will do it" (John 14:13–14). The goal of prayer is to bring glory to the Father. "This is to my Father's glory, that you bear much fruit" (John 15:8). As we pray and obey, he guides us on a fragrant, fruitful path.

In addition to our faith being built in God's character, he wants to equip us with faith to establish our confidence in the power we can possess when we believe. After Jesus' death, he sent his Holy Spirit to dwell within us, individually and corporately, to release his power of authority over all the earth when we pray in Jesus' name. Anyone who has faith in Jesus will do what he has been doing. He said we will do even greater things. I believe in the power and manifestation the Holy Spirit in a person who possesses a life of prayer.

Until we make prayer a priority, we will not know the power and passion we can possess by the Holy Spirit. He promises when we open wide our hearts and mouths for his purpose, he will fill them. We must trust with confidence that he will give us what we need to pray.

Let us not sin by failing to pray for one another due to our lack of confidence (1 Sam. 12:23). Since Jesus lives in me, when I am available, obedient, and allow the Holy Spirit to pray through me, the Holy Spirit delivers my prayers to Jesus, who takes my prayers and presents them as a pure fragrance unto Almighty God.

There is freedom in the realm of prayer. When we do not know what to say when we pray, we trust that Jesus and the Holy Spirit live to intercede and present our prayers perfected to the Father on our behalf. We must believe the truth that we have great help in this area by the Holy Spirit and Jesus, himself.

Do you think the prayers of those who are strong in the LORD are the only prayers God hears? In our weakness Christ's power rests on us more fully. In our humble, weak, and in our desperate cries, he is glorified. "The very weakness that drives us to pray becomes an invitation for God to respond with compassion and power."[4]

God is honored and glorified when we pray faithfully, humbly, specifically, and expectantly. God has affirmed his confidence in us as he has called us all to be intercessors. So we pray with confidence knowing that we have his approval. We have been made priests.

Pray according to what we know to be true about God. Pray for anything that will bring love, healing, forgiveness, and prominently pray for things that will bring God glory. "This is the confidence we have in approaching God: that if we ask anything according to his will, he hears us. And if we know that he hears us—whatever we ask—we know that we have what we asked of him" (1 John 5:14–15).

Here is something easy you can do. Ask for joy! Nehemiah 8:10 says, ". . . the joy of the LORD is our (your) strength." Our family went through a season when my husband encouraged us all to pray for joy. God heard and God answered. Joy came abundantly to us all. It was the sweetest time in our home. Strength comes as we find joy in times of prayer. God promises the blessing of strength and confidence to those who have set their hearts on a journey of communion with him (Ps. 84:5).

In the story of Queen Esther, we see a woman of outstanding confidence who through her devotion to God, her wisdom, and boldness saved the Jewish race.

As a beautiful Jewish girl, she was chosen to be queen to King Xerxes. Haman, an evil man, plotted to murder all the Jews. Mordecai, the queen's cousin, convinced her to save her people. Queen Esther decreed a fast among the people for three days to pray and ask God to prepare the king's heart for her request. Risking her life, Esther could only enter the presence of the king when his scepter was raised. Esther could then approach and touch the tip of the scepter. God had put her in royal position for "such a time as this" (Esther 4:14). The King granted her favor, served the justice of death to the evil Haman, and brought salvation to the Jewish nation.

Queen Esther's boldness exemplifies a life of prayer that is reverent and sensitive to God's leading and timing to enter the king's presence. Thankfully, the scepter is eternally raised for those who believe. It welcomes us to come forward into his presence beyond the veil at any time.

Discover Healing

God designed us with a need to talk, with a need for relationship. We have all experienced how helpful it is to talk about our own problems with others. How much more clearly will we see truth in our problems talking with God?! God wants us to come and release the burdens of our hearts in prayer so our bodies can be healed and we can live in supernatural grace.

The condition of our physical, spiritual, emotional, and mental health can be the result of our response to relationships and circumstances influencing our lives. Prayer has been scientifically proven to bring both physical and spiritual healing. Research shows a correlation between people who pray and people who have lower stress levels; with an overall link to better health and psychological well-being. Praying scripture helps us release anxiety, manage affliction, overcome temptation, gain spiritual strength, and provide freedom from addictions.

When relational conflicts or trauma arise, they are capable of adding stress to our lives. It is natural for most, out of desperation, to call on God for help. But when the crisis is a result from relationships of those who have hurt you, praying and seeking reconciliation is a true sign of maturity possessing the mind of Christ. As people witness our calm response, which is so radically different from those who do not possess or understand the supernatural grace for living, we will be a light of hope pointing to God's sufficiency.

In the book of Acts, as Stephen was being stoned, he prayed, "Lord Jesus, receive my spirit." Then he fell on his knees and cried, "Lord, do not hold this sin against them" (Acts 7:59–60). Stephen's last words before dying were prayers on behalf of others as he had seen in Jesus' example during the crucifixion. In response to Stephen's cries, Jesus was standing by the right hand of God awaiting Stephen's reception into the kingdom. This type of vicarious sacrificial prayer considers the condition of the hearts of others instead of being consumed with their own intense pain. You may not see it, but this type of redemptive prayer is sharing in God's work. You are helping to save a lost and hurting world.

Several years ago, my friend's nineteen-year-old son was jogging one afternoon. While he was on his run, a young boy nearby had accidentally let his dog out of the house. My friend's son stepped out into the street to avoid the attacking dog and was struck by a passing van. After rushing to the site, my friend immediately began praying over her son through her tears, but was asked to step aside by the paramedics. God provided comfort to her through another couple who began to intercede with her petitioning the throne of grace. The most amazing beauty and strength was exhibited by my friend. She responded with supernatural grace and forgiveness to the driver of the van, a forty-year-old woman. She wrote her a note assuring her of her forgiveness and asking that God be exalted in this tragedy.

Later at my friend's house, the investigating policeman came to report why her son had stepped out into the middle of the road. The policeman told of the anguish of the young boy's mother who had let the dog outside. My friend again sent a note to tell this young mom not to be disturbed or feel guilty. They did not hold her or the child responsible. My friend breathed grace, possessing no hard feelings in her heart toward any of the people involved. Giving all glory to God, she said, "Truly, God was manifesting his love and mercy through me to them!" This kind of gesture can only come about by the power of the Holy Spirit living within. In the midst of losing her son, she thought of the hurting hearts of the women involved.

Many college students attended the funeral and came to know God through this young man's death. The investigating police officer and the families involved attended the funeral. The bereaved mother courageously spoke at the funeral, touching us all with her astounding faith and strength. This young man was passionate for Jesus. His favorite verse comes from Philippians 1:21, "For to me, to live is Christ and to die is gain." The LORD allowed this young man's life to bear much fruit in his living and his dying. I have no doubt this young man is praising God and interceding with his angel armies.

Prayer helps us to overcome the temptation to be bitter and hate when we perceive we have been wronged. As we pray for people who are EGRs, (extra grace required)[5], we grow in grace and forgiveness. God is able to work a change in our hearts to see the other person with God's eyes. We must stay and abide, remaining connected with the Head for spiritual growth and wholeness to occur.

Reconciliation begins with Christ, believing by faith in his sacrifice, the bloodshed for us and his resurrected life. By prayer and delving into scripture we can be made whole. "Give ear and come to me; hear me that your soul may live" (Isa. 55:3a). Through prayer and obeying God's Word we can have hope that our earthly relationships can be reconciled and healed. But first we must be in a right relationship with God, daily abiding and obedient.

If we become fixated on our problem—controlled by fear—anxiety can cause or intensify many health problems like heart conditions, diabetes, and depression. In the temptation to be anxious about complicated circumstances in your life, remember to think about the reality of God's love. Think about what is true, right, and real at the present moment as we see in Philippians 4:8–9. You will achieve God's best for you in life by filling your minds and meditating on things upright, good, authentic, gracious—the best, not the worst; beautiful, not thoughts that are negative or demeaning. And the God of peace will be with you and his shield of love will surround you; a great guide for prayer.

Being empowered by the Holy Spirit in prayer with God's Word is the key to setting our minds on what is true, right, and excellent. Will you respond to the invitation to receive a focused and sound mind through his power? "The end of all things is near. Therefore be clear-minded and self-controlled so that you can pray" (1 Pet. 4:7).

Prayer brings rest to the weary, life to the soul, and healing to the body. Our lives would be healthier if we capture our thoughts of worry and fear, and immediately take our concerns to God. Turn your worries into worship through prayer. There is a vicious cycle when we think we are too busy to pray—right where the enemy would have us with our hands behind our backs.

When my soul becomes depleted, I am easily irritated and anything but gentle. I don't know about you, but when I get upset, focusing on the circumstances, gentleness, and peace are not apparent in my life. This is a great test for worry—like a worry barometer. Are you reacting like a bull in a china shop? The rampage is a check on my spirit and tells me, "It is time to feed the soul."

"Let your gentleness be evident to all. Do not be anxious about anything (*not one thing*), but in everything, by prayer and petition, with thanksgiving, present your requests to God. And the peace of God, which transcends all understanding, will guard your hearts and your minds in Christ Jesus" (emphasis mine) (Phil. 4:4–7). God's promise is that his perfect peace will come to those who pray instead of worry, keeping their mind on him, trusting in his love and plans by giving him thanks. Look for the good and thank him!

There's a hurting world out there. What a ministry we have in prayer for the sick. Scripture tells us when a person is sick, have those in authority pray for them. "Is any one of you sick? He should call the elders of the church to pray over him and anoint him with oil in the name of the Lord" (James 5:14). The sick person is responsible to initiate the need for prayer. The elders of the church gather to pray with anointing oil as a symbol of our reliance on Holy Spirit and to ask for wisdom to make the best decisions possible for our health while trusting God to respond according to his will with healing.

Several years ago my father had a herniated disk in his back from picking up a cement bird bath. It is hard to see your father, who could do anything he put his mind to, be instantly bedridden and in pain. Surgery was inevitable. The surgery seemed successful, but the pain continued debilitating him from all the things he loved in life: fishing, golf, Bridge, and even getting out for Bible study. During our family gathering at Easter, we felt led to pray for him.

Journal Entry April 1, 2002

Yesterday for Easter the family gathered around to pray for dad, to put our hands on him and bless him (Mark 10:16)—all the kids were with us. Right as we began to pray we heard a bird fly into the family room Palladian window. Poor thing was stunned and stayed still for a long time. We all went out to look at it on the deck and it still didn't stir. We gave it awhile to catch its breath and we noticed its right wing was bleeding. My oldest brother went to get a shovel to scoop up the sparrow and put it in the natural area so my parents wouldn't have to worry about it. While my brother was gone the bird miraculously flew away. My oldest daughter said, "It was like God scooped up the bird with his hand!"

We prayed for dad after the unusual occurrence. Later, riding back home in separate cars, my brother and I phoned one another. We both thought of Matthew 10:29–31. "Are not two sparrows sold for a penny? Yet not one of them

will fall to the ground apart from the will of your Father.
And even the very hairs on your head are all numbered.
So do not be afraid; you are worth more than many sparrows." We can learn so much from God's creation if we
stop, look, and listen. God cared for the little sparrow . . .
How much more will he uphold us created in his image
with his righteous right hand?! If I, (we) could just grasp
how much God really loves and cares for us!

The wait for our answer to prayer took many months. My dad
seemed to get worse before he got better. But I kept holding on
to the promise God sent our way—the wounded sparrow taking
flight. Oh, how much more I knew God loved my dad! Today, I
am thankful to say my dad is healed, playing golf again, and a
little more cautious about picking up weighty objects.

In God's presence through prayer we will find blessed rest for
our souls. For every decision and every prayer, God says, "Stand
at the crossroads and look; ask for the ancient paths, ask where the
good way is, and walk in it, and you will find rest for your souls"
(Jer. 6:16). As you understand the role of prayer, God's benefits for
you, and the investment you will be making in the lives of others,
his supernatural grace will be yours. "Dear friend, I pray that you
may enjoy good health and that *all* may go well with you, even as
your soul is getting along well" (3 John 1:2).

There are multiple health benefits and reasons to journal. Most
importantly as you write your prayers and how you see God working in your life, you are free to express your emotions and thoughts,
without causing damage to others or feelings of guilt. Write with
more honesty, more empathy, more of yourself, unburdening your
mind and heart. Try not to primarily record your problems in life,
but rejoice and give thanks for what God has done.

Journaling for me is simply writing out my dialogue with God.
Journaling links a connection between the spiritual, emotional, mental, and physical realms of the body. By writing out your feelings,
you can reduce stress, consequently lowering your blood pressure
and boosting the immune system. Many counselors use writing as
a form of therapy. When I record a conflict in a relationship, I begin
to see a different perspective. By having time to reflect, I begin to
understand the other person's point of view or heart motive.

We need God's help in looking with true perspective into our
hearts and the hearts of others. God created us with a wonderful

array of emotions. There is purpose in feeling and expressing them, and your written journal is a safe place to express them. Many restless nights, I have journaled the concerns of my heart when I have failed to release my anger before the sun went down (Eph. 4:26). By furiously writing out my emotions in my journal, a softening of my heart is fostered—transforming my response. My husband says he always knows when I am struggling with an issue, when he sees me soar through the pages of my journal.

After confessing and searching my heart, I have applied an idea from Joanna Weaver's book, *Having a Mary Spirit*, and I release the person and offense by writing "Forgiven" in red over the words in the entire entry concerning the situation that had caused my heart pain. In our fleshly nature, forgiveness may not always occur instantly, although we are commanded to forgive. As we acknowledge with our minds when we write "Forgiven," our hearts tend to follow by surrendering completely. Pray and say, "I release them to you" to be forgiven.

Trust God's heart and mind toward you. Then learn to trust yourself and your thoughts filtered through his Word. "We distrust ourselves because we value the perceptions of others over our own experiences."[6] As unique individuals, we are designed to communicate with God. We are invited to be who we are, authentic and transparent. As we fellowship with God, recording our spiritual journeys, we discover healing.

Today's Prayer Journal Task

- When situations disturb you repeatedly ask God:
- Help me to see the situation or person through your eyes.
- Give me the grace to forgive and find healing.
- Bless me with a desire to read your Word and let you bring healing to my pain.

Writing Clarifies

Journaling has many valuable benefits as we reflect on all the LORD has done for us. His great love is seen and experienced as we remember God is with us and he is faithful. Writing clarifies our thoughts. Those thoughts lead to actions. A periodic review of our journey with God renews our strength and increases our faith. Writing helps to clarify the work of God in our lives.

As I mentioned previously, journaling is an expression of who you are and who you are becoming. Not everyone enjoys writing, but all of us can record one thing God is revealing to us or one thing for which we are thankful. Our journey is the best determiner of our destination. As we write we can see more clearly the road God is leading us to travel and the place he has prepared for us. "Now the dwelling of God is with men, and he will live with them. They will be his people, and God himself will be with them and be their God . . . he who was seated on the throne said, 'I am making everything new!' Then he said, 'Write this down, for these words are trustworthy and true'" (Rev. 21:3–5). What Word of direction or hope has God given you that is trustworthy and true?

Moses had the responsibility of recording what God had said for the people, the Israelites. "When Moses went and told the people all of God's Words and laws, they responded with one voice, 'Everything the LORD has said we will do.' Moses then wrote down everything the LORD had said" (Exod. 24:3). As we recall Israelite history, God knew they would need help in remembering all the good deeds he had done.

If God places high value on our remembering what he has done, we should value it too. A journal is an object of remembrance to build our faith when the waves of doubt occur. In 1 Samuel, Saul and King Achish were pursing David's life. Before David escaped to the caves, he encountered a priest who offered David the bread of the Presence from the tabernacle and the sword of Goliath. "If you want it, take it; there is no sword here but that one," the priest said. David replied, "There is none like it; give it to me" (1 Sam. 21:9).

This sword was passed on as hope from one hand to another as a gift of assurance of God's personal faithfulness. The sword provides an object of remembrance to jolt David's memory of his victory with God over Goliath. God had kept his promise before and delivered David from his enemy. Surely, his God could deliver once again.

Imagine how massive the sword must have been, giving David strength and confidence, encouraging him to trust in the LORD as

Saul and his army loomed with mighty force. It was a physical reminder of all the might, power, and provision David knew about his God. David poured out his heart while hiding in the caves. "The righteous cry out, and the LORD hears them; he delivers them from all their troubles" (Ps. 34:17). So, "gird your sword upon your side!" (Ps. 45:3).

Your journal entries can be such a sword of hope and remembrance. When the mighty waves of doubt come over us, let us run back and grab our swords of hope, remembering the scriptures, the prayers, words, and presence of people that gave us strength to endure. Or when we doubt God's plan for our future, doubt that God has a purpose for our lives, doubt God could use us in building his kingdom, we need to remember what God has done. How strong our faith would be if we could remember all the times God affirmed his presence in our lives; "I AM with you." What God has done once, he can do again. He delivered the Israelites through the waters. He can do it again. He rescued us from evil. He can do it again. He values our remembering his good deeds.

Writing helps to apply God's Word and proclaim who he is. In the New Testament, James says, "Anyone who listens to the word but does not do what it says is like a man who looks at his face in a mirror and, after looking at himself, goes away and immediately forgets what he looks like. But the man who looks intently into the perfect law that gives freedom, and continues to do this, not forgetting what he has heard, but doing it—he will be blessed in what he does" (James 1:23–25). As we write down our lessons from scripture we are more likely to apply the new truth. By recording we can easily see God's redemption and be blessed—with joy and peace.

Job was such a man. He was faithful in his response to intense suffering and God blessed him. Job desired with all seriousness that the words from his mouth, overflowing from the depth of love in his heart, be permanently recorded and engraved on a rock forever. No matter what happens in our lives we long for these words from Job to ring true in our hearts, "I know that my Redeemer lives! In the end he will stand upon the earth. After my skin has been destroyed, yet in my flesh I will see God; I myself will see him with my own eyes—I and not another. How my heart yearns within me!" (Job 19:23–27). Little did Job know his words would be an everlasting witness.

Journaling can be a vital resource to record and reemphasize what we are learning, discovering, and applying in our lives. Years later, when we face the same experience or similar trial, we may need to renew our faith in recalling God's hand in the past circumstance to give us hope as we walk through the current test. We may want to glance back to know how to encourage or exhort a loved one with the same encouragement we received.

Outside of sharing a few entries with you in this book, I have only shared partial entries with those I felt God leading me to share. When a friend of mine miscarried, I went back and reread my journal to refresh what had happened in my life when I miscarried. I copied my journal entry to share with her—my thoughts, prayers, and struggles, along with the special moments when I sensed God's loving embrace through many others who encouraged me.

My hope was to comfort my friend, assuring her that God was there in the suffering. Your journal can be a source of faith, hope, and love. Taking the time to look back to see God's presence in your life, to reread prayers that were poured out, or recall a joyful victory won, helps to clarify your thoughts and trigger your memories on all that the LORD has done for you; this leads you to take action, renews your strength, and increases your faith.

PART IV

GLORY BEYOND THE SACRED TEMPLE

GOD COMMANDS US to maintain a consistent life of daily prayer because he knows our fleshly nature will allow discouragement. He originated the idea of sending the Encourager, the Holy Spirit, to help us stay confidently engaged in spiritual warfare around us.

Prayer is a valuable resource, utilizing the power and authority of the Father, Jesus, and the Holy Spirit, who are always working. Jesus said to the disciples that he and his Father are always at work (John 5:17). What do you think they are working on? Here are some ways the three persons of the Trinity are always at work. Every day the Three in One are all-powerful, holding the universe together—including every detail of our lives. Scientists say if the earth slipped one centimeter off its axis, the earth would spin out of orbit. On a more personal scale, God is all-knowing, keeping track of the number of hairs on our head. He stores the tears we have cried. He is drawing people to himself, enabling them to receive his grace, which accomplishes his will to build his kingdom. Jesus saves completely and lives to intercede. He's preparing a place for us. The Spirit is ever present, roaming the earth, searching for those who are the Lord's to counsel and administer heavenly riches; the Spirit guides our thoughts and actions by the spoken Word.

Joined with the Trinity we have nothing to fear. Believe that we have three agents at our side. We are admonished to be on guard, to stand firm in the faith, and be men and women of courage. Courage comes from the word *tharseo*, meaning take heart.[1] God sends his Holy Spirit to encourage us and boldly pursue the work of God with great passion. The Greek word for encourage is *parakaleo*, to call near, invite. The Holy Spirit is a *paraklete*, the one who comes alongside.[2] The Spirit has the work of ministering to our hearts the love, power, peace, fruit, and truth of God. The Spirit whispers in our ear, inviting us to come near.

God's promise for us today is that his power is at work within us. Prayer is the key that imparts power by the Spirit and moves us toward the work God has for us to do. Gird up and "strengthen your feeble arms and weak knees" (Heb. 12:12). As we ask for Jesus and the Holy Spirit to fill us, we are reminded that he is not a weak man outside of us, but a tremendous power that resides within (2 Cor. 13:3 PHILLIPS). Believing that God's power as at work in us; we keep praying and do not give up because God can do anything . . . more than we imagine.

One righteous, prayerful couple was Zechariah and Elizabeth. In the book of Luke, when the birth of John the Baptist was pronounced by an angel, a man named Zechariah from the priestly line of Aaron received the news. He was chosen by lot to go into the temple and burn the incense as a once-in-a-lifetime opportunity. This was not by chance or coincidence. God was in complete control—a divine incidence.

The assembled worshipers were praying outside when the time came for Zechariah to burn incense. In the meantime, while the people in the outer court were waiting for the priestly blessing from Zechariah, they continued to actively wait in prayer, perplexed why Zechariah had stayed so long in the temple. The incense could not be offered without prayer. Prayer was the primary service in which the people honored God. God utilized the delay of Zechariah to lengthen the call to prayer for the people ushering in the way for God's Son.

An angel of the LORD had detained Zechariah, standing at the right side of the altar of incense. Zechariah was startled to see the angel. His heart was gripped with fear. The angel immediately reassured him, "Do not be afraid, Zechariah; your prayer has been heard."

Some Jewish writers say the priests prayed for the salvation of the whole world as they offered incense. We do not know what Zechariah had prayed by the altar that day, but God had heard the couple's prayer for a child. God granted their request even in their older age. This child would "make ready a people prepared for the Lord" (Luke 1:13, 17). Zechariah responded in unbelief and the consequence was a loss of speech for nine months. A sign that the priesthood was soon to be silenced in the arrival of the New Covenant to come through Jesus.

Gabriel announced, "I stand in the presence of God, and I have been sent to speak to you and to tell you this good news which will come true at the proper time" (Luke 1:19). Zechariah had a lengthy wait and plenty of time to contemplate the divine occurrence in the temple. Once he could speak, he was filled with the Holy Spirit and a song of praise and blessing filled the air from his mouth, "Praise be to the Lord, because he has come . . . to guide our feet into the path of peace" (Luke 1:68, 79). Traditionally, he prayed over the people the priestly blessing after exiting the temple, "The LORD bless you and keep you; the LORD make his face shine upon you and be gracious to you; the LORD turn his face toward you and give you peace" (Num. 6:24–26).

Nine months before the miraculous arrival of John the Baptist and fifteen months before the glorious appearing of Jesus, God had caused his people to wait in intercession outside the tabernacle—preparing the way for Jesus. Through Elizabeth's perfect response the glory began to rise, "The LORD has done this for me!" she exclaimed (Luke 1:25). For everything there is a reason, there is a purpose; there is our God who is in complete control and designated a divine time for men and women to pray.

Journal Entry April 6, 1994

"And I will pour out on the house of David and the inhabitants of Jerusalem a spirit of grace and supplication. They will look on the One they have pierced, and they will mourn for him as one mourns for an only child, and grieve bitterly for him as one grieves for a first born son."

—Zechariah 12:10

This Easter was one I will never forget. After being three months pregnant, I miscarried my first child on Easter morning. The night was long . . . My faithful husband remained by my side and read me the Easter story from a magazine in the hospital. My body and my heart were in shock. But I remember throughout the night singing in my mind, "God is in Control," by Twila Paris. The doctors assured us there was nothing we did or didn't do to cause the loss. I know I took care of myself, but the mind always searches for reasons. There I must find peace. It is a mystery. God keeps encouraging me through the love and voices of many. I am not alone.

For those who have received the spirit of adoption, we are never left alone.

In the midst of my suffering and loss, I never before felt so strongly God's loving embrace. His caring hands came through many, to bring comfort and healing. My mother-in-law pampered me back to health after my much-needed rest and nourishment. Many flowers and touching cards were sent—flooding my heart with comfort . . . that I was not alone in my sorrow.

God is God over the joy and the sorrows. Be encouraged! We are not alone. We have been given a great Enabler! Jesus said anyone who has faith in him will not only do the same things he did here on earth, but he will do even greater things because he was going to the Father (John 14:12). Did you catch that? We are meant to do greater things than what Jesus did while he was in bodily form. I find it difficult to believe I would do greater works than Jesus. There had to be a reason for him to say we would do more. So what took place for this to be true? Jesus sent the Spirit to be present in everyone who believes, everywhere, at all times, and for more work to be accomplished. More healing could save lives. More love could be poured out. More power could be tapped. More freedom extended. More abundant life given—more of Jesus in us and more glory to God. Only after Jesus sacrificed his life and was taken up into heaven, and chose to sit right beside the Father, interceding for us forever. What comfort! Jesus added one more thing; he said he would do whatever we asked in his name so he can bring glory to God.

There is a time for everything . . . a needed time for prayer by God's ordained orchestration. Keep praying when life is sailing under blue skies and when storm clouds appear threatening. God is in control and he invites us to accomplish his mighty work with him through prayer, preparing for Jesus' return.

CHAPTER 11

ENGAGE IN
THE SPIRITUAL BATTLE

GOD LONGS FOR us to respond in prayer so he can infuse his strength in our weakness, and help us in our times of need. God desires to grow hearts of courage and valor as we engage in the spiritual battle looming around us. We live in a world where we experience life using our five senses. We are comfortable with our sight, hearing, taste, smell, and touch. By faith we believe in an unseen spiritual world. We engage this world through prayer. "So, we must fix our eyes not on what is seen, but what is unseen" (2 Cor. 4:18).

Open your eyes and do not be deceived; there is a battle taking place for God's glory and kingdom. The battle is for your heart and the hearts of those around you. Jesus taught, "The thief comes only to steal and kill and destroy; I (Jesus) have come that they may have and enjoy life, and have it in abundance" (to the full, till it overflows) (John 10:10 AMP).

As we look around, we see so much tragedy, violence, and suffering. Are we going to sit passively watching the wounded fall, or will we rise up victoriously and engage in the heat of battle? Again, I will say because it is worth repeating, *guard your heart above everything else*, for your heart determines the power of the words that you speak and course of your life. Scripture tells us, "The reason the Son of God appeared was to destroy the devil's work" (1 John 3:8). Jesus' chief purpose is to fully redeem, restore, and reconcile God's heart with man's, to bring God's Kingdom to earth, "as it is in heaven" (Matt. 6:10).

Why do you think Satan would want to destroy our relationship with God? Satan desires to keep us alienated from the heart of God, to keep us from living in God's power and fullness, from building God's Kingdom, and reflecting his glory. The enemy never wants us to believe we are loved and have a purpose.

Be heart-conscious of the enemy's many schemes and lies; he wants us to fall into sin . . . because the wages of sin is spiritual bondage. There must be an enemy because the scriptures tell us how to handle his attacks. I am referring to spiritual mind games . . . Like a thought enters your mind, *I can't go on* . . . Simply surrender to what you know to be God's will and pray to let him work in you to resist the assault. Say out loud against the thought, *"If God is for us, who can be against us!"* When you sense condemnation or face a temptation to do or think something that you know is not right, then speak out loud and command the devil to leave, and he will flee from you. Say it and pray it again. When you draw near to God in time of need, he promises to come near to you and be your Deliverer (James 4:7–8). I know it sounds easier on paper than in real life, but we can do this if we prepare our minds and hearts for battle.

Praying God's Word is one of the most powerful weapons God has given us to stand against the enemy. God's Word powerfully penetrates into the spiritual world. It is "alive and active, . . . sharper than a double edge sword . . . it judges the thoughts and attitudes of the heart" (Heb. 4:12). Jesus provided us with the example to use when he stood against the enemy by saying, "It is written . . . It is written . . . It says . . ." meaning Jesus repetitively quoted God's Word with authority (Luke 4:4, 8, 10).

Jesus said, "I have given you authority . . . to overcome all the power of the enemy; nothing will harm you. However, do not rejoice that the spirits submit to you, but rejoice that your names are written in heaven" (Luke 10:19–20). The authority is given to us in the powerful Name of Jesus; however, are you prepared for the many schemes and lies the enemy has for you with memorized scripture as Jesus exemplified?

As you pray, be careful that your focal point does not develop pride in your power of praying against the enemy. When we pray in the authority of Jesus, the Spirit of God drives away the enemy.

Focusing on the enemy in fear or in prayer, is giving him too much attention and credit. Determine your focal balance between complete awareness and not paying any attention to the enemy.

We are God's children and need to possess a childlike faith that *trusts* our heavenly Father's provision of his protection. We can learn from observing children by their nature of trust and honesty. Don't you love how children just tell it like it is? If someone around them is saying mean things, they stand up for themselves and just say, "Leave me alone!" Let us be bold and tell the enemy the way it is.

The adversary does not want you to be in alignment with the will and work of God. The thief will silently strike when we least expect it, attacking areas of our life where we are most likely to fail. His attempts will be to disrupt our times of prayer and fellowship in God's presence, creating isolation from others, and stifling our spiritual growth. The enemy—the devil—wants to defeat us through temptation of the "D" words . . . deceit, discouragement, doubt, depression, distraction, dissension, and disagreement. Take a stand and say, "No" to his subtle divisiveness.

When you are tempted to think, say, act something you know is not right or does not line up with God's ways, know that God is not tempting you. "God cannot be tempted by evil, nor does he tempt anyone" (James 1:13). But he promises to provide a way out of the temptation. Pray through the temptation, look for his "way out" and make the right choice. God promises: "I will contend with those who contend with you" (Isa. 49:25). God is mighty to save us!

There are discussions among struggling believers to discern if a trial is from the enemy or if it is discipline and refining from God. Praying through the trial, we acknowledge that whatever comes into our lives, the Almighty God, in his sovereignty, has allowed and promises to use it for our good to those who love him (Rom. 8:28). "Paul is not saying that God prevents his children from experiencing things that can harm them. He is rather attesting that the LORD takes all that he allows to happen to his beloved children, even the worst things, and turns those things into blessings."[1]

Henry Blackaby, the well-known author of *Experiencing God*, states that, "In every generation there seems to exist certain clichés used by members of the body of Christ. No doubt, on the top of the list for this generation are the words, 'I am under attack!' Every difficulty seems to be labeled 'spiritual warfare.' Without question we fight wars in the heavenlies; but before we can be sure it's spiritual warfare, we must be able to answer three questions negatively:

1. Am I living outside the will of God?
2. Do I have any unconfessed sin (*or willful disobedience in my life)?
3. Is God simply working his completion in me?

Far more often, our difficulties originate from one of these three realms."
*My addition to the quote

God designed us to be men and women of prayer to accomplish his purpose and participate in the spiritual battle. This battle is taking place for the manifestation of God's glory on earth, in and through the heart of mankind. Stand firm, dressed with God's armor and take hold of the sword of the Spirit, proclaiming the living Word of God in your hearts through prayer.

Today's Prayer Journal Task

- Are you under attack? Examine your difficultly and answer the questions 1–3 above.
- Relating to your struggle, find a verse in your Bible's concordance or in the back of the book, Praying God's Word A–Z. Pray through the verse several times.
- Memorize the verse you chose to give you strength in your struggle.

Pray God's Word

There is nothing more powerful to pray than God's very own Word back to him. It does not return without accomplishing God's will. God promises, "As the rain and snow come down from heaven, and do not return to it without watering the earth and making it bud and flourish, so that it yields seed for the sower and bread for the eater, so is my word that goes out from my mouth: It will not return to me empty, but will accomplish what I desire and achieve the purpose for which I sent it" (Isa. 55:10–11). ". . . The word of the Lord stands forever" (1 Pet. 1:25).

As we read and study God's Word we begin to discern God's voice of truth and the accuser's voice of lies. We can identify the counterfeit by studying the authentic. By faith we begin to gain full knowledge of the rightful place we have in Christ. His purpose for us as his children and heirs is to participate by learning here on earth the power of our authority.

The authority given us by grace is available for every believer. As we grasp this truth, our prayers begin to stand firm on God's promises and manifest his authority. Again, as we gain knowledge of God's Word, we should pray God's Word.

There is a great power, an invisible force that is set in motion when we speak God's Word out loud and proclaim his Word in prayer. "Let the word of Christ dwell in you richly . . ." so your prayer life can become fervent and effectual (Col. 3:16). When we pray, faith is not something we can muster up in our hearts, nor is it a substance we can manipulate to "control" God, but "consequently, faith comes from hearing the message, and the message is heard through the word of Christ" (Rom. 10:17). We possess the mind of Christ when we hear the Word of truth and believe it. As we pray scripture we uphold his thoughts and purposes. "It is written: 'I believed; therefore I have spoken.' With that same spirit of faith we also believe and therefore speak . . ." (2 Cor. 4:13). As you remain in Jesus and "as you remain in his Word, God will empower your prayer life. When we have been called to pray, yes, we can and do pray silently, but some of our most explosively powerful praying will be aloud."[2]

God's Word has no end. His Word has eternal ramifications for those who pray it. It is not burdensome, but energizes the soul. There are no words from human minds and mouths that can equal God's omnipotent and eternal Word. A *rhema*,[3] in the Greek is a word spoken or uttered, denoting the operative all powerful word or command of God—a message or word that is specific for you. When given a rhema claim it for yourself, claim it for others, and write it in your prayer journal until it becomes your own treasure hidden in your heart.

Reading the Bible, I pray through the scriptures with the LORD. There are three main questions you can ask yourself as you read and pray over God's Word. What does the passage tell me about God?

What does the passage tell me about myself? What does the passage tell me about others? If there is a verse that brings conviction of a wrong I've done, then I confess. Maybe a verse makes me think of the condition of my children's hearts; I pray for them. Often there is a verse about God's character I need to hear. I thank God for that reminder of who he is and what he says he will do. Then I share the passages with others in need as the opportunity arises.

"God can speak through any scripture, but the Psalms, Proverbs, Gospels, and Epistles are full of scriptures that can easily be turned into prayers."[4] The Gospels, the first four books in the New Testament, testify to Jesus' life of prayer. The Epistles are letters and prayers written to the church from Paul. The Psalms are full of praise and prayers mostly written by King David. The Proverbs were written by King Solomon and are full of wisdom for daily living. When you pray God's Word you cast the burden of responsibility to act on God and his Word, not your ability to pray.

Be energized by praying God's Word. "God's Word is not chained," but sets the captive free (2 Tim. 2:9). Let us internalize God's Word by listening, obeying, recording, and memorizing it every day. Digest it and let it become a part of who we are so we are equipped to pray. It is our sustenance. God asks that we ". . . listen carefully and take to heart all the words" he speaks to us (Ezek. 3:10).

When we pray it is good to come into his presence saying, "In Jesus name we come . . ." acknowledging and claiming his authority, righteousness, power, and promise to represent us as we pray. Again, it is not in our ability to pray, but in faith we release the prayer for God to act in power. Prayer can be explosive! Dynamite comes from the word *dunamis*[5] in the Greek, works of supernatural origin combining the Word and prayer together. "God has exalted above all things his name and his Word" (Ps. 138:2). Praying in Jesus' name with the Word releases his power and authority.

We come in prayer to surrender our hearts in an act of worship, acknowledging our dependence on God. Possessing a correct view of God and ourselves by faith and by praying God's Word, we participate in a holy work by faith. Energy and power are set in motion when we pray, trusting in the promises of God. Our deep spiritual thirst is quenched through spending time with God. There is power in speaking our prayers and scripture out loud. It keeps our minds focused and penetrates the invisible warfare. "The end of all things is near. Therefore be clear-minded and self-controlled so that you can pray" (1 Pet. 4:7).

Apply the Armor of God

WE HAVE GREAT help and hope! The Bible says, "The LORD is a warrior," our commander and chief. The LORD your God fights for you, just as he promised. So be very careful to listen to the LORD. He fights for us! (Exod. 15:3). Say in your battles, ". . . The LORD is with me like a mighty warrior" (Jer. 20:11). But he also commands us to be prepared and put on our armor! "We do not wage war as the world does" (2 Cor. 10:3). There is a battle for our hearts, minds, and anything that brings life to us and glory to God.

The enemy will use every tactic to silence our intercession and effectiveness, and attempt to lessen our desire to pray. What hinders our boldness in prayer? Satan's lies, temptations to sin, and pride are some of the root causes to apathy of prayer.

Although the battle has been won by Christ's death on the cross, the enemy fiercely desires to bring down as many with him as he can. The world is at war and "will continue until the end" (Dan. 9:26). In prayer, be prepared to engage in the battle and set your mind to stand against the enemy.

As I learned in my running class, running requires the right gear to achieve any distance before your knees or back start to ache. The right clothing, with wicking helps to pull away moisture from your body. Lightweight shorts are a necessity. But I am finding quality socks and shoes truly make the difference on my runs, but they can only handle so many miles before needing to be replaced. I know it is time for a new pair of shoes when I am no longer soaring on eagles' wings, but every step is greeted with aches and pain.

The same principle is spiritually applied with the armor that God provides for every believer. It is ours to apply daily for our own survival and protection so that we too can endure the trials and temptations in the journey of life. Let's put on our "camo" and engage the battle lines. Include in your daily prayer the principle of applying the armor of God. Visualize yourself and your loved ones applying each piece of the armor of God from head to toe; don't forget the shield of faith which can extinguish flaming arrows from the evil one. Go out today with confidence that you are prepared and never forget *God is with you!*

The victory over sin and death has been won through the gracious work of Christ on the cross. His blood screams and echoes from the mountain top . . . *Forgiven—and free!* But in the meantime we battle against evil until Jesus returns to establish his kingdom and meet his bride here on earth . . . We must fight for our freedom! "It is for freedom that Christ has set us free" (Gal. 5:1).

Stand firm against Satan and be coated daily by applying your spiritual armor. Let's find out how.

> Be strong in the Lord and in his mighty power. Put on the full armor of God so that you can take your stand against the devil's schemes. For our struggle is not against flesh and blood, but against the rulers, against the authorities, against the powers of this dark world and against the spiritual forces of evil in the heavenly realms. Therefore put on the full armor of God, so that when the day of evil comes, you may be able to stand your ground, and after you have done everything, to stand.
>
> Stand firm then:
>
> * With the belt of truth buckled around your waist
>
> * With the breastplate of righteousness in place
>
> * With your feet fitted with the readiness that comes from the gospel of peace.
>
> In addition to all this:
>
> * Take up the shield of faith, with which you can extinguish all the flaming arrows of the evil one.
>
> * Take the helmet of salvation and the sword of the Spirit, which is the Word of God.
>
> * And pray in the Spirit on all occasions with all kinds of prayers and requests. With this in mind, be alert and always keep on praying for all the saints.
>
> —Ephesians 6:10–18

'Stand firm' is mentioned four times in the Ephesians passage above. We stand firm against the enemy *with* all that we need. We are equipped with power by claiming God's promises in our position of authority in Christ, and by claiming the power of Christ's blood. We've been given God's Word of truth to guard us and Jesus' righteousness to coat us. We conquer the feeling of fear with peace. Holding up our shield of faith we protect our hearts, the core of what we believe. To combat the doubts that fly into our minds, we utilize the helmet of salvation. In essence, we replace negative and unconstructive thoughts with God's Word through the help of the Spirit—who is mighty to save us when we pray. (See companion journal for more scripture on each piece of armor).

Remember the battle with David and Goliath? King Saul quickly took David's brave proposal to fight the oversized Philistine for the Israelites' freedom. In dignity the king offered the shepherd boy his sturdy shining armor, the best shield, and protective covering. But David refused the offer. The king's armor was oversized and overwhelming for David's body and confidence.

A simple shepherd boy found courage to fight the big giant with a rock and a sling. David put on the armor he knew, was familiar with, and that fit him. Also, David knew his God who was *on his side*, was bigger than the giant as he proclaimed he came to fight in the Name of the Lord his God. Utilize the weapons you are familiar with, the sword of his Word that you know, and keep adding to your arsenal by memorizing more scripture. And remember *who* is on your side!

Does it mean God no longer loves us if we have trouble or calamity? . . . No, despite these things, overwhelming victory and life is ours through Christ, who loves us. Are you prepared to walk out the door today having applied God's armor that he provided for you?

What are we fighting for? We are created for God's eternal love. We are fighting for our relationship with God and for others. We are fighting for love. Love never fails and never gives up. Love never ends and always wins. . . . God is love. We cannot live without love (1 Cor. 13). May we be able to say, "Your troops will be willing on your day of battle" (Ps. 110:3). Strong and powerful men charge the throne, forcefully advancing the kingdom of heaven (Matt. 11:12).

Fight on the Frontlines

Our calling is straightforward; we are to protect our borders from any intrusion of the enemy. Be determined! Pray with everything you've got! Stand firm and fight for those you love. We are anointed to preach the good news, heal the brokenhearted, and set the captive free! Be alert and prepared for battle. Let us charge the throne, taking hold of heaven by force.

As I have shared throughout the book, entering into the writing arena was a slow, uncertain process for me. Several times I had this overwhelming sense of uncertainty as to whether I should continue writing. The unknown territory brought fear and the rejection seemed unavoidable.

I knew enough at this point, about doubt and my weaknesses, to open my Bible and battle my fears. I prayed through Psalm 144 and God impressed verses 1–2 in my spirit, "Praise be to the LORD my Rock, who trains my hands for war, my fingers for battle. He is my loving God and my fortress, my stronghold and my deliverer, my shield . . ." At first, I was comforted that God would be my helper in writing this book. But then I had a moment of revelation. The *training my hands for war*, *my fingers for the battle* was prayer (and ready access to his Word). I needed to press through the writing process with prayer, clinging to the scriptures, and leave the results—the "battle" of typing, editing, and marketing—to him. The disposal of the forces is totally in the hands of our Commander-in-Chief.

Do you possess a warrior's heart? Our families, relationships, and marriages are under attack in our society. Life itself seems to be falling apart; a breakdown of God's design for the family is rampant both inside and outside the church. Take a stand and pray. Engage in heart-to-heart combat for such a time as this.

Are you tired of seeing people hurt, sick, and defeated? Then, let us fervently pray for our homes, families, and friends. When our loved ones are down and defeated, the Holy Spirit's power through our prayers can pick them up to win their battles. Let us "charge" the throne on behalf of others who are down in the battle. I am asking you to beseech God concerning the needs of the hurting world around us. "Don't be afraid . . . Remember the Lord, who

The Lord will fight for you; you need only be still.
Exodus 14:14

is great and awesome, and fight for your brothers, your sons and your daughters, your wives and your homes" (Neh. 4:14). If you don't pray for those you love, who will?

Recently, one of my friend's sisters had made a series of poor choices and she was close to dying. Over time, my friend was too weary to stand in the gap to pray. Several of her friends and I felt convicted to enter boldly to the throne on her behalf. The act of "carrying each other's burdens" can be powerfully effective through prayer (Gal. 6:2). My friend sensed the presence of God through our prayers covering her as she was filled with unexplainable peace and was carried along by the power of the Holy Spirit. Weeks later her sister returned home from the hospital.

In Luke 5:17–26, there is a story about a time when Jesus was healing the sick. Men came carrying a paralytic friend on a mat. They attempted to get him to Jesus, but they could not find a way through the large crowds. The men came up with a bright idea and climbed up on the roof with the paralytic on his mat. I am sure it was a challenge to keep their friend from rolling off his mat. The friends detached the tiles and lowered their friend on the mat in the middle of the room right in front of Jesus. Can you imagine the effort, time, and care it took to hoist the paralytic up onto the roof, break through the roof, and then gently lower the man to Jesus? When Jesus saw their faith, he forgave and healed the paralytic due to the faith of his friends. Lesson learned: Do whatever it takes to get to Jesus! On behalf of yourself and friends, for those who are sick, are weary of praying, or who are not praying at all.

Pray for unbelievers in your sphere of influence. You should never give up praying that they will receive the grace of God. Pray for God's will in the lives of people you are concerned about. Pray as specifically as you know how and as the Holy Spirit leads. Pray that the bondage and stronghold of the enemy be torn down and demand he flee.

Pray for God to:

- "Open their *eyes* and turn them from darkness to light, and from the power of Satan to God, so they may receive forgiveness of sins and a place among those who are sanctified by faith" (Acts 26:18).
- "Open her *heart* to respond to the message" (Acts 16:14).

- "Open their *minds* to understand the scriptures," and may their *"hearts* burn within" (Luke 24:45, 32).

I enjoy music from a variety of composers. A song by Steve Camp called *Run to the Battle* rings loud and clear to the theme of this chapter. The lyrics bring a sense of conviction as they pierce the heart with truth that we are in the middle of a raging war and we often live in the security of our churches and our comfort zones. We need to zealously witness with everyone we meet, with urgency to share the love of Jesus—our time may be short and another soul may miss the grace that could have been theirs.

Are you reaching out beyond yourself to stand firm against the reality of the gates of hell? You have been trained to use his mighty sword and shield. Let's run to the frontlines of the battle! Shoulder to shoulder we are more than conquerors with the mighty LORD. As his assembled army, we are marching on our hands and knees. Our shields of faith held up together build a canopy of protection from the flaming arrows. March on, mighty prayer warriors, until the trumpet sounds the victory!

We not only fight against principalities, but devout men have also been known to wrestle with God in prayer. One of those men was Jacob. One night Jacob was alone sleeping. He presented his fears to God in prayer before resting. Jacob reminded God of his promises that God made to Abraham and Isaac, and now to him. He pleaded for deliverance from the hand of his brother, Esau, who was attempting to kill him. A man from God wrestled with him until daybreak. When the man saw that he could not overpower Jacob, he touched the socket of Jacob's hip and likely dislocated it. They brawled all night. Then the man requested to be released, but Jacob refused to let go of the angel until he received a blessing.

The man asked him, "What is your name?"

"Jacob," he answered.

Then the man said, "Your name will no longer be Jacob, but Israel, because you have struggled with God and with men and have overcome." Jacob called the place Peniel, saying, "It is because I saw God face to face, and yet my life was spared" (Gen. 32:22–30).

God can handle our "wrestling" prayers. He will bring about justice for his chosen ones who cry out day and night. Interceding for those we love—pouring out our fears for deliverance—takes unceasing exertion and strength. Jacob stood his ground and stayed put until he received his blessing. Do not fear, but choose faith to stay on the front lines in prayer until you see the white in his eyes and the victory banner waving over you with love. Wrestle with God; cry out for blessing! Help rescue others in prayer.

Today's Prayer Journal Task

- Who in your life are you committed to fight for using intercessory prayer?
- Is there an issue you need to "wrestle" with God in prayer about?
- Write down the name of an unbeliever and consistently pray for God to open their eyes, mind, and heart.

Keep an Object of Remembrance

AS STATED EARLIER, journaling is a work produced by faith as an object of remembrance. "The LORD places high value on our remembering what he has done."[6] Many God-fearing men in the Old Testament were honored for marking significant events in history on their journeys. As we look back to the Old Testament, what do you remember as one of the significant things God asked Moses to do after meeting with him on the mountain for forty days? The LORD asked Moses to write down his Words, his covenant he made with Israel—the Ten Commandments.

When Moses came down from the blazing mountain with the two tablets of the Covenant in his hands, he saw that the Israelites had sinned against the LORD, and made hideous idols. In anger he took the two tablets and threw them, breaking them to pieces. The LORD exhibited some tough love to Moses as I would to my children for thrashing about with some very valuable property! He had Moses return to the mountain and this time the LORD required Moses to participate in preserving God's Word. God commanded Moses to "chisel out two stone tablets like the first ones," and make a wooden chest to store them safely. This wooden chest became the Ark of the Covenant. Moses obeyed the LORD and put the tablets in the ark. Moses learned the hard way to highly value God's Word the second time around as he labored to preserve and protect it for generations to come.

Joshua, the successor of Moses, also learned the value of preserving God's Word and marking moments to remember. Joshua was commanded by God to lead the Israelites into the Promised Land. As the people of Israel were headed into unknown territory beyond the Jordan River, God assured Joshua of his continual presence; he would be with Joshua as he was with Moses. Amazingly, God performed a similar miracle as he did 40 years earlier with Moses when he delivered the Israelites out Egypt at the Red Sea.

The priests were commanded to carry the Ark of the Covenant while the soldiers were to keep a clear distance from it, about a half of a mile between them and the Ark. The priests arrived at the river bank and they were to "get their feet wet" by taking a few steps into the Jordan.

Can you imagine carrying the Ark of the Covenant, which represented the very presence of God and his Word, and taking that first step into the water? People had died from simply touching the Ark. These brave men stepped out into the uncertainty of their future and God stepped in with power.

Again we see God as their Deliverer; his promised presence leads them across into a free and fruitful land. After the priests obeyed and stepped into the water, God pushed back the water and held the waves up like a wall. With stamina and strength the priests stood in the middle of the dry river bed, standing in the gap as the entire Israelite nation successfully crossed the Jordan River headed toward the Promised Land.

From this event, we receive a great visual of the role of an intercessor. God's mercy met them in the middle! When the Israelites made it across, the LORD told Joshua to choose twelve men, one from each tribe of Israel. They were to take twelve stones, carry them on their shoulders from the middle of the Jordan where the priests stood to the other side. These stones were to be left as a landmark, a visual aid to help the people remember God's faithfulness. The stones were to serve as a sign among them for the future so when their children asked, "What do these stones mean?" (Josh. 4:21) they could tell them what the LORD had done. These stones were to be a memorial to the people of Israel, forever reminding them that God was with them.

Getting my feet wet in the writing arena has surely been one place I can identify with the priests in this story. I am challenged by the fact that these men of prayer were close to God and were faithful with such a huge responsibility! They chose to believe that God would grant them strength to hold the Ark for endless hours or days. His strength would hold back the waters from engulfing them and take care of any enemies on the other side. They just had to take one step. God had performed this miracle before and he could do it again. This story went down in the books forever, starting with stones of remembrance and then into the written Word. These men obeyed God and marked this significant moment in their lives with a visual reminder. Reading these stories brings hope to us and glory to God that will influence generations.

The Old Testament records some brutal, cold-blooded battles. I think many of them can leave an impression of how to properly handle our weapons in our spiritual battles. One more battle I would like to share that fuels my passion for prayer and journaling is the Battle of the Amalekites in Exodus 17. This particular battle teaches profound principles on the resource of prayer by hiding God's Word in your heart and writing them down for future generations.

Prior to the battle, God asked Moses to strike the rock with his staff to provide water for the grumbling Israelites. Water in the desert was a commodity worth fighting over, so the enemy, the Amalekites, who were well trained in battle, arrived thirsty. The Israelites were shaking with fear and God ordered Moses to send Joshua to fight the Amalekites.

So Joshua and his men fought the Amalekites as Moses had ordered. Moses, Aaron, and Hur went to the top of the hill. As long as Moses held up his hands, the Israelites were winning, but whenever he lowered his hands, the Amalekites were winning. When Moses grew tired, they took a stone and put it under him to rest on. Aaron and Hur held his hands up—one on one side, one on the other—so that his hands remained steady all day.

Joshua overcame the Amalekite army with the sword. Then the LORD said to Moses, "Write this on a scroll as something to be remembered and make sure that Joshua hears it because I will completely blot out the memory of Amalek from under heaven." Moses built an altar and called it, "The LORD is my Banner." He said, "For hands were lifted up to the throne of the LORD" (Exod. 17:10–15).

The principles demonstrated within this story exhibit power. The staff in Moses' hands can be inferred as the "rod" or sword of God's Word. Do you see what is within the word "sword"? Remove the "s" and you have the *Word*! Remember this rod parted the sea and split the rock—water gushed out to thirsty souls. This rod—thrown to the ground—turned to a snake that brought healing to the touch. The rod placed in Moses' insecure hands gave him power and assurance of God's confidence in him to set God's people free! Just as with Moses, we have been given the rod of God's Word. "Your rod and your staff they comfort me" (Ps. 23:4) because the Word brings boundaries in our lives, protection, guidance, authority, healing, wisdom, victory, and God himself. As Moses holds up the Word, to me it is a depiction of prayer; Joshua is overcoming the enemy with the sword. When Moses' hands grow tired, the battle is being lost. God provides family, Aaron and Hur, to help Moses' hands remain stable so he can continue in intercession and the battle be won.

Another point on prayer: Do you have some family or friends who can "hold up" your hands in prayer when you become weary? God always provides strength through prayer partners on earth to keep our hands and hearts lifted in prayer, as we proclaim his promises together. I have experienced throughout my lifetime intimate prayer with very committed, faithful prayer warriors who upheld my marriage, family, and children to the throne of grace. Not only do we need friends as prayer warriors, but God has placed Jesus and the Holy Spirit to faithfully intercede on our behalf. The Spirit holds up our hands in prayer when we are weary. Jesus is the Rock we can rest on to win the battle.

God, in his foreknowledge, instructs Moses to record the victory for Joshua and all the Israelites. God knows the condition of men's hearts—prone to wander and forget the One they love, their Deliverer. The Israelites were having a hard time remembering. Who doesn't have a hard time remembering? For that reason, their story was recorded to remind them (and us) of all the LORD had done for them. The day would come when the enemies' army would no longer exist.

This story seems to emphasize the power of lifting holy hands in prayer, standing on God's promises, and the authority given to us to overcome the enemy with the sword of truth. We also see God places importance on "writing this (victory) on a scroll as something to be remembered" for generations to come. Certainly that was a victory with no remnants to rise back up against them. A battle was won for the living water to flow freely to quench the thirst of the newly trained soldiers (Exod. 17:14–16).

We need to remember God's faithfulness and all the marvelous works his divine hands have done. "I have a good forgetter," my ninety-two-year-old grandmother used to say. Yes, I am right on her heels. Daily I struggle to remember what the Lord impressed on my heart from my morning quiet time. Whether it is applying what I've learned to everyday life or sharing the lessons with others, if I have not written it down, reviewed it, or carried it with me, I can easily forget. In retaining valuable lessons, studying, taking notes, repetition, and review works best for me.

Today's Prayer Journal Task

- Record an "object of remembrance" in your journal when you could confidently say, "My God is with me!"
- What "rod" do you cling to today?
- What scripture unleashes God's power to give you confidence?

CHAPTER 12

DISCOVER YOUR PURPOSE

> What we are is God's gift to us. What we become is
> our gift to God.
>
> —unknown author

A S WE HAVE explored throughout the book, God reaches out to us and initiates a relationship by welcoming us into his presence. Our response to God's love draws our hearts into a surrendered work of prayer. God's purpose is accomplished as he cultivates our hearts for growth, and we respond by engaging in the battle and building his kingdom to bring him glory. From the many efforts in coming before him, offering our countless prayers, and listening to his guidance, we discover our journey toward our life purpose.

What lasting legacy are you building for Jesus? Many times in life we are uncertain of our purpose. Discovering our unique and individual purpose can be a struggle, but consistent prayer, aided by journaling, can open our hearts to the opportunities God has planned. "For we are God's workmanship, created in Christ Jesus to do good works, which God prepared in advance for us to do" (Eph. 2:10). "He created us with a need to contribute and participate in the harvest. He created us to be most satisfied by diligent pursuit."[1]

Several years ago, I was asked to facilitate a MOMS (Mothers of Many Seasons) ministry at our former church. At the same time I had been given a little prayer book to read, *The Prayer of Jabez* by Bruce Wilkinson. As I prayed for clarification in making my leadership decision, I read that Jabez cried out to the God of Israel and asked for blessing, for his sphere of influence to grow, and God's hand to be with him. God used the prayer of Jabez found in 1 Chronicles 4:10 in my life. "Oh, that you would bless me and enlarge my territory! Let your hand be with me, and keep me from harm so that I will be free from pain. And God granted his request."

In my heart, I knew God was expanding my territory to lead these young mothers. Little did I realize that he would move our family three years later to another city and call me to establish and pilot another MOMS group. And, now, as I write, God is expanding the border a third time, reaching the hearts of many through the writing of this book. I prayed these verses over eight years ago and God keeps using them to fulfill his purposes in me. Continually, I ask the same request as Jabez, with a smile on my heart and a light-hearted laugh at God's sense of humor as I wait in expectation for his plan to unfold.

Jesus said, "My purpose is to give them a rich and satisfying life" (John 10:10 NLT). God has a redemptive plan for us through Jesus: life forever, free, and full. How is that accomplished? Three simple ways: loving God, loving ourselves, and loving people.

God created each of our lives specifically for a unique, special purpose and plan. We can find our adventure in life as we seek God's will through prayer, the study of God's Word, helping others, and recording his counsel by journaling. God has so much more to show you regarding his plans for your life.

As we abide in God's Word, which is setting forth his will, the Holy Spirit can work in our hearts. As we establish our identity in Christ, God can fully reveal our purpose. After years of prayer and study of scripture, I still seek God's continual revelation to the question of individuality, "Who am I?" and "What is my unique purpose?" God graciously supplies me enough light to see who I am today, with a vision of hope in who I am becoming; yet balanced with humility—accepting the fact that apart from him I am nothing.

As we read and believe his Word by faith, God blesses us with a core identity rooted in Christ and then he gives a sense of distinctiveness in our purposes. The acceptance of our identity in Christ affects all of our relationships and the ability to see God's purposes. We are led step by step. We do not need to see too far ahead, but believe and onward march! God does the rest.

The Father, Spirit, and Jesus are present together, working God's will and purpose in you to see God's Word fulfilled. "He who searches our hearts knows the mind of the Spirit, because the Spirit intercedes for the saints in accordance with God's will" (Rom. 8:27). God is deliberately holding the door open for you to discover his will for your life. "'For I know the thoughts and plans that I have for you,' says the Lord, 'thoughts and plans for welfare and peace and not for evil, to give you hope in your final outcome'" (Jer. 29:11 AMP).

God is patient with us. He knows we will speculate and doubt, and be "slow of heart to believe." What will happen when we walk through a door of uncertainty? . . . But it's good and pleases God when you walk through the doorway of faith, an entrance of no regrets. We leave a life of self-security and step into utter dependence. Let's make it our goal to "press on to take hold of that for which Christ Jesus took hold of (us)" (Phil. 3:12).

God is after our hearts. Go after his heart more than jobs, financial security, health, and happiness. As we seek him, we will find ourselves and our unique purpose. Here is the answer to our frustration in not finding direction for our lives . . . are we spending time with God, seeking first his Kingdom? Are we seeking where we can serve him and give him the most glory?

God's plan and purpose for our individual lives may not always be exactly what we might think. He sees us for who we truly are and with the potential for transformation. He desires to accomplish change within us using circumstances, people, and events on paths we would like to avoid. As we grow in intimacy with the LORD, he places his desires on our hearts. His Spirit prompts us to pray his purposeful petitions that he wants for us to partner with him to bring him glory.

Seeking God's will had been a challenge for me as I prayed for God's plan and the sale of my parents' home for over five years. My parents lived in a rural part of North Carolina and needed to travel for groceries and more frequently to doctor appointments. My heart desired for them to live nearby so I could be available to help in their later years. I was certain God was taking me through this long journey to teach me about prayer. I went through cycles of praying adamantly, remembering his promises, specifically asking for a buyer and for them to be located close by.

In an attempt to sell their home over the past five years, several deceitful transactions occurred, causing the sale to be terminated.

After months and years, my heart grew faint. I threw in the towel, not knowing how to pray, so out came, "Thy will be done!" as a reactive prayer thrown up in anger or apathy. Yet after time, deep down those words rang true in my heart. He would work all things, even the adversity, for their good, as promised for those who love him.

I remained faithful in prayer. I knew when I was weary of praying, others would be strong to intercede for them. I would keep on asking until we saw the fulfillment of his will and purpose.

Through prayer, surrender comes; a more active agreement with God's plan than a passive yielding to circumstances. God's way and timing is always best. "He determined the times set for them and the exact places where they should live. God did this so that men would seek him and perhaps reach out for him and find him, though he is not far from each of us" (Acts 17:26–27). The process of yielding to his will results in contentment. I kept running to God with my desires and trusted that the Father knows best.

Would you believe as I am finishing this book my parents received an offer on their house? In this difficult economy when the housing market struggles, the seemingly impossible was made possible. God's timing has proven perfect once again.

Whatever the prayer burden or purpose that God has put on your heart, the most important thing to remember is to pray for God's will—for his glory.

Come Alive!

One of my favorite quotations hanging in my kitchen is by John Piper. "God is most glorified in us when we are most satisfied in him." We are invited into God's presence and can stay until we are satisfied in him alone. Living in his fullness we find life and bring him glory.

In the movie *Chariots of Fire*, Olympian Eric Liddell said, "I believe God made me for a purpose . . . and when I run, I feel his pleasure." On a personal level, I have not felt that same sense of his pleasure when I run. But I do sense God's pleasure when I pray or discover his purpose for me, when he has led me to help others or to step out of my comfort zone in ministry.

We have all heard it said that life is best lived on purpose. Like everything else in the universe, our purpose originates in the heart of God. Whether you recognize it or not, God has a direction for your life, a divine calling, a path along which he intends to lead you.

When you welcome God into your heart and establish a genuine relationship with him, he will make his purposes known. Are you aware of his nudging presence? As you write and read through the prayer journal, and you are uncertain of your individual calling or purpose, keep looking for God's hand in your life. He will faithfully lead you in the direction you should go and you will discover the greatest journey of your life!

Your time in prayer, his Word, and journaling is vital. Writing gives us time to reflect and examine our hearts and purposes. Journaling is a paper trail of the history of our lives intervened by God's redemption and grace. God's callings need to be founded in prayer, maintained by prayer, and move forward with prayer. I have seen callings and ministries founded on scripture and bathed in prayer succeed.

There are wonderful materials available to help you discern God's purpose for your life. The book *SHAPE* by Erik Rees is a rich resource to obtain guidance. The acronym comes from Rick Warren's book, *The Purpose Driven Life*: S—spiritual gifts, H—heart, A—abilities, P—personality, E—experiences.[2] He says, as unique as our individual thumbprints are, so are our purposes and gifts.

You are SHAPE(d) to serve God and others. The great adventure is in discovering God's unique purpose for your life and doing it. Sincerely ask in prayer for the Holy Spirit to fill you with power and guide you, showing you who you are and who you will become. Enter into this time of prayer with no preconceived thoughts and trust God for your life purpose, one you may not have expected. It may have never occurred to you that you would become what God has called you to be. Most likely, it may seem impossible! But it is most likely a position of total dependence on him to fulfill this role; exactly where we need to be. Embrace it. Don't look back. "When the Spirit of the LORD comes upon you in power . . . you will be changed into a different person . . . Do whatever your hand finds to do, for God is with you" (1 Sam. 10:6–7). And be patient.

In scripture we are told to eagerly desire spiritual gifts. There are several passages and tests that can help you determine your spiritual gifts. "There are different kinds of gifts, but the same Spirit. There are different kinds of service, but the same Lord. There are different kinds of working, but the same God works in all of them in all men. Now to each one the manifestation of the Spirit is given for the common good—wisdom, knowledge, faith, and healing" to name a few (1 Cor. 12:4–7). A spiritual gift test that I have found helpful is from *INJOY*.

There is freedom to accept and not compare in God's kingdom of gift giving. He is God and can generously give us individual gifts in time of need to build our confidence, the church, and our spiritual growth.

Within the church the enemy uses the realm of spiritual gifts to bring division. Many issues arise when discussing the gifting of tongues. Scripture teaches, "The one who prays using a private 'prayer language' certainly gets a lot out of it, but proclaiming God's truth to the church in its common language brings the whole church into growth and strength. I want all of you to develop intimacies with God in prayer, but please don't stop with that. Go on and proclaim his clear truth to others. It's more important that everyone have access to the knowledge and love of God in a language everyone understands than that you go off and cultivate God's presence in a mysterious prayer language—unless, of course, there is someone who can interpret what you are saying for the benefit of all" (1 Cor. 14:4–5 MSG).

In college I had several friends who shared with me that they were given a personal prayer language. I felt a little "lesser than," and took my curiosity to God. I cried out to God, "Why wasn't I given a prayer language? I love to pray! Was I loved less?" As I waited in the quiet, the Holy Spirit brought comfort to my spiritual condition and reminded me, "If I (Sarah) speak in tongues of men and angels, but have not love, I (Sarah) am only a resounding gong or a clanging cymbal" (1 Cor. 13:1). I certainly didn't want to be a loud gong walking around. I was gently convicted that I needed to focus on love . . . that was the greatest gift and I needed to be content with the gifts God had given me.

Be on your guard not to compare yourself, your spiritual gifts, or service. It is not wise. It robs you of enjoying and accepting the gifts of others and diminishes your perception of those gifts you possess. Comparing can snatch your dreams! You have Jesus to offer and reflect in your own unique way. Read and reflect on Psalm 139, asking God to search you, know you, and show you.

Let's jump back to the tabernacle setting in the Old Testament. God used a story to gently bring me back into an attitude of contentment in accepting my purpose. The Kohathite tribe, descendants of the Levites, were assigned the crucial task of transporting the articles of the tabernacle. This was an important job; many were not able to enter in the tabernacle in the first place and they were commanded to transport the furniture on their shoulders without touching or looking at the articles or they would die. Envying Moses' position of authority, the Kohathites became resentful and rose up against Moses, accusing him of being too holy.

Journal Entry December 4, 2001

The tribes of Korah and Kohath (branch of the Levites) rose up against Moses because of pride and ambition. They wanted to be on top of the chain of command. Moses said to Korahites and their followers, "Now listen, you Levites! Isn't it enough for you that the God of Israel has separated you from the rest of the Israelite community and brought you near himself to do the work at the LORD's tabernacle and to stand before the community and minister to them? He has brought you and all your fellow Levites near himself, but now you are trying to get the priesthood too?" (Num. 16:8–10).

With integrity Moses seeks God's counsel and tells Korah and his followers to bring censors filled with fire, and incense before the LORD at the entrance to the Tent of Meeting for the morning offering. God's Divine glory appeared and Moses and Aaron cried out for mercy. God in his sovereignty had set apart the leaders of Israel. God speaks to Moses, pouring out his warning and grace . . . to separate themselves for salvation, to move out from the tents of the Korahites.

Isaiah 7:13 "Hear now, you house of David! Is not enough to try the patience of men? Will you try the patience of God also?"

I sometimes have thoughts—"Oh, I wish I could teach
like. . . ." or "Why didn't I get the talent to sing like. . . .?"
I often want to be more and have other spiritual gifts. The
answer was given to me by a question . . . *Isn't it enough,
Sarah? Is it too small a thing for you to be my servant?*

—Isa. 49:6

The God of Israel has separated me from the rest by
choosing me—to serve him and to be a faithful wife and
mom, to stand before the ladies at church (MOMS) to
encourage, love, and lead them.

Is it not enough to have Jesus alone? Forgive me, LORD,
for complaining, for comparing, for wanting *more* than
what you have given me and deemed best for me. Thank
you for showing me this in such a gentle and quiet way.
You are kind and loving. I am a daughter of the King! I
have eternal life with Jesus who dwells within me. How
privileged and blessed I am, my precious Jesus, my greatest treasure.

God poured out his judgment on the Korahites by allowing the
earth to swallow them and their possessions, and sending fire to
consume those offering the presumptuous incense. There is great
freedom and joy accepting the gifts God has given you. God has
given you these gifts for the common good of the church. When we
envy or look down on others' gifts, we are not sharing the love of
Christ. Be thankful for your unique purpose in serving him. Isn't it
enough, just to serve him wherever we are?

Our faith needs to put feet on! God asks us to love him with
our all hearts, all our souls, with our entire strength, and with our
complete minds; and love our neighbor as we would love ourselves
(Luke 10:27). Applying God's Word of what we know to do is always the right first step in finding our purpose. Nurture and allow
the seed God plants to produce the most fruit possible for God's
kingdom. The entry below occurred during a season of questioning
God's gentle "nudges" for me to step out of my comfort zone and
lead an outreach.

Journal Entry May 20, 2004

Bloom where you are planted. *I planted you as a choice vine of sound and reliable stock.*

— Jeremiah 2:21

What a word of affirmation to me! God planted me here—as his choice vine to bear fruit, fruit that will last—of sound and reliable stock—Oh, that the LORD would consider me faithful and reliable!—(and maybe a little crazy due to motherhood!)

Rick Warren's newsletter, The Ministry Tool Box, said this week, "Farmers know that seed must be given away for it to increase. If you keep a seed in a sack, it doesn't do any good. But when you plant it, it multiples." *Thank you, LORD, for planting me as a "seed" starting a new ministry. I don't want to be a seed left in a sack.*

You planted. You water it. You make it grow, LORD. Only because of you!

What are you planting today that will bear fruit for tomorrow, for eternity? "God can take what you have to offer and make a difference for eternity . . . If you want to walk on water . . . start praying."[3] What is interfering and distracting you from being all God made you to be? We each have significant purpose by reflecting Jesus. We just need to believe it! We are called and commissioned to tell the story of the gospel through our lives.

Time and again, God can use our human imperfections to reach others with his redeeming power. The manifestation of Jesus in us may come in many different facets and ways, communicating his love to meet the variety of hearts and needs in this world.

We each have a story to tell of God's great love. Your life, your story, is a message from God of his testifying power. Pray for opportunities to tell the world of the gospel of Jesus Christ and what he has done for you. You will face opposition, but your story is yours! No one can deny what Christ has done personally in your life.

Our lives through the spoken word of our testimonies and prayers are a weapon, instruments of righteousness. Deliver the message of love and power by the sword of his Word which penetrates the heart. Jesus said, "Anyone who accepts your message is also accepting me. Anyone who rejects you is rejecting me. Anyone who rejects me is rejecting God who sent me" (Luke 10:16 NLT). So take the risk and tell your story.

As we choose to hide God's Word in our hearts and pray through the scriptures we will be transformed by renewing our minds and we will see God's direction for our lives. "All Scripture is God-breathed and is useful for teaching, rebuking, correcting, and training in righteousness, so that the man of God may be thoroughly equipped for every good work" (2 Tim. 3:16–17). As we listen and obey, taking risky steps feels like taking a step off the zip line of faith; we will be able to determine God's individual will for our lives . . . receiving energy, joy, and peace.

In all things, God's will is that we bear much fruit, an outgrowth of love. Jesus said, "You did not choose Me but I chose you, and appointed you that you would go and bear fruit,—fruit that will last. Then the Father will give you whatever you ask in My name" (John 15:16). "He will lead you first to himself, and then with him, he will lead you into the world that he loves and needs you to love. It is by invitation."[4]

Jesus tells us that hearts are ready to reap for eternal life. Be glad and work together. One plants and another reaps. Let's enjoy laboring together in prayer, accomplishing God's purpose.

The temptation is to give up the work unfinished which he began within us. God has instructed us "that he who began a good work in you will complete it" (Phil. 1:6). God does the work through us! Stop straining, listen and obey for today. Move to the rhythms of his grace.

Paul encouraged the Corinthian church to be generous and finish his ministry; their eagerness and willingness to do the work gave them a sense of joy and accomplishment. He reminded them if the willingness was there, the gift was acceptable according to what one has to offer, not according to what he does not have (2 Cor. 8:11–12).

Are you struggling to find your purpose and come alive? Who do you know that really knows you, knows your heart and gifts? Use them as a resource to help you identify and affirm where God may be leading you.

Remember you are God's temple, his dwelling place. Isn't everything you have and everything you are gifts from God? So, why do we spend so much energy comparing and competing? Don't forget you already have all you need—you have more access to God than you can grasp. In the effort to seek fulfillment in our life purpose we can easily lose sight of the most important purpose of our lives. We need to pull back, revaluate, and embrace the reality that our first purpose and design in life is to love God. Do we love God above all? Then do we love our neighbor as ourselves? Love is the royal law that gives freedom.

In my drive to finish this book, it became apparent to me that I was trying so hard in my own strength to finally finish that I became consumed by the process, thinking about it day and night, stressing and feeling overwhelmed. I realized I had lost my focus on loving God and everybody around me. My attitude was less than desirable! God gently reminded me of the lessons I am sharing; he will do the work when I yield, placing my time to complete the task is in his hands.

As we love, serve, and "submit to one another out of reverence for Christ" (Eph. 5:21). God lives in us and his love is apparent to the world. When we trust and "know that in all things God works for the good of those who love him, who have been called according to his purpose" then we are living for his purpose giving him glory (Rom. 8:28). God wants us to be satisfied, fulfilled, and know that we have purpose. We are the apple of his eye.

A quote by Gil Bailie which I hold close to my finger tips on a bookmark is a true test in helping to discover our designed purpose and contribution for his glory and kingdom. "Don't ask yourself what the world needs, ask yourself what makes you come alive and do that, because what the world needs is people who have come alive." The answer to becoming alive is meeting with God, discovering your spiritual gifts, and using them to reach the world around you.

As Jesus once said, "Here I am . . . I have come to do your will, O God." To obey God's will by praying, acting and responding with a sincere heart is a supreme act of love that will graciously be rewarded in heaven. A cherished prayer I have written in my Bible is by Betty Stam, a young missionary woman who died as a martyr in China in the 1934.

> LORD, I give up all my own plans and purposes
> All my own desires and hopes
> And accept Thy will for my life.

I give myself, my life, my all
Utterly to Thee to be Thine forever.
Fill me and seal me with Thy Holy Spirit
Use me as Thou wilt, send me where Thou wilt
And work out Thy whole will in my life at any cost now
and forever.

Journal to Discover Your Unique Purpose

Journaling bestows at our fingertip an opportunity to remember and see God threading a theme, a passion in our lives, and leading us to our unique purpose. We see the fulfillment of his promises and provision of what we patiently waited for through prayer. Grace never shuts the door of discovery to a willing soul.

Never underestimate the power of prayer in finding your purpose. Never take too lightly the influence of your life in the life of another. One prayer may lead to one life that is changed forever. Each of us has an opportunity to be used by God to bless the world around us.

What drives us? Is it a desire to make a difference, to make a contribution by discovering our God-given passion? Desire . . . drives us! We were made with a capacity for a passionate prayer life because God is a passionate Intercessor and Communicator of his love. We are designed with competence to practice here on earth what we will do for eternity. "So love the Lord God with all your passion and prayer and intelligence and energy" (Mark 12:30 MSG).

Through prayer, studying his Word, obedience, and experience, God will increase your passion for your designed purpose. Please don't think you have strayed so far that the hand of God can't use you. Our God is a God of full redemption! "But God will redeem my life from the grave; he will surely take me to himself (Ps. 49:15). Previously, what did I say would occur in our hearts from being in his presence? Transformation—your story for his glory! Take heart and wait for the LORD.

Do you remember when God told Abraham to leave his country, his people and his father's household and to go into the land God would show him? This is when Abraham was given the promise of blessing. Abraham, Moses, the Israelites, and Jesus traveled from place to place following God. God often requires us to leave our comfortable places of ministry to broaden our territories so we do not become complacent.

Our journey in life can be made up of smaller destinations that lead us to a new assignment God has for us. We always need to stop, look, and listen to God's direction for our lives. However, we must rely on the promise God shares; God shares that he has great plans for us as co-laborers to give us hope.

King Hezekiah's life exemplified this promise. He honored the LORD during his twenty-nine year reign, and in all he did he never ceased to follow God and his commands. Scripture declares there was no other king like him among all the kings of Judah. God was with him; he was successful in whatever he did. When faced with a threat of being overtaken by the king of Assyria, Hezekiah chose to pray instead of fear. "Hezekiah received the letter from the messengers (concerning the encroaching enemy). He went up to the temple of the LORD and spread it out before the LORD."

And Hezekiah prayed to the LORD restating all he knew about God's mighty presence, "enthroned between the cherubim." He was God, creator over all the kingdoms of the earth. Hezekiah cried out to the LORD for his divine ear to hear, his eyes to see and to listen to the insulting words of the enemy concerning his God as he presented the letter. His final plea—deliverance for God's glory and his name to be known among the nations!

This is what God said in response: "I have heard your prayer concerning Sennacherib king of Assyria . . . For out of Jerusalem will come a remnant; he (king of Assyria) will not enter this city or shoot an arrow here" (2 Kings 19:20, 31–32). God heard the cry of Hezekiah and kept his Word by sending out an angel who put to death 185,000 men in the enemy's camp for his name sake and for the generational blessing of King David.

Prayer journaling or recording our prayer requests is a tangible way to spread out your prayer before the LORD. Spread out your concerns and inquire of him with holy boldness. "In everything you do, put God first (by praying); he will direct your steps and crown your efforts with success" (Prov. 3:6 TLB).

As we enjoy our journey with God, he will impart his desires to us that amazingly become our desires. As we commit these desires to God, he carries them out through us and promises us success. "Delight yourself in the LORD and he will give you the desires of your heart. Commit your way to the LORD; trust in him and he will do this" (Ps. 37:4–5). What desire has God placed on your heart? If your desire brings glory to God and builds his kingdom then trust by faith that he placed them there. Don't shut the door of your dreams by means of human reasoning. "The Lord works out everything for his own ends—In his heart a man plans his course, but the LORD determines his steps" (Prov. 16:4, 9). Trust God step by step . . . go through the door that makes you walk in the footsteps of faith. Hear the words, *Do not fear . . . I AM with you.*

> ### *Journal Entry March 2, 2008*
>
> Where would publishing this book lead me? Closer to God's heart in total dependence. Inviting others to life. John Eldridge in *Captivating*—"We can't wait until we feel safe to love and invite. In fact, if you feel a little scared then you're probably on the right path. . . . God calls us to stop hiding . . . to trust him and offer our true selves . . . to the world."
>
> LORD, I fear putting my life "out there." Jesus put his life out there, he laid it down. He was crucified. LORD, I know that you are glorified as we lay down our lives. You pick us up. You resurrect!

Ask yourself, how does what I am doing impact God's kingdom? The LORD designed you with a distinct purpose of giving him glory. Recording his leading and direction helps to clarify your gifts, abilities, and purposes. Once these are discovered, writing them down assists you to carefully "pay attention to the ministry you have received in the LORD, so that you can accomplish it" (Col. 4:17 HCSB).

To see a true reflection of who you are, you must look to him. To find your voice, you must find his. To discover your purpose, you must discover his. Ask to see with his eyes. To grasp this truth more vividly, there is a picture of a timid calico kitten looking in a mirror. In the reflection appears a strong impressive lion. I love the image! In our weaknesses, he is strong.

It is imperative that you grasp that God's purpose and pleasure is to be in a relationship with you for all eternity. Eternity with God starts when the Holy Spirit opens your eyes, mind and heart; stirring a desire to know, receive and believe in Jesus. To find and know him brings purpose from the empty way of life. Jesus brings you meaning and your purpose comes from him. Through the process of discovery, no matter how you feel . . . pray, trusting that every good purpose God starts, he holds together! (Col. 1:17).

Each of us who believes in Jesus carries an awesome responsibility to share the gospel with others. We have the love of Jesus in our hearts! "Be imitators of God, therefore, as dearly loved children and live a life of love, just as Christ loved us and gave himself up for us as a fragrant offering and sacrifice to God" (Eph. 5:1). We offer our lives as living sacrifices when we passionately pray, building a legacy by journaling, and living out our purpose.

> From the east I summon a bird of prey; from a far-off land, a man to fulfill my purpose. What I have said, that will I bring about; what I have planned, that will I do" (Isa. 46:11). "The Lord will fulfill his purpose for me; your love, O Lord, endures forever—do not abandon the works of your hands."
>
> —Psalm 138:8

After one full year of building the tabernacle, the Israelites had not abandoned the work of their hands. The tabernacle was built to perfect specification as God commanded Moses. It was time for the final inspection. Moses bowed and blessed the Israelites for their obedience. As God commanded, Moses set up everything in the tabernacle for ministering in the sanctuary. Moses anointed everything and consecrated it to the Lord. Moses finished his assigned work.

Jesus, the perfect tabernacle, cried out in his death on the cross, "It is finished." "With that, he bowed his head and gave up his spirit" (John 19:30). His obedience on earth invites us to come freely into God's presence. Will you obey and finish the work he has planned for you? His grace is sufficient . . . "Lord, you establish peace for us; all that we have accomplished you have done for us" (Isa. 26:12). What are your dreams? Invite God to do the impossible with your life; finish the work, and give him the glory.

CHAPTER 13

GOD'S KINGDOM COME

WOULD GOD really dwell in the human heart? Amazingly, he does! It's hard to comprehend that the God of the Universe dwells within me. Once more, God reveals his profound love and desire to be with us; by giving us an opportunity to invite him to dwell so close in the innermost part of us just as he desired to dwell in the innermost sacred part of the tabernacle. We are all *unworthy recipients, but* . . . the invitation stands open forever. "Come, you who are blessed by my Father" (Matt. 25:34). And when we come to him and settle down with him . . . we will receive the promised blessing of his goodness forever, just as he said.

God initiated a relationship with us from the very beginning in the Garden of Eden. When sin occurred and the garden was closed off from the human race, the need to fellowship with God remained. God established a place to be present with us by setting up the tabernacle. Now through his Son we can have continual fellowship. God invites us to his kingdom forever. We are a royal priesthood. God is pleased to give us his kingdom.

Embrace God's will and accept that you were created for a larger purpose. In Christ you have all you need to help establish God's kingdom here on earth. As we pray, "Your kingdom come, your will be done on earth as it is in heaven" (Matt. 6:10), that his dwelling place be in every heart on earth. God establishes a spiritual kingdom . . . "The kingdom of God is within you" (Luke 17:21). To expand the borders of this kingdom we are created to fulfill the great commission which must be accompanied by prayer. Prayer hastens the time for God's kingdom to come and prepares us for our imminent resurrection and perfect restoration with God on the New Earth. We are created eternal beings . . . designed for a life of communion.

Our life on earth is preparation for a continuous and harmonious relationship with God. Our obedient, faithful stewardship of our time and resources on earth correlates to our eternal riches in heaven. It is a mystery, but I do believe when Jesus teaches that those who are faithful with a few things will be put in charge of many things, not only is he talking about life here on earth, but our responsibility to help rule in the kingdom of heaven.

There are many passages in the Bible concerning Christ's return for his church. If you watch the media and know the scriptures, it appears the signs of Christ's return are intensifying. Time is of the essence for Christ's return. Agreeing with scripture, we do not know the day or the hour, but I sense in my heart that "for such a time as this," now is the time to make prayer your highest priority. God has called us to be engaged in prayer and find ourselves ready when he returns.

Are we doing our part to prepare for his kingdom to come? Pray for God to open doors for the gospel message to reach the world. "Devote yourselves to prayer, being watchful and thankful" (Col. 4:2). "The harvest is plentiful, but the workers are few. Ask the LORD of the harvest, therefore, to send out workers into his harvest field" (Luke 10:2). We are all commanded to participate and receive the promise of his presence as we go and make disciples by teaching them to obey everything he has commanded. His promise is sure as he confirms, "I am with you always, to the very end of the age" (Matt. 28:20).

The Bible makes it clear there will be an eternal kingdom. "His dominion is an everlasting dominion that will not pass away, and his kingdom is one that will never be destroyed" (Dan. 7:14). God promises as his name endures . . . so will his descendants as he establishes a new earth . . . "the home of righteousness" (2 Pet. 3:13). We need to live with a sense of urgency for Jesus declares, "Behold, I am coming soon!" (Rev. 22:7). Let us pray for his coming!

Prayer for the Church

Throughout the Bible we have seen God establish a dwelling place for worshiping him; first in the Garden of Eden, then the Tent of Meeting or tabernacle. In the new covenant, God lives in us through his Spirit. God founded his church for worshippers to gather together for love, support, strength, and to be a beacon of hope. The church was built on the man who by faith briefly walked on water: Peter. The disciple who answered correctly when Jesus questioned, "Who do you say that I am?"

Peter affirmatively pronounced Jesus' position, "You are the Christ, the Son of the living God . . ."

Jesus validates Peter's identity, "And I tell you that you are Peter, and on this rock I will build my church, and the gates of Hades will not overcome it" (Matt. 16:15, 18).

Although Peter's life had moments of merit, other moments were lacking perfection when in his fear he stumbled on the Rock. In Peter's boldness he had a tendency to blurt out responses based on his level of confidence. When Jesus had been arrested, fear gripped Peter and he denied association with Jesus. He abandoned Jesus at the pinnacle of his affliction. Peter's mission gives us hope to know that God sees our potential, and his love keeps no record of the failures that we make along the way. Peter's name meaning "rock" came to fruition as Peter built the early church after Jesus' ascension.

Again, I love how the Old and New Testament interlace God's truths! In the Old Testament, a passage in Genesis 28 brings a great foreshadowing of Jesus and the church being built on the rock. Abraham's grandson, Jacob, received the generational blessing of God's covenant. One night Jacob stopped during his travels to rest for the night. Jacob had a vivid dream. He saw angels on a stairway ascending and descending from heaven to earth. Above the stairs stood the LORD, saying, "I am the LORD, God of your father Abraham . . . I give you and your descendants the land . . . I am with you and will watch over you wherever you go" (Gen. 28:13, 15). Jacob woke and knew the Lord had been with him, although he was not awake. He made a memorial from the *stone* that was under his head called the place Bethel, meaning house of God, the gate of heaven. . . . Jesus told us we would see heaven open and we would see angels ascending and descending on the Son of Man (John 1:51). The Word descended and became flesh, and tabernacle among us . . . and we are members of God's household, built on the foundation with Christ Jesus himself as the chief cornerstone. In him the whole building, each of us as living stones, are joined together and rise to become a holy temple in the Lord (John 1:14, Eph. 2:19b–21). The blessing we receive is that there is now joy given in God's house of prayer . . . for all nations (Isa. 56:7).

God entrusts us with the responsibility to continue the building of the Christian church. We are intended for a life of prayer to build up and protect his church, the corporate body of Christ. We are encouraged to gather together for the purpose of edifying each other in faith and love as we wait for God's kingdom to come.

The signs of the end times are increasing with intensity and frequency—fires, wars, earthquakes and "in the last days there will be very difficult times. For people will love only themselves and their money. They will be boastful and proud, scoffing at God, disobedient to their parents, and ungrateful. They will consider nothing sacred. They will be unloving and unforgiving; they will slander others and have no self-control. They will be cruel and hate what is good. They will betray their friends, be reckless, be puffed up with pride, and love pleasure rather than God. They will act religious, but they will reject the power that could make them godly" (2 Tim. 3:1–5).

It's time for the church to rise to the occasion, stand strong, and look different than the world, diligently proclaiming the message of the Jesus Christ. We need to come together in close relationship; we do not need to stand alone in the last days. The enemy in his final plea will come against the church and not sit idly watching those who promote the name of Jesus.

It is often forgotten that "prayer is the greatest resource of the church."[1] Yet "prayer is the most underutilized tool we have in the church."[2] Yet scripture proves that Jesus was passionate for his church. "Jesus loved the church and gave himself up for it" (Eph. 5:25).

We serve the church with good intentions in its many activities, but do we sacrificially love the church? Do we serve the church through fervent prayer? As the church we have an awesome responsibility to protect, support, and build the church through intercession. We are encouraged by God's promise to be leaders for our nation of people who pray, "If my people, who are called by my name, will humble themselves and pray and seek my face and turn from their wicked ways, then will I hear from heaven and will forgive their sin and will heal their land" (2 Chron. 7:14).

How does the church, the Bride, make herself ready? Is the church ready for her wedding day? We are preparing for his return as we fellowship in prayer—the body made as one. We come together to worship One God, through One Spirit by the grace of One Savior.

The church's purpose is to know God and make him known. The body of Christ prepares for his return by looking to him and for him. In the "wait" we gather together for worship, prayer, receiving the "washing with water" (Eph. 5:26) through the study and exposition of scripture, ministering to one another, and reaching out to build his kingdom.

Our highest purpose is to love one another as Christ loved his disciples so the world will see we are one—unified, and sanctified. The church is intended to be a refuge and strength for those in need. The healthy do not need a doctor, but the sick (Matt. 9:12). Where do the sick and wounded go if not to the church?

God's intent was that, through the church, the multi-faceted character of God should be known to us and be made known through us to the world; and together we stand against "the rulers and authorities in the heavenly realms according to his eternal purpose which he accomplished in Christ" (Eph. 3:10–11). One important principle of prayer is for the strengthening of the church. The bride of Christ is the church and she is to be a Boulder; not easily moved nor tossed around by the ever-changing ways of world.

Pray that the Spirit of the Sovereign LORD would open wide the doors of opportunity for evangelism and for the Holy Spirit to be poured upon your church, that through us he may heal the brokenhearted, set the captive free, release people from darkness, give comfort to the hurting, provide for those who grieve, restore beauty from ashes, pour out gladness to those who mourn, and clothe those in despair with praise; then we will be called mighty oaks of righteousness, a planting of the LORD for the display of his splendor (Isa. 61:1–12). Jesus is our heavenly bridegroom coming to rescue his Bride!

The church is called to assemble the people for prayer. There are times in the Old Testament that a trumpet sounded when God's people were in great need. The priests would declare a holy fast and call a sacred assembly. The people gathered together and consecrated themselves; the elders, women, and children. With such seriousness and humility they would gather for prayer that scripture implies to leave whatever is important at the moment and pray. "Let the priests, who minister before the LORD, weep between the temple porch and the altar. Let them say, 'Spare your people' and in his mercy . . . The LORD will reply to them: 'I am sending you grain, new wine and oil, enough to satisfy you fully; surely he has done great things'" (Joel 2:17–19). God honored the sincerity of their united cry.

God's presence is among us when we gather to pray corporately. "Where two or three come together in my name, there am I with them" (Matt. 18:20). As we come together to pray as a whole, we are knit together as a temple, the body of Christ. His glory is manifested as we intercede on behalf of one another. We are stronger standing together! God originated the design of the church. He arranges each part of the body exactly as he wants them to be and holds it together. Prayer assists God in building his kingdom and church. Pray for the leaders and staff of your church. The enemy knows the heart of our Savior and he will go right where it hurts; remember . . . *Jesus gave himself up* for the church.

Today's Prayer Journal Task

- Are you committed to attend, serve, and pray with a body of believers?
- What can you do today to passionately love the church despite its imperfections?

Prayer for Jerusalem

Isaiah's Prayer for Jerusalem is in italics below: Isaiah 62:1–12 (NLT). Each section is supported by reference verses for further prayer. Let us join Isaiah in prayer for peace in Jerusalem; to become a light to the world, preparing for Jesus' second coming, and building God's kingdom for his glory. We are commanded to pray for peace in Jerusalem (Ps. 122:6).

Until then, the Lord is holding open the door of opportunity for salvation for all to hear the gospel. His astonishing patience is toward all he made, not desiring that any should miss his marvelous grace, but that everyone turn to repent and live (2 Pet. 3:9). Jesus' second coming could happen tomorrow or in another decade. It is not for us to know when, but to be concerned about being ready. It is not so much the delay of his coming for the church, as it is giving every chance possible for the gospel to be heard by all, according to his promise. As with Jesus' first coming, it shall be with his second, God moves hearts to pray, preparing the way for his arrival. For such a time as this we are called to pray—for Jerusalem. And this can be prayed for the church.

> Because I love Zion, because my heart yearns for Jerusalem, I cannot remain silent. I will not stop praying for her until her righteousness shines like the dawn, and her salvation blazes like a burning torch.

"Therefore, as we have opportunity, let us do good to all people, especially to those who belong to the family of believers," by praying for one another (Gal. 6:10).

> The nations will see your righteousness. Kings will be blinded by your glory. And the LORD will give you a new name. The LORD will hold you in his hands for all to see— a splendid crown in the hands of God. Never again will you be called the Godforsaken City or the Desolate Land. Your new name will be the City of God's Delight and the Bride of God, For the LORD delights in you and will claim you as his own.

Pray for the next generation to pursue righteousness. "So then, just as you received Christ Jesus as Lord, continue to live in him, rooted and built up in him, strengthened in the faith as you were taught, and overflowing with thankfulness. See to it that no one takes you captive through hollow and deceptive philosophy, which depends on human tradition and the basic principles of this world rather than on Christ" (Col. 2:6–8).

Your children will care for you with joy, O Jerusalem, just as a young man cares for his bride. Then God will rejoice over you as a bridegroom rejoices over his bride.

Pray for the his kingdom to come. "My food," said Jesus, "is to do the will of him who sent me and to finish his work. Do you not say, 'Four months more and then the harvest?' I tell you, open your eyes and look at the fields! They are ripe for harvest" (John 4:34–35).

O Jerusalem, I have posted watchmen on your walls; they will pray to the Lord day and night for the fulfillment of his promises. Take no rest, all you who pray. Give the Lord no rest—remind the Lord until he makes Jerusalem the object of praise throughout the earth. The Lord has sworn to Jerusalem by his own strength: "I will never again hand you over to your enemies. Never again will foreign warriors come and take away your grain and wine. You raised it, and you will keep it, praising the Lord. Within the courtyards of the Temple, you yourselves will drink the wine that you have pressed; you will eat the grain with thankful hearts.

Pray and ask God to open the eyes of hearts in all nations to see their need for Jesus.

Go out! Prepare the highway for my people to return! Smooth out the road; pull out the boulders; raise a flag for all the nations to see. The Lord has sent this message to every land: "Tell the people of Israel, 'Look, your Savior is coming. See, he brings his reward with him as he comes.'" They will be called the Holy People and the People Redeemed by the Lord. And Jerusalem will be known as the Desirable Place and the City No Longer Forsaken.

Our Rich Inheritance

RESPONDING TO THE invitation through prayer we can learn to persevere through our problems in this life, and gain a renewed perspective while we expectantly wait for what the Bible calls our rich inheritance. Jesus said whatever our heart is paying attention to, there our treasure will be found. This is a profound mystery, but we can store up treasures in heaven through prayer. "We have a priceless inheritance—an inheritance that is kept in heaven, pure and undefiled, beyond the reach of change and decay. And through your faith, God is protecting you by his power until you receive this salvation, which is ready to be revealed on the last day for all to see" (1 Pet. 1:5 NLT).

Do you know that God is preparing a place for us because he wants us to dwell with him forever? Remember God established the garden and then, because of sin, he required the building of the tabernacle as a place for his presence to dwell. These physical dwellings represented the heavenly eternal dwelling. Only God can ". . . make known the end from the beginning, from ancient times, (to) what is still to come. His purpose will stand, and he will do all that he pleases. What he has said, that will he bring about; what he has planned, that will he do" (Isa. 46:9–11). God is the ultimate covenant keeper. God promises to dwell with us forever.

The morning of my first race, butterflies were swirling in my stomach. The adrenaline was rushing through my veins. As we were closing in on the start time, one of the guys in our training group decided to take us down toward the front of the race. I could not believe I was stationed at the front of the pack. The advanced runners were waiting with pep in their step. In my nervous anxiety I attempted to look confident and started to trot in place. The timer went off. We patiently crossed the starting line and began to spread out on the course.

As my friend and I rounded the first corner, to my surprise my husband and children were holding up huge bright signs that said, "Run, Joanie, Run!" "Run, Sarah, Run!" They were yelling and screaming and cheering for us! The adrenaline rush warmed me up quickly. But the last mile was all downhill, and my legs felt like Jell-O®. Not knowing the course and exactly how much farther I had to run, I was holding back energy to reserve my legs. The location of the finish line was not in my radar scope and I assumed we had another half of a mile to run. But the finish was down the hill, around the corner, and closer than I expected.

My husband always says, "Run the mile you're in." I think that philosophy is true in running as well as in life. Be present in the now, but focus on seeing the horizon. I think knowing the location of the finish line is crucial to finishing the race strong. During the race, when my friend finally said, "There's the finish line!" I let go of my reservation and ran with all my strength. Finishing was my goal. Finishing was victory enough for me! I surprised myself and ran a 29.30 for my first 5K!

The same is true for prayer. "Let us fix our eyes on Jesus, the author and perfecter of our faith . . ." (Heb. 12:2). This goal will carry us through the days on earth until we see him face to face. Read scripture and seek to understand, accept, and believe the rich inheritance we have in Christ.

Heaven will be more magnificent than we can ever imagine. But, even more importantly, God says, "I AM . . . your very great reward" (Gen. 15:1). Can you imagine the joy as you see Jesus standing before you with his arms open wide, once again welcoming you into his presence forever?

Our highest goal, to know God and to love him in everything we do and all that we are, should drive us to think eternally. What more could there be? His Word tells us his power is at work in us to do immeasurably more than all we can ask or imagine (Eph. 3:20).

So as we focus on eternity, "Whatever you do, work at it with all your heart, as working for the Lord, not for men, since you know that you will receive an inheritance from the Lord as a reward. It is the Lord Christ you are serving" (Col. 3:23–24). God has given us a living hope through the resurrection of Jesus. He eagerly longs with anticipation to bless us with the riches of his inheritance that can never be stolen, destroyed, or faded—kept in heaven for us (1 Pet. 1:4).

In the meantime, we should be careful how we spend our lives, making sure our center of attention, our hope, is on Jesus Christ. If we build our security using the temporary things of this world, our work will be shown for what it is, because the Day of Judgment will bring it to light. As we look at prayer, we must look beyond the momentary and see the eternal value. As Jesus shares the Sermon on the Mount and talks about praying sincerely and in secret, he says,

> And when you pray, do not be like the hypocrites, for they love to pray standing in the synagogues and on the street corners to be seen by men. I tell you the truth, they

have received their reward in full. But when you pray, go into your room, close the door and pray to your Father, who is unseen. Then your Father, who sees what is done in secret, will reward you. And when you pray, do not keep on babbling like pagans, for they think they will be heard because of their many words. Do not be like them, for your Father knows what you need before you ask him. Do not store up for yourselves treasures on earth, where moth and rust destroy, and where thieves break in and steal. But store up for yourselves treasures in heaven, where moth and rust do not destroy, and where thieves do not break in and steal. For where your treasure is, there your heart will be also.

—Matthew 6:5–8, 19–21

Through prayer, "Seek first his kingdom and his righteousness," and all that we need on earth and in heaven will be given to us (Matt. 6:33). To strip away the busyness and distractions of life and seek God first, it is a good discipline to consider a time of prayer and fasting periodically—from food, sweets, television, or something we think we cannot live without.

When we pray with endurance inspired by the hope of eternal life, storing up treasures through prayer, may we know that when the Son of Man comes in his glory, and all the angels with him, he will rule on his heavenly throne in glory. All the nations will be gathered before him. May we be found praying with passion when Jesus returns.

Then the King will say to those on his right, "Come, you who are blessed by my Father; take your inheritance, the kingdom prepared for you since the creation of the world.

—Matthew 25:34

Often we get comfortable and safe in our own world. We can fail to be transformed by the truth that it is more blessed to give than receive. There are so many needs to meet in the global problems of this world—the poor, the hungry, the AIDS epidemic, war, floods, and fires—so many that we feel overwhelmed and do nothing.

These are some of the daily realities of human, individual lives. We think we are only one person and wonder how can we make a difference? Each of us has been blessed with time, talents, and treasures. Our efforts may seem small or insignificant, but we have been given the gift of prayer. Prayer can touch the world. Prayer can help the hurting and hungry. If we touch one life of another human being, we make a difference.

We can care about others throughout the world by giving of our time in prayer for the poor and oppressed. When we pray for others on the other side of the world or in our own city, we become more mindful of the needs of others and begin to realize we are truly blessed.

Today, commit to pray for one city or one missionary—globally and locally. Pick a neighbor and pray for them. My pastor encourages our congregation to take a prayer walk around our neighborhoods praying for each individual household. Through prayer God can lead us to use other resources to minister to those we are praying for and to build bridges between us. There are many resources available to help you pray for the world in need. (See appendix for resources). The companion journal also provides weekly space to pray for these concerns.

"One thing God has spoken, two things have I heard: that you, O God, are strong, and that you, O Lord, are loving. Surely you will reward each person according to what he has done" (Ps. 62:11–12). May the endurance it takes to store up our treasures in heaven through prayer be inspired by hope. Our reward is eternal life: that we may know and live in the presence of the only true God and his Son, Jesus Christ. To see his face!

Jesus longs for us to be with him where he is (John 14:3). Any further reward will be "icing on the cake."

Today's Prayer Journal Task

- Do you know and focus on your final destination?
- Are you finishing faithful and strong to the very end, persevering in prayer?
- What steps do you need to take to finish the race strong?
- Commit to pray for his kingdom to come, for the church, and for Jerusalem.
- Are you inquisitive and longing for a better country—a heavenly one? For he has promised and prepared a city for us.

God's Glory Revealed

As we pray to God in Jesus' name and authority, we become one in Spirit and purpose. Loving and living our lives to please him, reaching others to build his kingdom, his glory is revealed.

Recalling the tabernacle, do you remember where God's glory settled? God's glory was contained in the Most Holy Place, which enclosed the golden altar of incense and the gold-covered Ark of the Covenant. Above the Ark were the cherubim of the divine Glory, whose wings overshadowed the atonement cover (Heb. 9:1–5).

Once the tabernacle reached completion, Moses gave the final inspection. To show his approval God came down in a cloud and "the glory of the LORD filled the tabernacle" (Exod. 40:34). Over the Ark of the Testimony, God agreed, "There . . . I will meet with you" (Exod. 25:22).

The Ark of the Testimony was given this name for a special purpose. The word testimony means "witness." The Ark's covering was called the mercy seat, the place of the ministry of reconciliation. It contained items that bore witness to God's faithfulness to the Israelites. The Ark contained the tablets of stone (Ten Commandments), the omer of manna, and the budding rod of Aaron. All three artifacts represent the grace of God's living Word that guides, feeds, protects, and produces fruit in us.

Our lives now bear witness of God's promise fulfilled in us as we receive the invitation behind the veil, to enter the Holy of Holies at the mercy seat of reconciliation. "For all have sinned and fall short of the glory of God, and are justified freely by his grace through the redemption that came by Christ Jesus. God presented Jesus as a sacrifice of atonement, through faith in his blood. He did this to demonstrate his justice, because in his forbearance he had left the sins committed beforehand unpunished" (Rom. 3:23–25).

We possess free access into the presence of a holy God. We need to take hold of this confidence that is ours for the taking. We come because Jesus is our confidence! We enter by grace into the Most Holy Place. But we only come by faith in the blood of Jesus and through his purified prayers. He provided a new, fresh,

and living way for us to approach the Holy of Holies through the sacrifice of his body. The place where we meet with God now is in our hearts. On this earth you are a Holy Place. And since Jesus lives to pray for us, we have an advocate on our behalf; let us not fear, but draw near to God with all our heart.

Prayer brings glory to God. When we pray for things with the pure motive to give God glory, we will see answers to prayer. Jesus says, "I will do whatever you ask in my name, so that the Son may bring glory to the Father. You may ask me for anything in my name, and I will do it" (John 14:13–14). The more we pray, praise, and worship God, the more we see God work causing us to exalt and glorify him. Could this be our purpose? "I raised you up for this very purpose, that I might display my power in you and that my name might be proclaimed in all the earth" (Rom. 9:17). In creating us to glorify him, God is inviting us to enjoy him.

After all he has provided, are you devoted to enjoying him, to giving God the most glory? You are his testimony. "Christ in you, the hope of glory" (Col. 1:27).

Is there a way to show the passion in your heart? Go and bear the most fruit possible for God's glory. Believe and receive the invitation. Receive God's love. Let him love on you because your life depends on it. Through love by faith there is hope for you and all of us. You only need to come into his presence believing. Believing without seeing is not always easy, but as we continue to faithfully pray and journal, he gives us eyes to see his work. Jesus said it best, "Did I not tell you if you believed you would see the *glory* of God?" (John 11:40).

In this present world we see small glimpses of God's glory. For me these snap shots of heaven have been during miraculous moments, the joy of holding my newborn babies or being captivated by the sunrise in the Colorado mountains. These brief encounters give us hope for a future life full of beauty.

During Jesus' second return to earth I would think there would be a myriad of angels, if not more than there were announcing his first coming. I still ponder this awesome sight . . . How will it be that all over the world we will see his coming together? The internet maybe? Or an awesome, mind-boggling revelation? Jesus will come again in all his glory with a mighty trumpet sound announcing his return with strength and power. He will come as a King.

Be dressed in righteousness—ready with the light on—so when Jesus comes you can open the door and receive him. We who are still alive will be caught up together to meet the Lord in the air. We will be called priests of God and we will reign with him. "And so we will be with the Lord forever" (1 Thess. 4:17).

As we view the glorious heavenly temple and God's emerald throne, "The LORD God Almighty and the Lamb are its temple. The city does not need the sun or the moon to shine on it, for the glory of God gives it light, and the Lamb is its lamp. The nations will walk by its light, and the kings of the earth will bring their splendor into it. On no day will its gates ever be shut, for there will be no night there" (Rev. 21:22–23).

Come to the King's banqueting table to taste and see that the LORD is good. He offers himself.

> The night of the LORD's Supper "while they (the disciples) were eating, Jesus took bread, gave thanks and broke it, and gave it to his disciples, saying, 'Take and eat; this is my body.' Then he took the cup, gave thanks and offered it to them, saying, 'Drink from it, all of you. This is my blood of the covenant, which is poured out for many for the forgiveness of sins. I tell you, I will not drink of this fruit of the vine from now on until that day when I drink it anew with you in my Father's kingdom.'"
> —Matthew 26:26–28

Jesus is the great Host of Hosts. We are asked to practice communion as a reminder of the grace given us, his life paid for our sins by the One who longs for us to enjoy his company. Jesus wants us to be with him in heaven so we can see and share his glory. In heaven we will partake of this blessed communion with him. He will gather his own and serve them with gracious hospitality at his banqueting table. "It will be good for those servants whose master finds them watching when he comes. Truly, I tell you, he (Jesus) will dress himself to serve, will have them recline at the table and will come and wait on them" (Luke 12:37).

In the book of Revelation, John the apostle had visions with eternal implications for those who believe, giving us hope for an everlasting kingdom. Our prayers by faith do indeed have eternal ramifications. Our prayers are received through the eternal incense of Jesus' life and his intercessory prayers being offered. "When he had taken the scroll, the four living creatures and the twenty-four elders fell down before the Lamb. Each one had a harp and they were holding golden bowls full of incense, which are the prayers of the saints" (Rev. 5:8). From this passage we receive a glimpse of our prayers being stored in golden bowls arising like incense.

In heaven I believe we will see golden bowls full of incense, overflowing with our prayers as a sweet aroma unto God. Then we will fully see the glory and power of prayer and see that we have been participants of building God's kingdom.

Since time will have no bounds, I wonder if Jesus will sit with us and show us each prayer we offered by faith and the impact that prayer made on our lives by others, as well as the ramifications of our touching the world through prayer.

Seeing that we respond to the invitation by the King to come, we will be the honored guests at the banqueting table of his kingdom forever; a kingdom full of his eternal fellowship, luscious foods, and new wine. He is a King who has made evident extension of his hand in an eternal covenant of friendship and love. Let us allow his Spirit to stir in us anticipation of our magnificent future. Our award awaits us . . . GLORY!

CHAPTER 14

GRACE FOR THE JOURNEY

A RE YOU READY to pray and journal the rest of your life
journey with God?

As you have witnessed in this book, God's desire is to dwell with
us! Since the Garden of Eden and even after the broken fellowship
by sin, God reveals his timeless presence to us. God pursued mankind with whom he made covenants of love and promises of his
presence. God shared his glory in the earthly tabernacle; purposely
designed and built to meet with him. Now under the new covenant
as we respond in prayer by faith and accept Jesus, the Holy Spirit
abides much more closely in our hearts. What an awesome privilege
to be welcomed into his presence. Be intentional as you receive his
invitation and approach the throne with reverence.

The mind is a powerful resource. As you pray, picture yourself
entering into the earthly tabernacle. Remember in the new covenant
Jesus is the culmination of all that the sanctuary represents. Enter
through his gates with thanksgiving and his courts with praise, walk
by the bronze altar, and accept the sacrifice of the Lamb. Cleanse off
your sins in the bronze basin as you confess and accept his cleansing
power and forgiveness. Bring your prayers to the altar of incense,
releasing the concerns of your heart as they rise to heaven as a continuous aroma. Enter the Holy of Holies beyond the torn veil and
bow humbly in his holy presence, the place of pure intimacy.

THE INVITATION

As you come into God's presence daily ask God these questions and listen for his gentle reply—your grace for the journey!

Daily Prayer Journal Task

- LORD, am I praising you no matter what?
- Search me and show me the sins I need to confess.
- Are all my relationships healthy and right?
- Am I surrendering to your will in all areas of my life?
- Am I seeking to glorify and please you above all others?
- Am I depending on the Holy Spirit's guidance?
- LORD, do I trust you despite what I see?

The invitation from God is all about love. Conversation with God is all about relationship. It is about the One who created our souls, who longs for our intimate communion.

The journey is lonely without someone to pour out your heart. "There is a friend who sticks closer than a brother" (Prov. 18:24). He understands you better than you understand yourself because he created you. Listen, listen, and listen some more! God longs to tell you . . . he loves you with an everlasting, unconditional, unmerited love. Write it down when he woos you. He is gentle and desires to share his heart with you—If you will only stop and listen.

Circumstances in life may not be on our timetable or agenda, but God is pouring out his love on us. It may not look like love. Love may come delivered in different packages than we could ever imagine. Remember, his ways are not our ways; his thoughts are not like man's thoughts (Isa. 55:8–9). His ways are so much higher than our minds can conceive. He sees the realm of the whole kingdom.

It comes down to believing God. He proclaims that he will remain with us and speak tenderly to us. He will betroth us to him forever in righteousness, justice, compassion, and faithfulness. He indeed has shown us his love. He says, "You are my people." Let us respond, "You are my God" (Hosea 2:14, 19, 23). Let us remain committed to communion with God.

"Where is this 'coming' he promised?" God is not slow in keeping his promise, but patient so that everyone will come to him. The day he comes will be quick and we are told to be ready; to know him, actively waiting through a life of prayer and discovered purpose utilizing our gifts. God proclaims, "You will be for me a kingdom of priests" (Exod. 19:6). With urgency it is time for God's people to rise up, to watch, and to pray.

Recorded is a dialogue between Habakkuk and God; a conversational prayer to give us hope. Habakkuk cries out, "How long, Oh LORD must I call for help?" The LORD replies, "Look at the nations and watch—and be utterly amazed. For I am going to do something in your days that you would not believe, even if you were told" (Hab. 1:1, 5).

Believing the promise, Habakkuk commits, "I will stand at my watch and station myself on the ramparts; I will look to see what he will say to me" (Hab. 2:1). God has something to say! Are we listening with tender, responsive hearts?

Then the LORD replied: "Write down the revelation and make it plain on tablets so that a herald may run with it. For the revelation awaits an appointed time; it speaks of the end and will not prove false. Though it linger, wait for it; it will certainly come and will not delay . . . The righteous will live by faith. For the earth will be filled with the knowledge of glory of the LORD . . . The LORD is in his holy temple; let all the earth be silent before him" (Hab. 2:2–4, 14, 20).

Remember the tabernacle of his presence, God said to Moses, "Have them make a sanctuary for me, and I will dwell among them" (Exod. 25:8).

In the final stages of this book and my study of the tabernacle, my husband played a song for me by Kutless called *"Take Me In."* It was affirmation to my soul. The words of this song were a clear picture of so many truths that I have learned in my life and shared with you in this book. This song became a cry of my heart in prayer.

Take Me In

Take me past the outer courts
Into the holy place
Past the brazen altar
LORD I want to see your face
Pass me by the crowds of people
And the priests who sing your praise
I hunger and thirst for your righteousness
But it's only found in one place

Chorus
Take me in to the Holy of Holies
Take me in by the blood of the Lamb
Take me in to the Holy of Holies
Take the coal, touch my lips, here I am.[1]

Each part of the earthly sanctuary points to the perfect fulfillment in Jesus.

- Enter his courts with praise. He alone is worthy.
- Enter his gates with thanksgiving. He opens the door. "I am the gate; whoever enters through me will be saved" (John 10:9).
- He lays down his life. He is the permanent sacrifice on the bronze altar. "Jesus suffered to make the people holy through his own blood" (Heb. 13:12).
- He is the bronze basin, "Unless I wash you, you have no part with me" (John 13:8).
- He says "Come" to the table, "I am the bread of life. He who comes to me will never go hungry and he who believes in me will never be thirsty" (John 6:35).
- He is the lampstand. "I am the light of the world. Whoever follows me will never walk in darkness, but will have the light of life" (John 8:12).
- He is the altar of incense ". . . he always lives to intercede for them" (Heb. 7:25).
- He is the veil that was torn and "we have confidence to enter the Most Holy Place by the blood of Jesus, by a new and living way opened for us through the curtain, that is, his body" (Heb. 10:19–20).
- He is the mercy seat. "God raised us up with Christ and seated us with him in the heavenly realms in Christ Jesus" (Eph. 2:6).
- He is the true tabernacle. "He made his dwelling (tabernacle) among us and we have seen his glory" (John 1:14). "You

yourselves are God's temple and God's spirit lives in you" (1 Cor. 3:16). "On that day you will realize that I am in my Father, you are in me, and I am in you" (John 14:20).

- He is the manifestation of God's glory—"And now, Father, glorify me in your presence with the glory I had with you before the world began" (John 17:5).

The realization that all Old Testament principles and symbols align with present and future promises—were and are being fulfilled *completely* through Jesus—these revelations were overwhelming to me. Jesus represents everything in the tabernacle and he is everything to me.

> That is what he is when I am running . . . he's everything I need, the water I thirst for, the ground beneath my feet, the wind against my face, the next breath of air that I breathe, my next heartbeat. This is what he is to me. Prayer is like running: the more you pray, the more you can pray, and the more you realize how desperately you need him.

We are all called to be runners in the race of faith. "Since we are surrounded by such a great cloud of witnesses, let us throw off everything that hinders and the sin that so easily entangles, and let us run with perseverance the race marked out for us" (Heb. 12:1). This verse spoke volumes to me, during the Columbus, Ohio Half Marathon.

It was a cool fall morning at the beginning of the race—beautiful blue skies with the sun peeking over the horizon sending warmth on its way. I stood behind thousands of people who were waiting for the race to start. The moment the horn blew, clothes went flying into the air: coats, hats, gloves, jackets, long-sleeve t-shirts—all were shed. The impression left on me was such a vivid picture of "throwing off everything that hinders." A serious runner does not want to be burdened with extra—anything!

The "great cloud of witnesses" were everywhere, on every corner and every mile. I knew Columbus, Ohio had spirit, but that spirit was for a whole different sport. Strangers were cheering at the top of their lungs, "Go! Go! Go!" "You can do it!" Musicians were playing in bands. Individual guitarists, a bagpiper, a young man playing "Rocky" on a boom box, and blaring music screamed through the wide open windows of their homes. Homemade signs were held up high.

These encouragers along the way made me persevere when the going got tough. About mile ten or eleven, my legs felt like they might buckle underneath me. I looked up and saw people, complete strangers, cheering for us. Not just for me to succeed, but for every single one of us, whether we were full marathoners, half, or walkers, it didn't matter. Their purpose was to encourage the participant to reach the goal—to finish.

Another essential lesson during that marathon that came to me; the "witnesses" are often the ones closest to us. God has put some of us together in this journey of life who are not strangers, but who run the race with us. My family was a huge support. My sister-in-law ran the race with us. I can still hear her say, "What are you afraid of? You can do it, Sarah." My brother-in-law brought our kids to cheer us on at the finish. Knowing my kids were there made me want to finish all the more. I knew deep down that the prayers of many friends were being said.

My husband, who has successfully run three other half marathons, stayed right by my side speaking positive words over me, "Breathe deep. Stay strong. Be courageous." Crossing the finish line with him was the greatest gift celebrating our fifteen years of marriage. The day before the race, as I was reading my Beth Moore Bible study, I discovered a truth: "God has chosen that our victories are sweetest when shared."[2]

Thankfully, I persevered through my first half marathon. My hat goes off to those who can successfully run a full marathon. This season of my journey, learning to run and gaining insight into prayer has made it clear to me that with God all things are possible. With God a man or woman can change and do things they never imagined in their wildest dreams they would accomplish. "Father, your will be done on earth as it is in heaven" (Matt. 6:10). Through prayer may we accomplish the impossible and bring heaven to earth. Will you join me in the marathon for Life?

Let us "run in such a way as to get the prize." Run to win and "to get a crown that will last forever" (1 Cor. 9:24–25). Run to receive a crown to present at Jesus' feet. Press on toward the goal of a heavenly prize. God is calling us through Christ Jesus . . . "Come to me!" (Phil. 3:14).

May this book (and journal) help to keep you running into his presence. Know that I am coming alongside of you through prayer, and passionately cheering for you at the top of my lungs, "You can do it! Run, *your name*, Run!" More importantly than my cheers, Jesus comes beside you, praying for you with all his heart—talking straight to the Father. With authority he speaks the same words of life over you, but with a greater passion because he truly knows you and loves you with an everlasting love.

In the race of life, remember to rest in his presence in prayer, record his Word and work in your life; for this is the sustenance for life and energy to finish strong. It is not important where you have come from, how many times you have fallen, but that you get back up, and know where you are going from this day forward. Strive to reach the goal for his presence and glory; move toward it step by step, choosing faith over fear, hope over despair, and perseverance over apathy.

Whatever you are looking for—you will find the answers in the presence of Jesus. Our great reward stands victoriously at the finish line with his arms wide open to welcome you. Jesus leaves an impression; everything about him invites you in—his voice, his face, his aroma! He longs to spend eternity with you.

All of this? . . . . Because of *love*. . .

"This is what the LORD says—he who created you, he who formed you, 'Fear not, for I have redeemed you; I have summoned you by name; you are mine. Since you are precious and honored in my sight, and *because I love you* . . . Do not be afraid, for I am with you; everyone who is called by my name, whom I created for my glory, whom I formed and made. You are my witnesses,' declares the LORD, 'and my servant whom I have chosen, so that you may know and believe me and understand that I am he'" (Isa. 43:1, 4–5, 7, 10).

God loves us with an everlasting love. We were designed for a life of eternal sweet communion. We have Jesus, our great High Priest, providing ready access to God—let us not let it slip through our fingers. We do not have a priest who is out of touch with reality (Heb. 4:4 MSG). Jesus has brought us to a place of undeserved privilege—into God's presence—where we can now stand, boldly and joyfully as we look forward to sharing God's glory. He is reality—he invites us . . . *Come with me. I have prepared a place for you. I have placed before you an open door that no one can shut.*

THE INVITATION

My heart has heard you say, "Come and talk with me." And my heart responds, "LORD, I am coming!" (Ps. 27:8).

In your unfailing love you will lead the people you have redeemed. In your strength you will guide them to your holy dwelling . . . to the secret place of your heart. Blessed are those who are invited to the wedding supper of the Lamb! (Rev. 19:9).

Your invitation awaits . . . *Come to me! Come boldly to the throne of grace!*

Today's Prayer Journal Task

- Are you entering boldly to the throne of grace?
- List how you have grown spiritually confident in prayer and journaling from reading this book and spend time thanking God.
- Are you running in such a way as to obtain your rich inheritance?
- Write a prayer committing to stay close to God.

The Invitation

In the palace in the land of mercy
The King looked out from his throne
He saw the sick, the homeless, and hungry
He saw me lost and without hope
And moved with compassion
He sent out his only Son
With the invitation to come
This is your invitation
Come just the way you are
Come find what your soul has been longing for
Come find your peace
Come join the feast
Come in, this is your invitation
So I stood outside the gates and trembled
In my rags of unworthiness
Afraid to even stand at a distance
In the presence of holiness
But just as I turned to go
The gates swung open wide
And the King and his only Son
They invited me inside
So now will you come with me
To where the gates swing open wide
The King and his only son
Are inviting us inside.[3]

THE INVITATION

Example from the companion journal *Grace for the Journey*

Daily

(My Personal Example)

Praise and Proclaim, Offer Thanks, Search and Confess,
Listen, Apply Armor

Date 1/17/08

Personal Needs

Trust in the LORD with all your heart and lean not on your own understanding; in all your ways acknowledge him and he will direct your paths. (Prov. 3:5–6).

LORD, I seek your will in these next steps. You tell me to ask, seek, and knock. Please open the best door for me to publish this book when the time is right.

Immediate Family

"May (_____) pursue righteousness, godliness, faith, love, endurance, and gentleness" (1 Tim. 6:11).

May my children and husband, (list by name, put in the prayer and add anything specific.) Give my children an awareness of your presence.

My Activities Today

"Now to him who is able to do immeasurably more than we all can ask or imagine, according to his power within us, to him be the glory" (Eph. 3:20).

Use me, LORD, as I go about my day. Bless the work of my hands and my mind with instruction for the details of this book. Open the doors of opportunity.

Special Concerns

You who daily bear our burdens, encourage the marriages that are hurting, P&J, S&K, friends who have come to us. Bring your love and reconciliation (Ps. 68:19).

Missionary

Protect Kelly and Ralph. Help them not to fear, but to share the gospel in power.

Ask and it will be given to you; seek and you will find; knock and the door will be opened to you.

Matthew 7:7

(My Personal Example)

Dear LORD,   4/7/07

Thank you for the grace given me in Christ Jesus. For in him I have been enriched in every way. Therefore, I do not lack any spiritual gift as I eagerly wait for our Lord Jesus Christ. He will keep me strong to the end . . . God who has called me into fellowship with his Son is faithful! (1 Cor. 1:4–8).

Thank you, LORD, for leading me to these verses today as a reminder that you do all things through me. As I complete this book, you have given me much grace and knowledge. You have enriched me in every way that I do not lack what I need to complete this. Because you are faithful! I must choose to trust and believe. I needed this boost of confidence!

As we returned from our trip with the kids, it was all about making our dreams come true. My heart was moved as I watched 71,000 people at the parks, that the possibility of that many people getting this book in their hands and using it, actually praying . . . that is my dream come true!! For God to use it and encourage people into a new or deeper relationship with him, increasing their prayer lives, building their faith, to help build up his Kingdom . . . that would delight my heart!!!

Give me clarity, focus, the ability to hear your voice and what you want in this book. I so desire that every pen stroke, every word and thought, please you. Bless those who have read the book and have given up their time to give me feedback. Give them abundant time back. Give them joy! Thank you for calling me into fellowship with your Son. There is no greater gift of grace! I in return give this gift, this prayer journal, this offering of sacrifice. I lay it at the foot of the cross, as well as my life. Take it, LORD. Not my will, but yours be done.

In the precious name of Jesus,

I love you!

Sarah

THE INVITATION

Sample of Daily Prayer Page / Journal Entry from *Grace for the Journey*

Praise and Proclaim, Offer Thanks, Search
and Confess, Listen, Apply Armor

Personal Needs   Date _____

"Taste and see that the LORD is good; blessed is the man who takes refuge in him. Fear the LORD, you his saints, for those who fear him lack nothing" (Ps. 34:8–9).

_____

_____

Immediate family

May your eyes watch over (_____) for their good, and bring them back to this land. You build them up and do not tear them down; you plant them and not uproot them. Please give them a heart to know you, that you are the great, I AM, the LORD (Jer. 24:6–7).

_____

_____

My Activities Today

"Search me, O God, and know my heart; test me and know my anxious thoughts. See if there is any offensive way in me, and lead me in the way everlasting" (Ps. 139:23).

_____

_____

Special Concerns

_____

_____

Missionary

_____

_____

GRACE FOR THE JOURNEY

*"These I bring to my holy mountain and give
them joy in my house of prayer."*
Isaiah 56:7

Praying God's Word A–Z

Identify a need that has caused you concern for yourself, family member, friend or coworker. Write out a prayer based on the promises given below from the Bible in your journal. A concordance may be helpful.

Anger—Prov. 15:1, Rom. 12:19, Eph. 4:26–27, 31, Col. 3:8
Bitterness—Eph. 4:31–5:2, Col. 3:13
Contentment—Phil. 4:11–12, 1 Tim. 6:6–8, Heb. 13:5,
Depression—Ps. 3:3–5, Ps. 147:3, 2 Cor. 1:3–4
Discouragement—Rom. 15:4–5, Heb. 13:20–25
Eating—1 Cor. 10:31, Rom. 14:17, 1 Cor. 3:16–17
Finances—Prov. 11:28; 16:16, Matt. 6:24, 31–33, 1 Tim. 6:17–19
God's Will—Col. 1:9–10, Heb. 13:20–21, 1 Thess. 4:1–12
Healing—Exod. 15:26b, Jer. 17:14, Jer. 33:6, Matt. 9:22
Integrity—1 Kings 9:4, Job 2:3, Prov. 10:9; 11:3, Titus 2:7
Jealousy—Exod. 20:5, 2 Cor. 11:2, 1 Cor. 3:3, Gal. 5:20
Knowledge—Prov. 1:7; 10:14; 13:16, Rom. 11:33, Col. 2:3, 2 Pet. 3:18
Lust—Prov. 6:25, Eph. 5:3, Col. 3:5–6, 1 John 2:16
Marriage—Gen. 2:24, 1 Cor. 7:3–5, John 13:34–35, Heb. 13:4
No to Ungodliness—Titus 2:12, Rom. 12:1–2
Opportunity—Rom. 7:11, Gal. 6:10, Eph. 5:16, Col. 4:5
Peace—Ps. 34:14, Ps. 85:10, Ps. 119:165, Isa. 26:3, John 14:27,
    1 Cor. 7:15, Eph. 2:14
Quarrelsome—Prov. 15:18; 17:14,19; 19:13, 2 Tim. 2:24, 1 Tim 3:3
Resisting the Enemy—James 4:7, 1 Pet. 5:9
Strength—2 Sam. 22:33, Neh. 8:10, Ps. 28:7, Isa. 40:31, Phil. 4:13,
    2 Pet. 4:11
Treat with Respect—Lev. 22:2, 1 Tim. 5:1, 1 Pet. 3:7
Unity—Ps. 133, Eph. 4:29–32
Value—Matt. 13:46, 1 Tim. 4:8, Heb. 11:26
Worry—Matt. 6:25–27, Matt. 10:19, Phil. 4:6–8
eXcel—Phil. 4:8, 1 Cor. 14:12, 1 Cor. 12:31, 2 Cor. 8:7, Titus 3:8
Your Name and Identity—Prov. 3:3–4; 10:7; 22:1, Song of Sol. 7:1,
    Isa. 43:1
Zion—Rom. 9:33; 11:26

Significant Prayers in the Bible

Pray one a day

Genesis

Abraham for Sodom—Gen. 18:17–33
Abraham's Chief Servant for Favor—Gen. 24:12–15a
Isaac's Blessing—Gen. 27:28–29
Jacob's Deliverance—Gen. 32:9–12; 32:24–30

Exodus

The Song of Moses—Exod. 15:1–18
Moses Seeks Direction—Exod. 33:12–18

Numbers

Aaron's Blessing—Num. 6:24–26
Moses for Healing of Miriam—Num. 12:13
Moses for Israelites—Num. 14:13–19

Deuteronomy

Moses and the Promised Land—Deut. 3:24–29
Moses' 40 Day Prayer—Deut. 9:18–20; 19:25–29
Moses for Israelites—Deut. 9:26–29
The Song of Moses—Deut. 32:1–43
Moses Blesses the Israelites—Deut. 33:1–29

Judges

The Song of Deborah—Judg. 5:1–31
Gideon for Signs—Judg. 6:36–40
Samson for Strength—Judg. 16:28

THE INVITATION

1 Samuel

Hannah for a Child—1 Sam. 1:10–18
Hannah for Thanksgiving—1 Sam. 2:1–10

2 Samuel

David for Thanksgiving—2 Sam. 7:18–29
David's Praise for Deliverance—2 Sam. 22:1–51

1 Kings

Solomon for Wisdom—1 Kings 3:6–9
Solomon for Dedication—1 Kings 8:22–61
Elijah for Widow's Son—1 Kings 17:20–22
Elijah on Mount Carmel—1 Kings 18:36–39

2 Kings

Elijah for Sight and Blindness—2 Kings 6:15–18
Hezekiah for Deliverance—2 Kings 19:14–19
Hezekiah for Healing—2 Kings 20:1–11

1 Chronicles

Prayer of Jabez—1 Chron. 4:10
David's Thanksgiving for Ark—1 Chron. 16:8–36
David for Solomon—1 Chron. 29:10–20

2 Chronicles

Jehoshaphat for Deliverance—2 Chron. 20:5–19

Ezra

Ezra for Safe Journey—Ezra 8:21–23
Ezra Confesses the Nation's Sin—Ezra 9:5–15

Nehemiah

Nehemiah for his People—Neh. 1:3–11
The Israelites Confess their Sin—Neh. 9:1, 5–37

Esther

Esther Proclaims Fast for Israel—Esther 4 & 5

Job

Job Mourns—Job 1:20–21; 13:20–14:22

Psalm

In Troubled Times—Ps. 34; 46
In Times of Grief—Ps. 23
For Praise and Thanksgiving—Ps. 33; 67; 145–150
In Times of Waiting—Ps. 13; 27
When Seeking Guidance—Ps. 5; 25
Prayer and Fasting—Ps. 35
About God's Word—Ps. 19; 119
For God's Protection—Ps. 3; 91; 121
About God's Love and Care—Ps. 89; 103; 107
Requesting Forgiveness—Ps. 51; 32

Isaiah

Isaiah Praises God—Isa. 25:1–10
Hezekiah for Healing—Isa. 38
Prayer and Praise—Isa. 63:7–64:12

Jeremiah

Jeremiah's Complaint—Jer. 20:7–18
Jeremiah's Trust in God—Jer. 32:17–25

Lamentations

Lamentations for the Fall of Jerusalem—Lam. 1–4
Prayer for Jerusalem's Restoration—Lam. 5, Isa. 62:1–12

Daniel

Daniel's Praise—Dan. 2:20–23
Daniel for Mercy—Dan. 9:4–19

The Invitation

Jonah

Jonah Inside the Fish—Jon. 2:1–10

Habakkuk

Habakkuk's Prayer—Hab. 3:2–19

Prayers of Jesus

The Lord's Prayer—Matt. 6:9–13, Luke 11:2–4
Praises for Revelation to Children—Matt. 11:25–26, Luke 10:21
Jesus for Lazarus—John 11:41–42
Jesus Before His Death—John 12:27–28
For Himself—John 17:1–5
For His Followers—John 17:6–19
For all Believers—John 17:20–26
In Gethsemane—Matt. 26:36–44
On the Cross—Luke 23:34.46; Matt. 27:46

Luke

Mary's Song—Luke 1:46–55
Zechariah's Prayer—Luke 1:68–79
Simeon's Prayer—Luke 2:29–32
Tax collector—Luke 18:13

Acts

Apostles for Divine Direction—Acts 1:24–25
For Believers—Acts 4:24–31
Stephen Martyred—Acts 7:59–60
Paul and Ananias—Acts 9:3–19; 40
Cornelius' Prayer—Acts 10:30–33
For Sending Barnabas and Paul—Acts 13:1–3

1 Peter

Peter for Thanksgiving—1 Pet. 1:3–5

Jude

Doxology—Jude 1:24–25

The Prayers of Paul

For Rome—Rom. 1:8–10
For Israel—Rom. 10:1
For Early Church—Rom. 16:25–27
For Thanksgiving—1 Cor. 1:4–9
For Corinthians—2 Cor. 13:7–9
For Ephesians' Wisdom and Spiritual Growth
    Eph. 1:16–23; 3:14–21
For Philippians' Ministry—Phil. 1:3–11; 4:20
For Colossians Knowing God's Will—Col. 1:3–14
Thanksgiving for Thessalonians—1 Thess. 1:2–3; 2:13; 3:9–13; 5:23
Thanksgiving, Love and Peace for Thessalonians—2 Thess. 1:3;
    2:13, 16–17; 3:1–5, 16
For Timothy—2 Tim. 1:3
For Sharing Faith—Philem. 4–6

Recommended Reading/ Bibliography

Allen, Leonard, *The Contemporary Meets the Classics on Prayer*, West Monroe, Louisiana: Howard Books, 2003.

Bounds, E M, *Power through Prayer*, Grand Rapids, MI: Baker Books, 1991.

Chapell, Bryan, *Praying Backwards*, Grand Rapids, MI: Baker Books, 2005.

Duewel, Wesley L., *Touching the World through Prayer*, Grand Rapids, MI: Francis Asbury Print (imprint of Zondervan Publishing House), 1986.

Foster, Richard J., *Prayer: Finding the Heart's True Home*, San Francisco: Harper-Sanfrancisco (a division of HarperCollins Publishers), 1992.

Jeremiah, David, *Prayer—the Great Adventure*, Sisters, OR: Multnomah Publishing, Inc., 1997.

Johnstone, Patrick and Mandryk, Jason, *Operation World—21st Century Edition, When We Pray God Works*, Waynesboro, GA: Paternoster Publishing, 2001.

Kelly, Douglas, *If God Already Knows, Why Pray?* Brentwood, TN: Wolgemuth & Hyatt, Publishing, Inc., 1989.

Moody, D L, *The Joy of Answered Prayer*, New Kensington, PA: Whitaker, 1997.

Moore, Beth, *Breaking Free from Spiritual Strongholds Praying God's Word*, Nashville, TN: Broadman & Holman Publishers, 2000.

Murray, Andrew, *With Christ in the School of Prayer*, Springdale, PA: Whitaker House, 1981.

Omartian, Stormie, *Power of a Praying Wife*, Eugene, OR: Harvest House Publishers, 1997.

Power of a Praying Parent, Eugene, OR: Harvest House Publishers, 1995.

Power of a Praying Husband, Eugene, OR: Harvest House Publishers, 2001.

Sangster, W.E., *Teach Me To Pray*, Nashville, TN: The Upper Room, previously published in Great Britain by the Epworth Press, 1959.

Wallis, Arthur, *God's Chosen Fast*, Ft. Washington, PA: CLC Publications, 1968

Wallis, Arthur, *Pray in the Spirit*, Ft. Washington, PA: CLC Publications, 1970

ENDNOTES

Introduction

1. Text: Lucy A. Bennett (1850–1927) Music: T. A. Willis

Chapter 1

1. http://bible.crosswalk.com/Lexicons/Greek

Chapter 2

1. *Merriam Webster Inc.*, (Philippines, Library of Congress Cataloging in Publication Data, Webster's Ninth New Collegiate), p. 300.
2. Brennan Manning, *The Ragamuffin Gospel*, (Colorado Springs, CO: Multnomah Publishers, 2005), p. 101.

Chapter 3

1. Beth Moore, *A Woman's Heart, God's Dwelling Place*, (Nashville, TN: LifeWay Press, 2007), p. 10. Reprinted and Used by Permission.
2. G.K. Beale, *The Temple and the Church's Mission: A Biblical Theology of the Dwelling Place of God*, (Downer's Grover, IL: Intervarsity Press, 2004), p. 66.

3. *Merriam Webster Inc.*, (Philippines, Library of Congress Cataloging in Publication Data, Webster's Ninth New Collegiate), p. 113.
4. Matthew Henry's Commentary, http://bible.lifeway.com/crossmain.asp, Luke 1:18.
5. Beth Moore, *A Woman's Heart, God's Dwelling Place*, (Nashville, TN: LifeWay Press, 2007), p. 10. Reprinted and Used by Permission.
6. The Three Achers Co., Ltd., *Spikenard Magdalena*, Manger Street, Box 214, Bethlehem, Via Israel.

Chapter 4

1. Erik Reese, *SHAPE*, (Grand Rapids, MI: Zondervan, 2006), p. 212.
2. Simon, Tobin & Metcalf, Linda, *Writing the Mind Alive the Proprioceptive Method for Finding Your Authentic Voice*, (New York: Ballentine Publishing Corp, 2002), p. 28.
3. Ken Helser, *Keys to Journaling*, (Sophia, NC), p. 10.
4. *Merriam Webster Inc.*, (Philippines, Library of Congress Cataloging in Publication Data, Webster's Ninth New Collegiate), p. 879.
5. Mark Walter, *Prayer Made Easy*, (Peabody, MA: Hendrickson Publishers Inc., 1999), p. 28.

Part II Responding to the Invitation

1. Brennan Manning, *The Ragamuffin Gospel*, (Colorado Springs, CO: Multnomah Publishers, 2005), p. 46.

Chapter 5

1. *Vine's Complete Expository Dictionary*, W.E.Vine, (Nashville, TN: Thomas Nelson, Inc., 1996), p. 530.
2. Brennan Manning, *The Ragamuffin Gospel*, (Colorado Springs, CO: Multnomah Publishers, 2005), p. 240 Ref. Karl Barth.
3. Steve Lynam, First Love, Producer Bobby Kelly, The Process Recording Studios, GSO, NC 1987 Grace Productions, 610 Simpson St., 27401.
4. *Heritage Builders/Bible Stories for Preschoolers, Family Nights Tool Chest*, Jim Weidmann and Kirk Weaver, (Colorado Spring, CO: Chariot Victor Publishers, 1999), p. 10.

ENDNOTES

5. David Beaty, Message: "Why Pray?" River Oaks Community Church, (Lewisville, NC) May 2, 2004.
6. J.H., *Runner's World Magazine*, The Weight of Water, Aug. 2007, p. 72.
7. Elizabeth Elliot, *Passion and Purity*, (Old Tappan, NJ: Fleming H. Revell Company, 1984), p. 23.

Chapter 6

1. Fern Nichols, *Heart to Heart*, MITI, Spring '07, Vol. 19, No. 1.

Part III You Are a Sacred Temple

1. E. Sangster, *Teach Me to Pray*, (Nashville, TN: The Upper Room, 1959), p. 13.

Chapter 7

1. John and Staci Eldredge, *Captivating*, (Nashville, TN: Nelson Books, Thomas Nelson, Inc., 2005), ref. Brent Curtis, p. 57.
2. Edward Goodrick and John Kohlenberger III, *The Stongest NIV Exhaustive Concordance* (Grand Rapids, MI, Zondervan, 1999), p. 1556.

Chapter 8

1. Beth Moore, *Believing God*, (Nashville, TN: Lifeway Press, 2002), p. 67. Reprinted and Used by Permission.
2. Simon, Tobin & Metcalf, Linda, *Writing the Mind Alive the Proprioceptive Method for Finding Your Authentic Voice*, (New York: Ballentine Publishing Corp, 2002), p. 115.
3. Ken Helser, *Keys to Journaling*, (Sophia, NC), p. 10.

Chapter 9

1. Max Lucado, *A Love Worth Living* (Nashville, TN: W Publishing Group, a Division of Thomas Nelson, Inc.), p. 57.
2. Scotty Smith, *Speechless*, (Grand Rapids, MI: Zondervan Publishing House, 1999), p. 149.
3. Beth Moore, *Believing God*, (Nashville, TN: Lifeway Press, 2002), p. 176. Reprinted and Used by Permission.

4. Beth Moore, *To Live is Christ*, (Nashville, TN: Lifeway Press, 1997), p. 43. Reprinted and Used by Permission.

5. Brennan Manning, *The Ragamuffin Gospel*, (Colorado Springs, CO: Multnomah Publishers, 2005), p. 84.

6. Text: Joseph Scriven (1820–86) *The Book of Hymns*, I. Bradley, Ian (Woodstock, NY: Overlook Press, 1989), p. 449, 451 music by Charles Converse (1832–1918).

7. Beth Moore, *Believing God*, (Nashville, TN: Lifeway Press, 2002), p. 198. Reprinted and Used by Permission.

8. B John Calvin, *Sermons on the Epistle to the Ephesians*, (Edinburgh, Scotland: Banner of Truth Trust, 1975), p. 683.

Chapter 10

1. Readings from Amy Carmichael, *Learning of God*, compiled by Stuart and Brenda Blanch (Fort Washington, PA: CLC Publications, 1985/2000), p. 50.

2. David Beaty, Message on Moral Impurity, (Riveroaks Community Church, Winston-Salem, NC) Aug. 7, 2005.

3. Brennan Manning, *The Ragamuffin Gospel*, (Colorado Springs, CO: Multnomah Publishers, 2005), p. 155.

4. Philip Yancy, *Prayer Does It Make Any Difference?*, (Grand Rapids, MI: Zondervan, 2006), p. 36.

5. Rick Warren, *The Purpose Driven Life*, (Grand Rapids, MI: Zondervan, 2002), p. 149.

6. Simon, Tobin & Metcalf, Linda, *Writing the Mind Alive the Proprioceptive Method for Finding Your Authentic Voice*, (New York: Ballentine Publishing Corp, 2002), p. 115.

Part IV Glory Beyond the Sacred Temple

1. Edward Goodrick and John Kohlenberger III, *The Stongest NIV Exhaustive Concordance*, (Grand Rapids, MI: Zondervan, 1999), p. 1557.

2. *Vine's Complete Expository Dictionary*, W.E. Vine, (Nashville, TN: Thomas Nelson, Inc., 1996), p. 111.

Chapter 11

1. John F. MacArthur, *The MacArthur New Testament Commentary, Romans 1–8* (Chicago: Moody Press, 1991), p. 473.

ENDNOTES

2. Beth Moore, *Believing God*, (Nashville, TN: Lifeway Press, 2002), p. 124. Reprinted and Used by Permission.
3. *Vine's Complete Expository Dictionary*, W.E. Vine, (Nashville, TN: Thomas Nelson, Inc., 1996), p. 683.
4. Beth Moore, *Believing God*, (Nashville, TN: Lifeway Press, 2002), p. 135. Reprinted and Used by Permission.
5. *Vine's Complete Expository Dictionary*, W.E. Vine, (Nashville, TN: Thomas Nelson, Inc., 1996), p. 478.
6. Tuttle, Wes, Message: "Memory Stones of Marriage," (River Oaks Community Church, Winston Salem, NC), May 6, 2007.

Chapter 12

1. Beth Moore, *Believing God*, (Nashville, TN: Lifeway Press, 2002), p. 79. Reprinted and Used by Permission.
2. Rick Warren, *The Purpose Driven Life*, (Grand Rapids, MI: Zondervan, 2002),p. 236.
3. John Ortberg, *If You Want to Walk on Water You've Got to Get Out of the Boat*, (Grand Rapids, MI: Zondervan Publishing, 2001), p. 51.
4. John and Stasi Eldredge, *Captivating*, Nelson Books, (Thomas Nelson, Inc., Nashville, TN 2005), p. 217.

Chapter 13

1. Wesley L. Duewel, *Touching the World through Prayer*, (Grand Rapids, MI: Francis Asbury Press), p. 13.
2. David Beaty, "Why Pray?" River Oaks Community Church, (Lewisville, NC) May 2, 2004.

Chapter 14

1. Kutless Strong Tower, Producer Aaron Sprinkle, (A&R BEC Recordings Seattle, Washington, 2005).
2. Beth Moore, *A Woman's Heart, God's Dwelling Place*, (Nashville, TN: LifeWay Press, 2007), p.130. Reprinted and Used by Permission.
3. The Invitation/Speechless, Steven Curtis Chapman, (Brown Bannister and Steven Curtis Chapman, 1999 Nashville, TN).

ABOUT THE AUTHOR

Sarah Bush is currently a prayer consultant and speaker for Stonecroft Ministries—Christian Women's Clubs. She is a member of Moms in Touch International, a women's ministry leader and speaker, and an active participant on the prayer team at her church. Formerly an elementary education teacher, she currently serves on a board for a small non-profit foundation, Youth Ministry, Inc. and manages a busy home of three children and her husband. A native of North Carolina, her family resides in Winston-Salem. Sarah enjoys running, water sports, and biking with her family. In her free time she escapes by reading in the sun, scrapbooking, and traveling to the mountains or beaches of NC.

Sarah has had a habit of journaling for over twenty-five years, recording what God teaches her and how he reveals his work in her life. She passionately desires to deliver a practical tool and message into the hands of others to help them commune with God. She teaches, shepherds, and leads others through the disciplines of prayer and journaling including a variety of topics; listening, overcoming unbelief, spiritual confidence, and more. She continues her mission with the release of her first companion set.

For information about Sarah's books or speaking ministry, or to share how God has used this book in your life, please write to Sarah at:

Sarah Bush
http://sarahbush.authorweblog.com